Wishart Bell
Feb 2010

The Plainsong Psalter

Edited by James Litton

CHURCH

Church Publishing Incorporated, New York

To the memory of The Rev. Dr. Norman Mealy,
who through his love of the Church's music
and his many years of setting preliminary and
final texts of *The Book of Common Prayer*
to traditional unison chant, has provided Christians
a wealth of liturgical song so that they may
enlarge their daily round of prayer and praise.

10 9 8 7 6 5 4

Contents

Preface

The Standing Commission on Church Music of the Episcopal Church has requested that the collection of plainsong *Gradual Psalms* which was prepared by Richard Crocker and Ronald Haizlip be expanded to include the entire Psalter of *The Book of Common Prayer.* In addition, the Commission has directed that the antiphons which were selected and compiled by Howard E. Galley, Jr. and published in The Psalter section of his *The Prayer Book Office* (The Seabury Press, New York, 1980) be included with each psalm. The inclusion of these antiphons set to traditional office antiphon plainsong melodies makes this plainsong psalter unique. As far as it can be determined this is the first complete English plainsong psalter which has been published with antiphons for each psalm. The singing of antiphons with the psalms restores the complete musical form of the psalm tones. Divorced from the antiphons these plainsong tones are but a musical fragment.

In setting the antiphons I have followed the work of Dr. Crocker in his edition of *Gradual Psalms* with little or no change, and when an antiphon text is not included in *Gradual Psalms* I have tried to follow the spirit of Dr. Crocker's adaptations of the plainsong antiphon melodies.

Following the request of the Standing Commission on Church Music I have also tried to follow Dr. Crocker's choice of psalm tones as well as his method of pointing the psalm texts. Where this has not been possible, many plainsong psalters have been consulted, from Helmore's *A Manual of Plainsong,* 1850 to Willan's *The Canadian Psalter,* 1963.

Because of the revised translation of the psalms in *The Book of Common Prayer* the choice of tones and the pointed text of earlier psalters have been considered a guide and a starting point. The final choice of tones and the pointing of the psalm verses have been determined by either the unchanged decisions and solutions by Dr. Crocker and Mr. Haizlip, by a revision of the same, or finally, by original work. In all cases decisions were made after weekly singing of the Gradual Psalms with students, choirs, cantors and congregations over a decade of regular services in various churches and during many workshops throughout America and in England.

The section of Performance Notes which concerns antiphons is essentially the work of Howard E. Galley, Jr., and is taken from the Introduction to his monumental *The Prayer Book Office.* This information is included with the generous permission of Mr. Galley. Other parts of Performance Notes in this psalter are a revision of sections of Performance Notes prepared by the SCCM in *The Hymnal 1982.*

It would be impossible to adequately express appreciation to all who have helped in the preparation of this edition of the *Plainsong Psalter.* The many members and consultants of the Standing Commission on Church Music during the past eighteen years have generously contributed time and talent so that all of us can sing liturgical songs and hymns with "spirit and understanding."

In addition to those mentioned above who have provided practical experience in singing the psalms, deepest appreciation must be expressed to many friends and colleagues who have helped in countless ways to make this psalter possible. First of all I am grateful to Elizabeth Downie, the current Chair of the SCCM (1988) for her keen interest, support, patience and thorough knowledge of liturgical song. I am also grateful to her for her contribution to the Performance Notes in *The Hymnal 1982.*

During the many years that I had the honor of serving on various committees and subcommittees of the Standing Commission on Church Music and the Standing Liturgical Commission which dealt with liturgical song, liturgical texts, and especially the psalms, I learned a great deal from the scholars, clergy and musicians who served with distinction on those committees. Canon Charles

Mortimer Guilbert, Dr. Alec Wyton, Dr. Marion Hatchett, Dr. Raymond Glover, The Rev. Sherrod Albritton, Mr. Mason Martens and the late Rev. Leo Malania have all served on these many committees during the past fifteen years and have provided instruction, inspiration and helpful advice. During my last several years at Trinity Church in Princeton the late Dr. Erik Routley often was among those in the congregation who sang psalms. His delight in the opportunity to join the singing and his many helpful suggestions after each service will long be remembered with gratitude.

Much work on pointing the psalms for this psalter was accomplished during summer teaching sessions at The University of the South in Sewanee, Tennessee and at the Royal School of Church Music in England. I am grateful to these institutions for the use of their libraries and the cheerful assistance provided by the library staff of both institutions during the many hours of research and study. I am especially grateful to Dr. Lionel Dakers, the Director of the Royal School of Church Music for access to that institution's extensive collection of nineteenth and early twentieth century psalters.

Frank Hemlin and the entire staff of The Church Hymnal Corporation have provided detailed and able assistance in the preparation of all parts of this edition. Most of all I must thank them for their patience when the demands on the time of a practical musician and teacher strained proofreading and publication deadlines.

Shirley Hill was always available to type manuscripts—even at the last minute, and I also deeply appreciate her able help in checking final details of the pointing of the psalms.

I would be remiss not to have mentioned Dr. Allan Wicks, who awakened my interest in the singing of psalms during the daily round of Matins and Evensong week after week and month by month so many years ago in Canterbury Cathedral.

Finally, I must not neglect to express deepest thanks to my wife and family who suffered through many a late night of the drone of plainsong psalms drifting through our home from my study corner as I sought a solution to a particularly difficult pointing problem. I am especially appreciative for those moments when they joined in the psalm singing and helped solve many of those pointing problems.

James Litton
Eastertide, 1988

Introduction

Singing Psalms in Christian Worship

An important aspect of liturgical renewal has been the increased use of psalmody in our worship. The Psalter is the "liturgical hymnal of the people of God, of the Old Covenant first, but also of the New Covenant—the Christian Church."[1] It "has been shaped and molded, and its interpretation enriched, by long liturgical use, in temple, synagogue, and church, so that it emerges as a body of praise and prayer suited to the varying but recurrent needs and aspirations of the worshipping community."[2]

The Psalter, an anthology of religious verse, was the hymn book of the Second Temple, collected and edited to meet the liturgical requirements of the Temple liturgy.

In the oldest form of the daily offices the psalms were selected according to the time of day and/or the season of the liturgical year as they were used in temple and synagogue worship. In later monastic communities the entire psalter was sung within a specific period of time—daily, weekly, or fortnightly. In the 1549 *Book of Common Prayer,* Cranmer assigned the psalms to a monthly recitation with proper psalms for Christmas, Easter, Ascension, and Whitsunday. Later revisions of the prayer book added additional proper seasonal psalms.

In the 1979 *Book of Common Prayer* the Psalter is given a seven week pattern of recitation in the daily offices except for the weeks before and after Christmas Day, for Holy Week and for the week following Easter Day. Special attention has been given to include appropriate psalms for the time of day, the day of the week, and the season of the liturgical year. Alternatively, the prayer book also provides for the traditional anglican cycle of monthly recitation of the psalms.

Psalms have been sung in the Eucharist since at least the fourth century—during the Entrance Rite, as an introit; following readings; at the Offertory, and during the Communion. The normal practice in the Eucharist has been to sing psalms responsorially as opposed to the antiphonal or direct psalmody in the daily offices. An appropriate selection of psalms or selected verses of psalms from *The Plainsong Psalter* used in conjunction with the *Gradual Psalms* (Church Hymnal Corporation) provides a complete proper Eucharistic psalmody—Introit, Gradual, Offertory, and Communion.

The psalter, included in every prayer book of the Anglican Communion from 1549 to 1928 was based on the translation by Miles Coverdale for the Great Bible of 1539–1541. Coverdale translated the psalms in 1535. His translation was not based on the original Hebrew but upon the Latin translation of the Greek translation from the Hebrew. "The psalter of the Great Bible was, in other words, a translation from a Latin translation of a Greek translation of a Hebrew original."[3] In addition, Coverdale had reference to Luther's German translation of 1524, an English translation by Tyndale of a 1528 Latin translation of the Old Testament, and the Zürich Bible of 1529.

The current Prayer Book Psalter is in the "spirit of Coverdale" and is a more complete revision of that begun in the 1928 American prayer book. Although the vocabulary has been restricted to that used by Coverdale, this translation is the result of a more detailed "re-examination of the Hebrew text in the light of recent scholarship."[4] "Obsolete and archaic words have been removed and inaccurate renderings emended, but the rhythmic expression which characterized Coverdale's work has been carefully preserved."[5]

For a complete history and description of the liturgical psalter and of the 1979 Prayer Book translation, one is urged to study the introduction by Charles Mortimer Guilbert to *The Psalter—A New Version for Public Worship and Private Devotion.* (The Seabury Press—New York, 1978)

The plainsong psalm tones are among the oldest music of the Christian Church and certain forms of some can be traced to the liturgical music of the synagogue. The Latin translation of the psalms has been sung to these tones from earliest centuries of the Christian Church. Following the publication of the 1549 *Book of Common Prayer* very little plainsong survived in the English liturgy with the exception of remnants of liturgical song used by Merbecke in *The Book of Common Prayer Noted* (1550). In addition, the eight psalm tones continued to be sung in some form with the English prayer book psalter well into the eighteenth century. In some places the psalm tones were sung in harmonized versions, and these four-part settings became the basis of Anglican Chant. As Anglican Chant developed and came to be accepted as the norm for singing the psalms, especially in cathedrals, the Chapel Royal and collegiate chapels, the psalm tones came to be rarely used until revived in the mid-nineteenth century.

During the 1840s there were several attempts to revive the practice of singing the psalms in English to the eight traditional psalm tones, but it was Thomas Helmore who provided the first influential and widely used English plainsong psalter, *The Psalter Noted* of 1849. This was followed by *The Canticles Noted*. After 1850 both collections were published together as *A Manual of Plainsong*.

Helmore's edition was the result of many years of singing the plainsong psalms in the daily offices at St. Mark's College, Chelsea in London. Even though *A Manual of Plainsong* became the definitive English psalter for over fifty years, many other plainsong psalters appeared during the last three decades of the nineteenth century and well into the early twentieth century. The revival of singing the psalms to the psalm tones, however, took place mainly in parish churches while cathedrals and collegiate chapels held on to the practice of singing the psalms with Anglican chant.

A Manual of Plainsong was revised and re-edited by H.B. Briggs and W.H. Frere in 1902 and has continued to be used throughout this century. In North America this edition influenced both Canon Charles Winfred Douglas' *The Plainsong Psalter*, 1932 and Healey Willan's edition of *The Canadian Psalter*—Plainsong Edition, 1963. For a complete study of the revival of singing the psalms to the psalm tones, readers are referred to *The Choral Revival in the Anglican Church* by Barnarr Rainbow, London 1970 and *The Hymnal 1982 Companion*.

Notes

1 Charles Mortimer Guilbert, *The Psalter, A New Version for Public Worship and Private Devotion* (New York, 1978), Introduction, p. VI.

2 *Ibid.*, Introduction, p. VI and VII.

3 Marion J. Hatchett, *Commentary on the American Prayer Book* (New York, 1980), p. 551.

4 *Ibid.*, p. 551

5 *Ibid.*, p. 551

Concerning the Psalter

The Psalter is a body of liturgical poetry. It is designed for vocal, congregational use, whether by singing or reading. There are several traditional methods of psalmody. The exclusive use of a single method makes the recitation of the Psalter needlessly monotonous. The traditional methods, each of which can be elaborate or simple, are the following:

Direct recitation denotes the singing or reading of a whole psalm, or portion of a psalm, sung or read together by the entire congregation. It is particularly appropriate for the psalm verses suggested in the lectionary for use between the Lessons at the Eucharist, when the verses are recited rather than sung, and may often be found a satisfactory method of chanting them.

Antiphonal singing or recitation is the verse-by-verse alternation between groups of singers or readers; e.g., between choir and congregation, or between one side of the congregation and the other. The alternate recitation concludes with the Gloria Patri, or with a refrain (called the antiphon) sung or recited by all. This is probably the most satisfying method for singing or reciting the psalms in the Daily Office.

Responsorial singing or recitation is the name given to a method of psalmody in which the verses of a psalm are sung by a solo voice, with the choir and the congregation singing a refrain or antiphon after each verse or group of verses. This was the traditional method of singing the Venite and other Invitatory Psalms. The restoration of Invitatory Antiphons for the Venite and Jubilate Deo makes possible a recovery of this form of sacred song in the Daily Office. It was also a traditional manner of chanting the psalms between the Lessons at the Eucharist (especially after the Old Testament Reading.) It is a method of psalmody increasingly favored by modern composers.

The version of the Psalms which follows is set out in lines of Poetry. The lines correspond to Hebrew versification, which is not based on meter or rhyme, but on parallelism of clauses, a symmetry of form and sense. The parallelism can take the form of similarity (The waters have lifted up, O Lord/the waters have lifted up their voice;/the waters have lifted up their pounding waves. *Psalm 93:4*), or of contrast (The Lord knows the ways of the righteous;/but the way of the wicked is doomed. *Psalm 1:6*) or of logical expansion (Our eyes look to the Lord our God,/until he show us his mercy. *Psalm 123:3*).

The most common verse is a couplet, but triplets are very frequent, and quatrains are not unknown; although quatrains are usually distributed over two verses. An asterisk divides each verse into two parts for singing or reading. A distinct pause should be made at the asterisk.

Three terms are used in the Psalms with the reference to God: *Elohim* ("God"), *Adonai* ("Lord") and the personal name YHWH. The "Four-letter Name" (Tetragrammaton) is probably to be vocalized Yahweh; but this is by no means certain, because from very ancient times it has been considered too sacred to be pronounced; and, whenever it occurred, *Adonai* was substituted for it. In the oldest manuscripts, the Divine Name was written in antique and obsolete letters; in more recent manuscripts and in printed Bibles, after the invention of vowel points, the Name was provided with the vowels of the word *Adonai*. This produced a hybrid form which has been translated "Jehovah."

The Hebrew reverence and reticence with regard to the Name of God has been carried over into the classical English versions, the Prayer Book Psalter and the King James Old Testament, where it is regularly rendered "Lord." In order to distinguish it, however, from "Lord" as a translation of *Adonai*, YHWH is represented in capital and small capital letters: LORD.

From time to time, the Hebrew text has Adonai and YHWH in conjunction. Then, the Hebrew custom is to substitute Elohim for YHWH, and our English tradition follows suit, rendering the combined title as "Lord God."

In two passages (Psalm 68:4 and Psalm 83:18) the context requires that the Divine Name be spelled out, and it appears as YAHWEH. A similar construction occurs in the Canticle, "The Song of Moses."

The ancient praise-shout, "Hallelujah," has been restored, in place of its English equivalent, "Praise the Lord." The Hebrew form has been used, rather than the Latin form "Alleluia," as being more appropriate to this context; but also to regain for our liturgy a form of the word that is familiar from its use in many well-known anthems. The word may, if desired, be omitted during the season of Lent.

Performance Notes

Singing the Chant

Good chanting is good singing. Chant is a musical medium for the clear and expressive singing of the psalms. Word accents create the rhythm in chant, and the lines and verses of the text determine the shape of the chant's musical phrase. Single-line melodic chant (Plainsong) should be sung as song, whether lyrical or declamatory, as the words require.

When singing plainsong, special attention must be paid to the words sung to the reciting note. The recitation must not be rushed and is governed by the rhythm and flow of the words. Mediant cadences (the musical change at mid-point) and final endings or cadences should never slow down or speed up. This results in a false metrical emphasis which distorts the natural word accents and rhythm of the phrase. The established and recurring tempo of the recitation remains the same throughout the psalm tone, including the intonation, reciting notes, the mediant and final cadences. On the other hand, the text is not to be sung with a mechanical, unbending pulse. Certain words will be gently moved along; others will be slightly stressed or prolonged. Care is to be taken, however, not to sing the text with unnatural dotted rhythms.

Unaccented words or syllables at the beginning of lines should be treated in an anacrustic manner, moving directly to the first primary accent in the line. In general, accents should be created by lengthening the word or syllable (agogic accent) rather than by a sudden dynamic stress. Tempo and dynamics are to be determined by the meaning of the text, the number of singers, and the size and resonance of the space where the psalms are being sung.

If singers read the text in an expressive but not exaggerated manner, and then sing the words to the chant with the same rhythmic flow, they will discover how plainsong can unify the Christian community's singing of the psalms.

Notation

Plainsong is essentially melody heightening a text. The notation used in this book is intended to facilitate congregational participation.

Some notational symbols are peculiar to chant:

1. Noteheads without stems indicate pitch; the word accent determines duration, the white or open noteheads used at the ends of phrases (and occasionally elsewhere) are longer, approximately twice the lenth of black noteheads.

2. A lozenge or rectangular note symbol indicates a reciting note. The number of words and syllables and the natural word rhythm in the recitation determines its duration.

3. Notes slurred together indicate one syllable sung to two or more notes:

Al - le - lu - ia,

or:

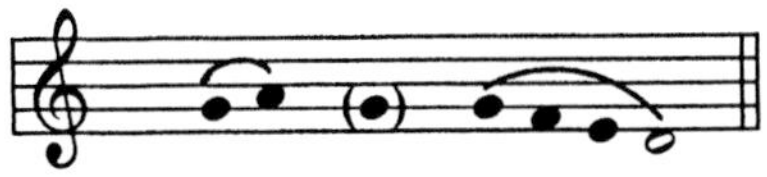

...for - ev - er.

Psalm Tones

A Psalm Tone has five parts, as shown in this example:

Tone VI

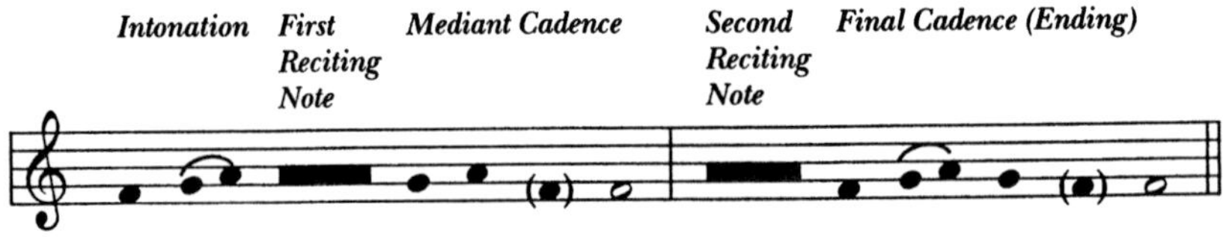
Intonation
First Reciting Note
Mediant Cadence
Second Reciting Note
Final Cadence (Ending)

The *Intonation* is sung to the first two syllables or first two single syllable words of the first verse of the psalm following the antiphon. It is indicated in the text by italics. Successive verses of the psalm begin on the first reciting note unless the antiphon is sung after certain verses in the course of the psalm. The intonation is always sung to the first two syllables of a verse following the singing of the antiphon.

The *First Reciting Note* is used for all words and syllables of the first half of the psalm verse which are not sung to the intonation or to the mediant cadence.

The *Mediant Cadence* is sung before the asterisk in the psalm text, and consists of one or two accented syllables and one, two or three preparatory syllables. Accent marks in the psalm text (´) correspond to accent marks under the notes in the psalm tone (´). The notes in parenthesis are used only when needed. Preparatory syllables follow the diagonal bar (/) in the text; they are sung to the notes following the diagonal bar under the notes of the psalm tone.

In a few cases, the first half of the verse ends with an accented syllable. In many cases this should be sung to the final accented note in the first half of the psalm tone, omitting the note in parenthesis and the last note of the mediant cadence. (When this happens, it is considered an abrupt mediation.)

In some psalm tones, two (and in some cases, three or four) notes are slurred together. These should never be divided between two syllables. Words or syllables requiring two or more notes are indicated by dots over the syllables in the pointed text [e.g., set upón your thrö̈ne (for Psalm Tone Id)].

The *Second Reciting Note* is used like the first, and the *Final Cadence* is used like the *Mediant Cadence.* The remainder of the psalm verse following the asterisk is sung to the *Second Reciting Note* and to the *Final Cadence* or Ending.

In a few cases in some psalms, due to the shortness of the half verse, the Intonation or the Reciting Note is omitted. This is indicated in the pointed text by the use of a dash (—) (e.g., O Lord—God of hosts).

In some cases, it has not been possible to align the real accents of the English texts with the accented notes of the Psalm Tone. The accent mark over the syllable in the pointed psalm text always indicates that such a syllable is sung to the accented note of the Psalm Tone.

Antiphons

In accordance with the rubrical suggestions on pages 141 and 935 of *The Book of Common Prayer*, the *Plainsong Psalter* provides general and seasonal antiphons for use with each psalm. Only one antiphon is used with a given psalm on any particular occasion. During the "green seasons" of the year, and at other times when antiphons of "ordinary time" are appointed, the reference is to the antiphon indicated "on other Sundays and Weekdays" or "Antiphon" provided for each psalm.

The usual practice is to have the entire appointed antiphon sung before the first verse of the psalm. The verses of the psalm are then sung full, by all, or antiphonally—verse by verse, from side to side, between women's and men's voices or between congregation and choir (or cantors). The psalm verses may also be sung by cantor, cantors or choir. The antiphon is repeated by all at the end of the psalm or after the Gloria Patri, when it is used. The antiphon is never sung both after the last verse of the psalm and also after the Gloria Patri. There are times when it may be desirable to sing a psalm responsorially, as at the Gradual in the Eucharist: the verses being sung by a cantor or a small group, and the antiphon sung by the congregation after each group of verses.

The antiphons should be sung in a natural, flowing manner, without strong accents or change of pace. They can be sung faster or slower, somewhat louder or softer in accordance with the text, the season, or the occasion. Many antiphons can be sung as one phrase without stopping for a breath. Others have a natural division, marked in the music by a quarter, half or whole bar, where a breath may be taken. Antiphons should be sung immediately after the psalm verses without hesitation.

Choosing a comfortable pitch for cantors, choir and congregation is very important. In the *Plainsong Psalter* antiphons and psalm tones often have been transposed into a comfortable range, but, in some situations, additional transposition might be necessary.

Antiphon Texts

Ordinarily the text of the antiphon is taken from a verse of the psalm, and serves to underscore the basic theme of the psalm or the reason it has been chosen for the particular occasion. Some historic antiphons, however, are taken from other parts of Scripture. Those for the season of Advent, for example, are frequently taken from the writings of the Prophets. Still other classic antiphons are non-scriptural. To have rejected these would have been a considerable impoverishment, since the majority of them draw upon recognizable biblical imagery and are frequently of great beauty. In choosing antiphons of this kind from the ancient repertory, care has been taken to see that they conform to the Prayer Book requirment for "anthems," namely, that they are congruent with the teaching of Holy Scripture.

On some occasions the first verse or first line of a psalm is used as the antiphon. In such cases (see, for example, Psalm 81) the text of the antiphon is followed by the symbol (†). This serves to indicate that the singing of the psalm is to begin, not at the first verse, but at the point indicated by the corresponding symbol (†) in the left margin.

Antiphons in Easter Season

In keeping with ancient western tradition, alleluiatic antiphons are appointed for the psalms during the fifty days of Easter. In some instances, this is simply the antiphon used at other times with Hallelujah added. More frequently, a proper antiphon is provided. The only exceptions are a few psalms whose nature is such that the use of Hallelujah would be incongruous.

Music for the Antiphons

Proper plainsong antiphon melodies, especially the ancient graduals, are usually extremely ornate, and unsuitable for typical modern parish use. In searching for a practical congregational psalmody, the simpler, less elaborate plainsong melodies provide an answer to the quest for easily learned liturgical song. Such melodies have been preserved from ancient times, mainly in music for the offices (Matins, Lauds, Vespers, etc.) and not for the Holy Eucharist, and in the style of antiphonal psalmody, not responsorial psalmody. The antiphon melodies used in the *Plainsong Psalter* are, therefore, most appropriately sung with the psalmody in the daily offices, but they may also be used to enlarge the repertory of Gradual Psalms in the Holy Eucharist.

The daily office antiphon melodies represent one of the most ancient traditions of Christian musical experience in a compact and accessible form. This repertory of office antiphons (dating from the period circa A.D. 400–700), which is used as the source of the antiphons in the *Plainsong Psalter,* consists of melodies that are used again and again throughout the Latin offices and for many different texts. This fact indicates that these melodies are a broad and deep foundation of Christian song. These priceless jewels of pure melody, many so short as to be sung in a single breath, are easily adaptable for modern English liturgical translations.

Possible Accompaniments

Traditionally plainsong has been sung without accompaniment, and in a favorable acoustical environment, such singing is very beautiful and is to be encouraged. When an instrumental accompaniment is felt to be necessary, the simplest keyboard solution is to play the plainsong melody in octaves. This is also an effective way to teach antiphons to a congregation.

Bell ringing is an excellent support for singing plainsong. Handbells may be used in various ways to accompany the singing of psalms:

1. Cluster chords may be rung at the mediant and/or final cadences of each psalm verse.
2. An ostinato pattern may be rung throughout the singing of the antiphon and/or verses of the psalm. The pattern should be rung freely, making no attempt to synchronize with special points in the antiphon melody or psalm tone.
3. Bells may be rung at random during the singing, creating a spontaneous accompaniment. Ringers must be sensitive to the overall sound; the bell sonorities should not dominate. Intervals of the fourth, fifth, octave, and major second provide the most satisfactory bell accompaniments for plainsong psalms.

The pitch and tempo of the antiphon and psalm tone may be introduced by bells or other instrument(s) in a brief intonation.

The Congregation, Cantors and Choir

The psalms are to be sung by the entire community—congregation, cantor(s) and choir. In many situations it will be best to have antiphon and psalm verses sung full by all. At other times and in other places it will be desirable to alternate the singing between solo voices (cantors), choir, and congregation.

Many parishes have rediscovered the important role of cantors in the singing of liturgical song, and especially in other singing of the psalms. A cantor may introduce the singing of the antiphon, which is then repeated by all—congregation and choir. In some places, and during certain times of the year, it may be preferable to have the psalm verses sung by a single cantor, or by a small group of cantors. This is an ideal manner of teaching the singing of psalms. When all have heard the psalm verses sung by a single cantor or small group, it will become easier for the entire congregation to join in singing the verses of familiar and more frequently used psalms.

The psalms and antiphons have been sung by the Church for many centuries, and it is hoped that this music will continue to be sung for years to come.

Gloria Patri

In the daily offices Gloria Patri is always sung at the conclusion of the entire portion of the Psalter; and may be used after each psalm, and after each section of Psalm 119. The antiphon is sung after the Gloria Patri.

Listed below is a chart of the Gloria Patri set to each psalm tone. The chart includes one ending for each tone. Different endings can be pointed based on the examples given in the chart.

Tone 1

Glory to the Fa - ther, and to the Son, and to the Ho - ly Spi - rit:

As it was in the be - gin - ning, is now, and will be for ev - er. A - men.

Tone 2

Glory to the Father, and to the Son, and to the Ho - ly Spi - rit:

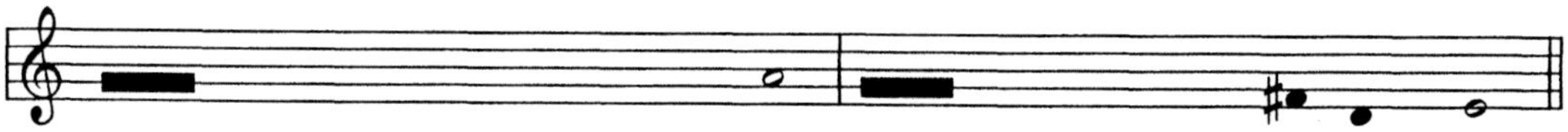

As it was in the beginning, is now, and will be for ev - er. A - men.

Tone 3

Glory to the Fa - ther, and to the Son, and to the Ho - ly Spi - rit:

As it was in the be - gin - ning, is now, and will be for ev - er. A - men.

Tone 4

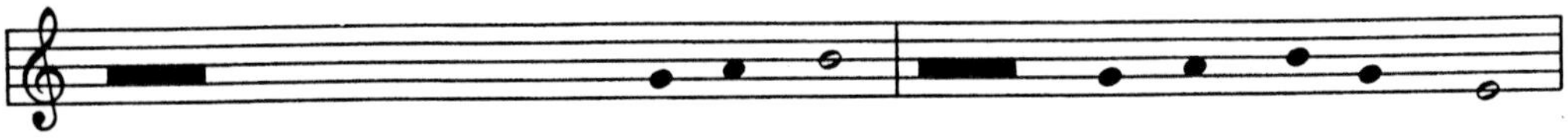

Glory to the Father, and to the Son, and to the Ho - ly Spi - rit:

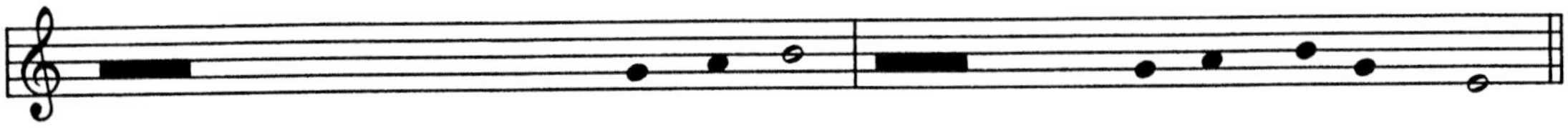

As it was in the begin - ning, is now, and will be for ev - er. A - men.

Tone 5

Glory to the Father, and to the Son, and to the Ho - ly Spi - rit:

As it was in the beginning, is now, and will be for ev - er. A - men.

Tone 6

Glory to the Fa - ther, and to the Son, and to the Ho - ly Spi - rit:

or

Glory to the Father, and to the Son, and to the Ho - ly Spi - rit:

As it was in the be - gin - ning, is now, and will be for ev - er. A - men.

or

As it was in the begin - ning, is now, and will be for ev - er. A - men.

Tone 7

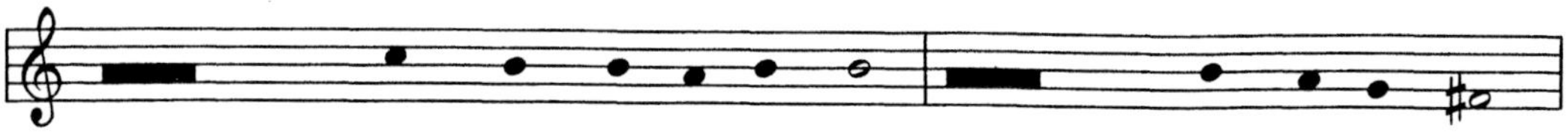

Glory to the Fa - ther, and to the Son, and to the Ho - ly Spi - rit:

As it was in the be - gin - ning, is now, and will be for ev - er. A - men.

Tone 8

Glory to the Father, and to the Son, and to the Ho - ly Spi - rit:

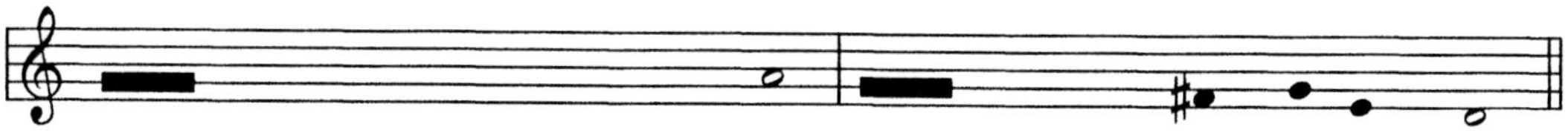

As it was in the beginning, is now, and will be for ev - er. A - men.

Tonus Peregrinus

Glory to the Fa - ther, and to the Son, and to the Ho - ly Spi - rit:

As it was in the be - gin - ning, is now, and will be for ev - er. A - men.

The Plainsong Psalter

1

In Easter Season

The LORD knows the way of the righ - teous, hal - le - lu - jah.

On other Sundays and Weekdays

Hap - py are they whose de - light is in the law of the LORD.

Psalm 1 *Beatus vir qui non abiit* *Tone V.1*

1 *Happy* are they who have not walked in the counsel of the wicked, *
nor lingered in the way of sinners,
nor sat in the seats of the scornful!

2 Their delight is in the law of the LORD, *
and they meditate on his law day and night.

3 They are like trees planted by streams of water,
bearing fruit in due season, with leaves that do not wither; *
everything they do shall prosper.

4 It is not so with the wicked; *
they are like chaff which the wind blows away.

5 Therefore the wicked shall not stand upright when judgment comes, *
nor the sinner in the council of the righteous.

6 For the LORD knows the way of the righteous, *
but the way of the wicked is doomed. *[Ant.]*

On the Twelve Days of Christmas

You are my Son; this day have I be - got - ten you.

In Easter Season

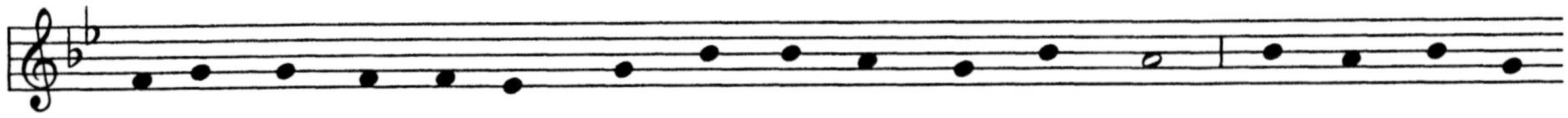

I will give you the na - tions for your in - her - i - tance, and the ends of

the earth for your pos - ses - sion, hal - le - lu - jah.

On other Sundays and Weekdays

I my - self have set my king up - on my ho - ly hill of Zi - on.

Psalm 2 *Quare fremuerunt gentes?* *Tone VIII.1*

1 *Why are* the nations in an uproar? *
  Why do the peoples / mutter empty threats?

2 Why do the kings of the earth rise up in revolt,
and the princes plot together, *
  against the LORD and against / his Anointed?

3 "Let us break their yoke," they say; *
  "let us cast / off their bonds from us."

4 He whose throne is in heaven is laughing; *
  the Lord has them / in derision.

5 Then he speaks to them in his wrath, *
  and his rage fills / them with terror.

6 "I myself have sét my king *
upon my holy / hill of Źion."

7 Let me announce the decree of the LÓRD: *
he said to me, "You are my Son;
this day have / I begótten you.

8 Ask of me, and I will give you the nations for your inhéritance *
and the ends of the earth for / your possésion.

9 You shall crush them with an irón rod *
and shatter them like a / piece of póttery."

10 And now, you kíngs, be wise; *
be warned, you / rulers óf the earth.

11 Submit to the LÓRD with fear, *
and with trembling / bow befóre him;

12 Lest he be angry and you pérish; *
for his wrath is / quickly kíndled.

13 Happy are they áll *
who take / refuge ín him! *[Ant.]*

3

In Easter Season

De - liv - erance be - longs to the LORD, hal - le - lu - jah.

On other Sundays and Weekdays

You, O LORD, are a shield a - bout me; you are the one who

lifts up my head.

Psalm 3 *Domine, quid multiplicati* *Tone II.1*

1 *LORD, how* many adversaries I have! *
how many there are who rise up / against me!

2 How many there are who say of me, *
"There is no help for him / in his God."

3 But you, O LORD, are a shield about me; *
you are my glory, the one who lifts / up my head.

4 I call aloud upon the LORD, *
and he answers me from / his holy hill;

5 I lie down and go to sleep; *
I wake again, because the LORD / sustains me.

6 I do not fear the multitudes of people *
who set themselves against / me all around.

7 Rise up, O LORD; set me free, O my God; *
surely, you will strike all my enemies across the face,
you will break the teeth of / the wicked.

8 Deliverance belongs to the LORD. *
Your blessing be upon / your people! *[Ant.]*

4

In Easter Season

You have put glad - ness in my heart, O LORD; hal - le - lu - jah.

On other Sundays and Weekdays

Have mer - cy on me, O LORD, and hear my prayer.

Psalm 4 *Cum invocarem* *Tone IV.1*

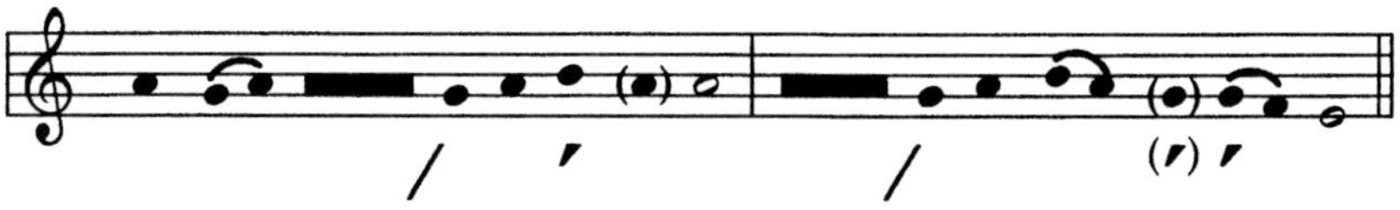

1 *Answer* me when I call, O God, defender / of my cause; *
you set me free when I am hard-pressed;
have mercy on / me and hear my prayer.

2 "You mortals, how long will you disho/nor my glory; *
how long will you worship dumb idols
/ and run after false gods?"

3 Know that the LORD does wonders / for the faithful; *
when I call upon the / LORD, he will hear me.

4 Tremble, then, and / do not sin; *
speak to your heart in / silence upon your bed.

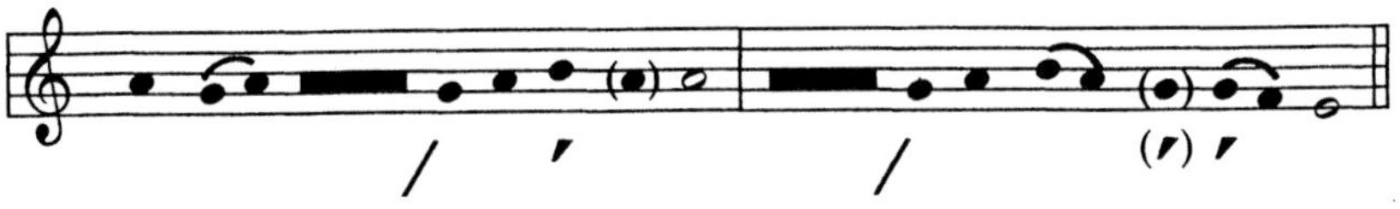

5 Offer the appointed / sacrifices *
and / put your trust in the LORD.

6 Many are saying,
"Oh, that we / might see better times!" *
Lift up the light of your counte/nance upon us, O LORD.

7 You have put gladness / in my heart, *
more than when grain and / wine and oil increase.

8 I lie down in peace; at once I / fall asleep; *
for only you, LORD, / make me dwell in safety. *[Ant.]*

5

In Easter Season

Those who love your Name will ex - ult in you, hal - le - lu - jah.

On other Sundays and Weekdays

I make my mor - ning prayer to you; for you, O LORD, will hear my voice.

Psalm 5 *Verba mea auribus* *Tone VI*

1 *Give ear* to / my words, O LORD; *
consider my / meditation.

2 Hearken to my cry for help, my King / and my God, *
for I / make my prayer to you.

3 In the morning, LORD, / you hear my voice; *
early in the morning I make my ap/peal and watch for you.

4 For you are not a God who takes pleasure / in wíckedness, *
and evil / cannöt dwéll with you.

5 Braggarts cannot stand / in yóur sight; *
you hate all those / who wörk wíckedness.

6 You destroy those / who spéak lies; *
the bloodthirsty and deceitful, / O LÖRD, yóu abhor.

7 But as for me, through the greatness of your mercy I
will go in/to yóur house; *
I will bow down toward your holy tem/ple ïn awé of you.

8 Lead me, O LORD, in your righteousness,
because of those who lie / in wáit for me; *
make your way / straight bëfóre me.

9 For there is no / truth ín their mouth; *
there is des/tructiön ín their heart;

10 Their throat is / an ópen grave; *
they / flattër wíth their tongue.

11 Declare them guil/ty, Ó God; *
let them fall, / becaüse óf their schemes.

12 Because of their many transgres/sions cást them out, *
for they have re/belled ägaínst you.

13 But all who take refuge in / you wíll be glad; *
they will sing out their / joy för éver.

14 You / will shélter them, *
so that those who love your Name / may ëxúlt in you.

15 For you, O LORD, will bless / the ríghteous; *
you will defend them with your favor / as wïth á shield. *[Ant.]*

6

In Holy Week

In the time of my trou - ble, I sought the LORD.

In Easter Season

The LORD has heard my sup - pli - ca - tion; the LORD ac - cepts

my prayer, hal - le - lu - jah.

On other Sundays and Weekdays

Save me, O LORD, for your mer - cy's sake.

Psalm 6 *Domine, ne in furore* — *Tone II.1*

1 *LORD, do* not rebuke me in your anger; *
do not punish me / in your wrath.

2 Have pity on me, LORD, for I am weak; *
heal me, LORD, for my / bones are racked.

3 My spirit shakes with terror; *
how long, O / LORD, how long?

4 Turn, O LORD, and deliver me; *
save me for your / mercy's sake.

5 For in death no one remembers you; *
and who will give you thanks / in the grave?

6 I grow weary because of my gróaning; *
every night I drench my bed
and flood my / couch wíth tears.

7 My eyes are wasted with griéf *
and worn away because of all / my énemies.

8 Depart from me, all evildóers, *
for the LORD has heard the sound of / my wéeping.

9 The LORD has heard my supplicátion; *
the LORD ac/cepts mý prayer.

10 All my enemies shall be confounded and quáke with fear; *
they shall turn back and suddenly be / put tó shame. *[Ant.]*

7

In Easter Season

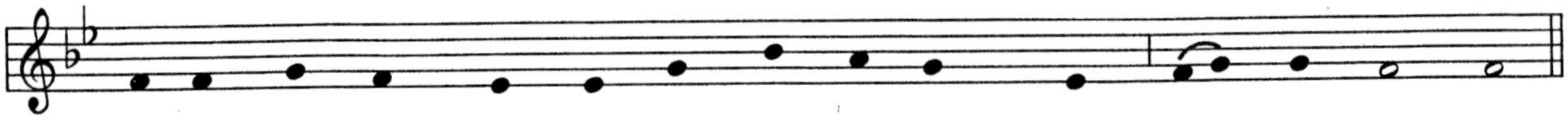

I will bear wit - ness that the LORD is righ - teous, hal - le - lu - jah.

On other Sundays and Weekdays

God is a righ - teous judge; he is the sav - ior of the true at heart.

Psalm 7 *Domine, Deus meus* *Tone VIII.1*

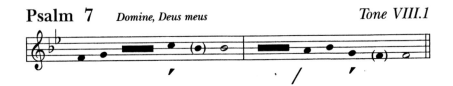

1 *O LORD* my God, I take refuge in you; *
save and deliver me from all / who pursue me;

2 Lest like a lion they tear me in pieces *
and snatch me away with none / to deliver me.

3 O LORD my God, if I have done these things: *
if there is any wicked/ness in my hands,

4 If I have repaid my friend with evil, *
or plundered him who without cause / is my enemy;

5 Then let my enemy pursue and overtake me, *
trample my life into the ground,
and lay my / honor in the dust.

6 Stand up, O LORD, in your wrath; *
rise up against the fury / of my enemies.

7 Awake, O my God, decree justice; *
let the assembly of the peoples / gather round you.

8 Be seated on your lofty throne, O Most High; *
O LORD, / judge the nations.

9 Give judgment for me according to my righteousness, O LÓRD, *
and according to my inno/cence, O Móst High.

10 Let the malice of the wicked come to an end,
but establish the ŕighteous; *
for you test the mind and / heart, O ŕighteous God.

11 God is my shield and defénse; *
he is the savior / of the trúe in heart.

12 God is a ŕighteous judge; *
God sits in / judgment évery day.

13 If they will not repent, God will whét his sword; *
he will bend his bow and / make it réady.

14 He has prepared his weapons of déath; *
he makes his / arrows sháfts of fire.

15 Look at those who are in labor with ẃickedness, *
who conceive evil, and give / birth to á lie.

16 They dig a pit and máke it deep *
and fall into the / hole that théy have made.

17 Their malice turns back upon théir own head; *
their violence / falls on théir own scalp.

18 I will bear witness that the LORD is ŕighteous; *
I will praise the Name / of the LÓRD Most High. *[Ant.]*

8

In Advent

The LORD is at hand; go out and meet him and say: Great is

his do - min - ion, and of his king - dom there shall be no end:

The migh - ty God, the Ru - ler, the Prince of Peace, hal - le - lu - jah.

In Lent

God has put all things un - der his feet, and made him the head of the

Church, which is his bod - y.

In Easter Season

We see Je - sus, who for a lit - tle while was made low - er than

the an - gels, crowned with glo - ry and hon - or, hal - le - lu - jah.

On other Sundays and Weekdays

How ex - alt - ed is your Name, O LORD, in all the world.

Psalm 8 *Domine, Dominus noster* *Tone VII.3*

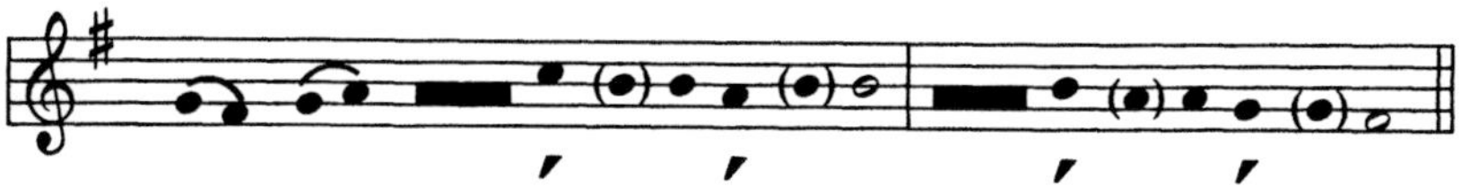

1 —O LÓRD our Góvernor, *
how exalted is your Náme in áll the world!

2 Out of the mouths of ínfants and chíldren *
your majesty is praised abóve the héavens.

3 You have set up a stronghold agaínst your advérsaries, *
to quell the enemy ánd the avénger.

4 When I consider your heavens, the wórk of your fíngers, *
the moon and the stars you have sét in their cóurses,

5 What is man that you should be míndful óf him? *
the son of man that yóu should séek him out?

6 You have made him but little lower thán the ángels; *
you adorn him with glóry and hónor;

7 You give him mastery over the wórks of yóur hands; *
you put all things únder hís feet:

8 All shéep and óxen, *
even the wíld beasts óf the field,

9 The birds of the air, the físh of thé sea, *
and whatsoever walks in the páths of thé sea.

10 O LÓRD our Góvernor, *
how exalted is your Náme in áll the world! *[Ant.]*

9

In Easter Season

I will tell of all your prais - es in the gates of the cit - y of Zi - on,

hal - le - lu - jah.

On other Sundays and Weekdays

The LORD is a ref - uge for the op - pressed; a ref - uge in time

of trou - ble.

Psalm 9 *Confitebor tibi* *Tone I.1*

1 *I will* give thanks to you, O LORD, with my whole heart; *
I will tell of / all your marvelous works.

2 I will be glad and rejoice in you; *
I will sing to your / Name, O Most High.

3 When my enemies are driven back, *
they will stumble and perish / at your presence.

4 For you have maintained my right and my cause; *
you sit upon / your throne judging right.

5 You have rebuked the ungodly and destroyed the wicked; *
you have blotted out their name for / ever and ever.

6 As for the enemy, they are finished, in perpetual ruin, *
their cities plowed under, the me/mory of them perished;

7 But the LORD is enthróned for éver; *
he has set up his / throne for júdgment.

8 It is he who rules the wórld with ríghteousness; *
he judges the peo/ples with équity.

9 The LORD will be a refuge fór the óppressed, *
a refuge in / time of tróuble.

10 Those who know your Name will pút their trúst in you, *
for you never forsake those who / seek you, Ó LORD.

11 Sing praise to the LORD who dwélls in Zíon; *
proclaim to the peoples the / things he hás done.

12 The Avenger of blood wíll remémber them; *
he will not forget the cry of / the afflícted.

13 Have píty on mé, O LORD; *
see the misery I suffer from those who hate me,
O you who lift me up / from the gáte of death;

14 So that I may tell of all your praises
and rejoice in yóur salvátion *
in the gates of the ci/ty of Zíon.

15 The ungodly have fallen intó the pít they dug, *
and in the snare they set is / their own fóot caught.

16 The LORD is known by his ácts of jústice; *
the wicked are trapped in the / works of théir own hands.

17 The wicked shall be given óver tó the grave, *
and also all the peoples / that forgét God.

18 For the needy shall not álways be fórgotten, *
and the hope of the poor shall not / perish fór ever.

19 Rise up, O LORD, let not the ungodly háve the úpper hand; *
let them be / judged befóre you.

20 Put fear upón them, Ó LORD; *
let the ungodly know / they are bút mortal. *[Ant.]*

10

In Easter Season

The LORD will judge the poor with righ - teous - ness, hal - le - lu - jah.

On other Sundays and Weekdays

Sure - ly, O LORD, you be - hold trou - ble and mis - er - y.

Psalm 10 *Ut quid, Domine?* *Tone IV.1*

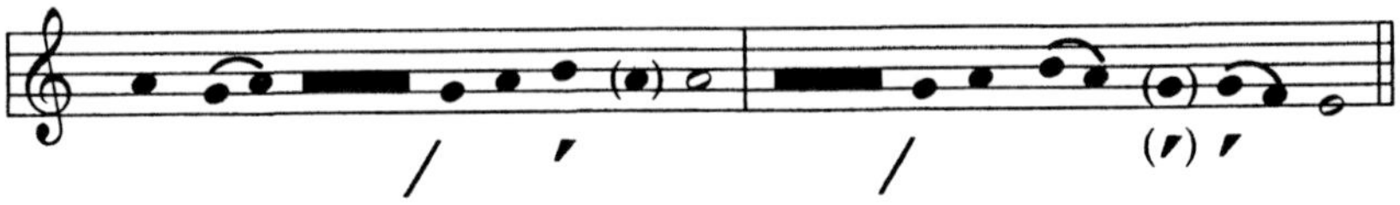

1 *Why do* you stand so / far off, O LORD, *
and hide your/self in time of trouble?

2 The wicked arrogantly perse/cute the poor, *
but they are trapped in the / schemes they have devised.

3 The wicked boast of their / heart's desire; *
the covetous / curse and revile the LORD.

4 The wicked are so proud that / they care not for God; *
their only thought is, / "God does not matter."

5 Their ways are devious at all times;
your judgments are far above / out of their sight; *
they defy / all their enemies.

6 They say in their heart, "I shall / not be shaken; *
no harm shall / happen to me ever."

7 Their mouth is full of cursing, deceit, / and oppression; *
under their / tongue are mischief and wrong.

8 They lurk in ambush in public squares
and in secret places they mur/der the innocent; *
they / spy out the helpless.

9 They lie in wait, like a lion in a covert;
they lie in wait to seize up/on the lówly; *
they seize the lowly and drag / them awäy in theïr net.

10 The innocent are broken and hum/bled befóre them; *
the helpless / fall befö̈re their pöwer.

11 They say in their heart, "God / has forgótten; *
he hides his face; / he will nëver nötice."

12 Rise up, O LORD;
lift / up your hánd, O God; *
do not / forget thë afflïcted.

13 Why should the wick/ed revíle God? *
why should they say in / their heart, "Yöu do nöt care"?

14 Surely, you behold trou/ble and mísery; *
you see it and take it / into yöur öwn hand.

15 The helpless com/mit themsélves to you, *
for you are the / helper öf örphans.

16 Break the power of the wick/ed and évil; *
search out their wickedness / until yöu fïnd none.

17 The LORD is King for ev/er and éver; *
the ungodly shall / perish frö̈m hïs land.

18 The LORD will hear the desire / of the húmble; *
you will strengthen their heart / and your eärs shäll hear;

19 To give justice to the / orphan ánd oppressed, *
so that mere mortals / may strike tërror nö more. *[Ant.]*

11

In Easter Season

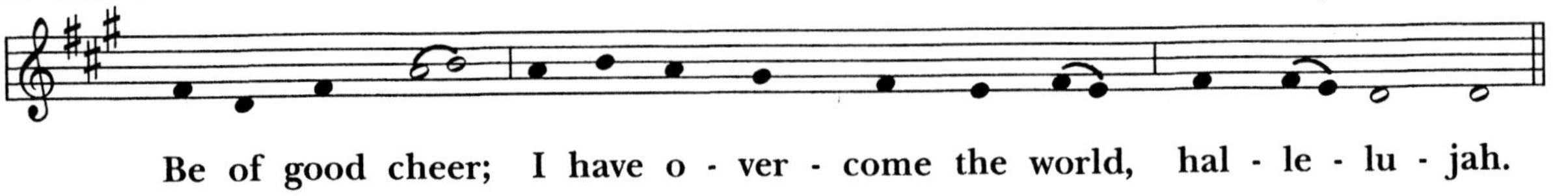
Be of good cheer; I have o - ver - come the world, hal - le - lu - jah.

On other Sundays and Weekdays

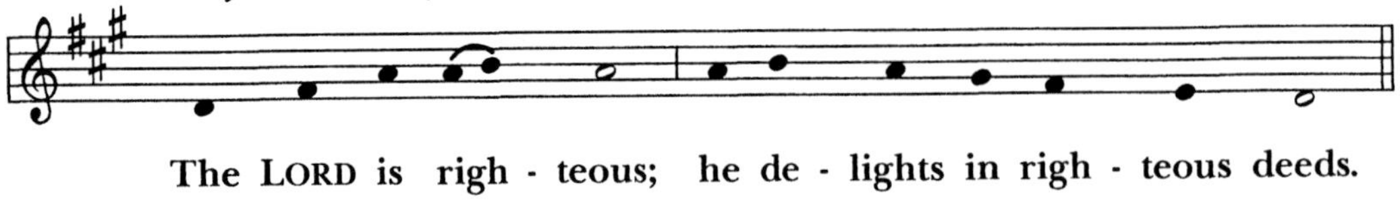
The LORD is righ - teous; he de - lights in righ - teous deeds.

Psalm 11 *In Domino confido*

Tone V.1

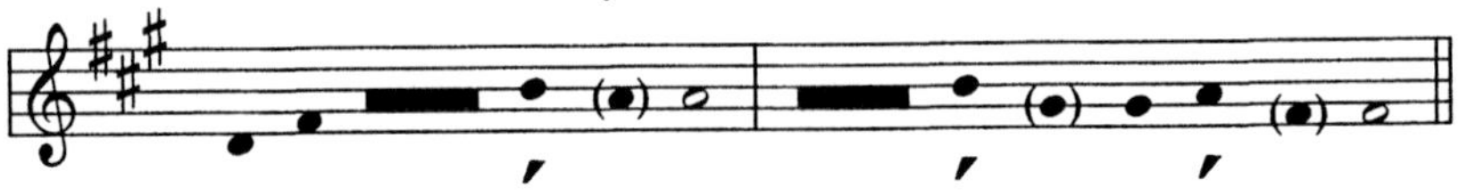

1 *In the* LORD have I taken refuge; *
how then can you say to me,
"Fly away like a bird to the hilltop;

2 For see how the wicked bend the bow
and fit their arrows to the string, *
to shoot from ambush at the true of heart.

3 When the foundations are being destroyed, *
what can the righteous do?"

4 The LORD is in his holy temple; *
the LORD's throne is in heaven.

5 His eyes behold the inhabited world; *
his piercing eye weighs our worth.

6 The LORD weighs the righteous as well as the wicked, *
but those who delight in violence he abhors.

7 Upon the wicked he shall rain coals of fire and burning sulphur; *
a scorching wind shall be their lot.

8 For the LORD is righteous;
he delights in righteous deeds; *
and the just shall see his face. *[Ant.]*

12

In Holy Week

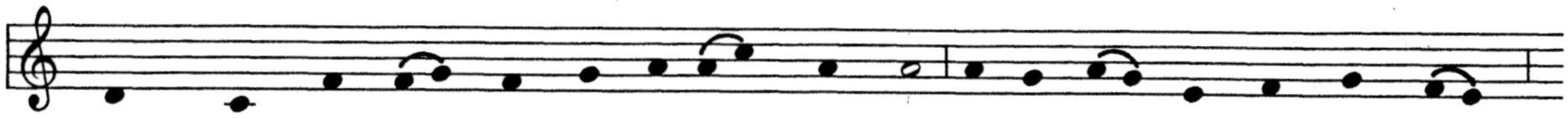

Be - cause the poor cry out in mis - er - y, I will rise up, says the LORD,

and give them the help they long for.

In Easter Season

The words of the LORD are pure words, hal - le - lu - jah.

On other Sundays and Weekdays

The words of the LORD are pure words, like sil - ver re - fined from ore.

Psalm 12 *Salvum me fac* *Tone I.2*

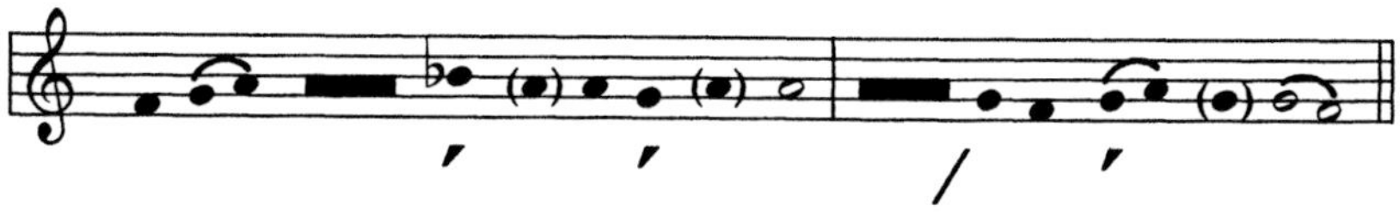

1 *Help më,* LORD, for there is no gódly óne left; *
the faithful have vanished / from amóng üs.

2 Everyone speaks falsely wíth his néighbor; *
with a smooth tongue they speak / from a dóuble hëart.

3 Oh, that the LORD would cút off all smóoth tongues, *
and close the lips that / utter próud böasts!

4 Those who say, "With our tongue wíll we prévail; *
our lips are our own; who / is lord ´över üs?"

5 "Because the needy are oppressed,
and the poor cry óut in mísery, *
I will rise up," says the LORD
"and give them the / help they lóng för."

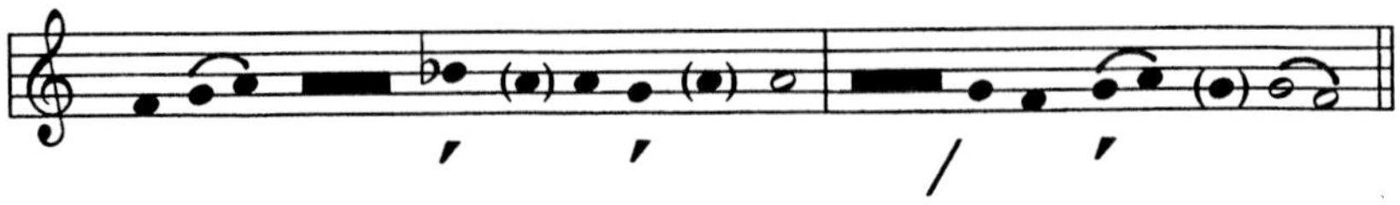

6 The words of the LORD are pure words, *
like silver refined from ore
and purified seven / times in the fire.

7 O LORD, watch over us *
and save us from this gene/ration for ever.

8 The wicked prowl on every side, *
and that which is worthless is highly / prized by everyone. *[Ant.]*

13

In Easter Season

My heart is joy - ful be - cause of your sav - ing help, hal - le - lu - jah.

On other Sundays and Weekdays

I will put my trust in your mer - cy.

Psalm 13 *Usquequo, Domine?* *Tone VI*

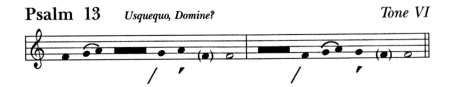

1 *How long,* O LORD?
will you forget me / for ever? *
how long will you / hide your face from me?

2 How long shall I have perplexity in my mind,
and grief in my heart, / day after day? *
how long shall my enemy / triumph over me?

3 Look upon me and answer me, / O LORD my God; *
give light to my eyes, / lest I sleep in death;

4 Lest my enemy say, "I have pre/vailed over him," *
and my foes rejoice that / I have fallen.

5 But I put my trust in / your mercy; *
my heart is joyful because / of your saving help.

6 I will sing to the LORD, for he has dealt with / me richly; *
I will praise the Name / of the Lord Most High. *[Ant.]*

14

In Easter Season

The LORD will re - store the for - tunes of his peo - ple,

and we will be glad, hal - le - lu - jah.

On other Sundays and Weekdays

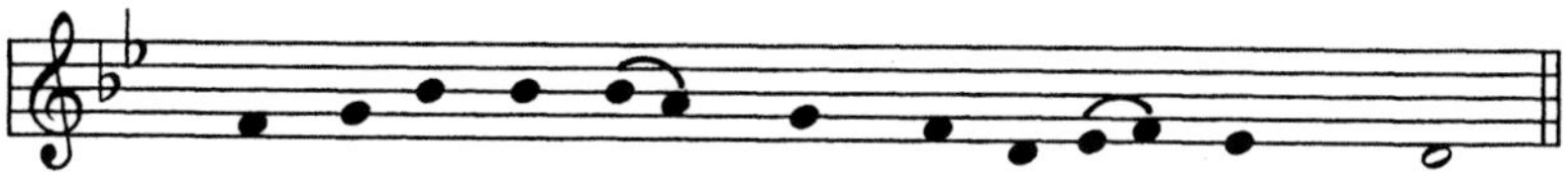

God is in the com - pa - ny of the righ - teous.

Psalm 14 *Dixit insipiens* *Tone III.4*

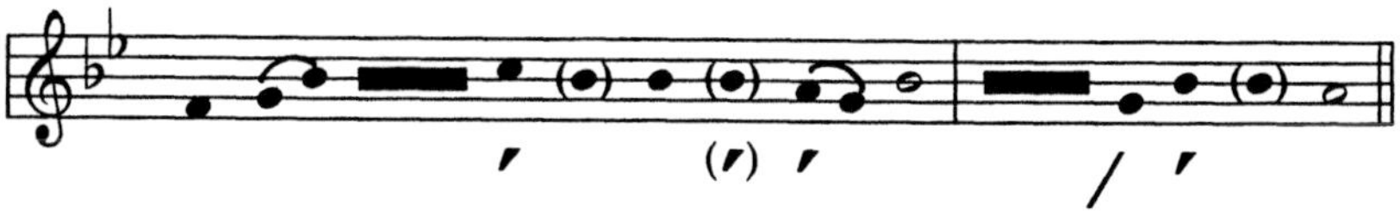

1 *The fool* has said in his heart, "There is no God." *
All are corrupt and commit abominable acts;
there is none who / does any good.

2 The LORD looks down from heaven upon us all, *
to see if there is any who is wise,
if there is one who / seeks after God.

3 Every one has proved faithless;
all alike have turned bad; *
there is none who does good; / no, not one.

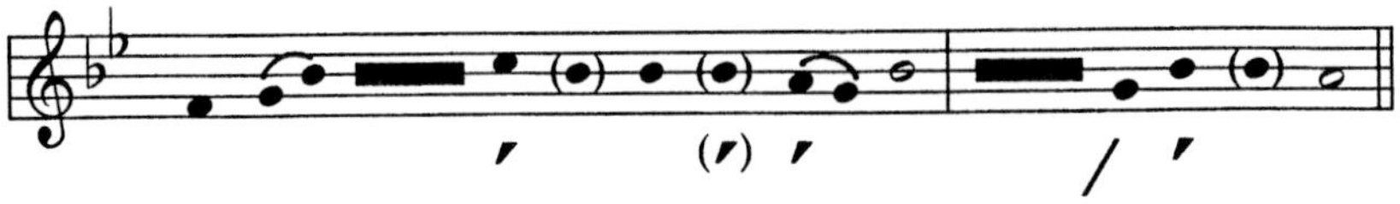

4 Have they no knowledge, all those evildoers *
who eat up my people like bread
and do not call / upon the LORD?

5 See how they tremble with fear, *
because God is in the company of / the righteous.

6 Their aim is to confound the plans of the afflicted, *
but the LORD is / their refuge.

7 Oh, that Israel's deliverance would come out of Zion! *
when the LORD restores the fortunes of his people,
Jacob will rejoice and Isra/el be glad. *[Ant.]*

15

In Easter Season

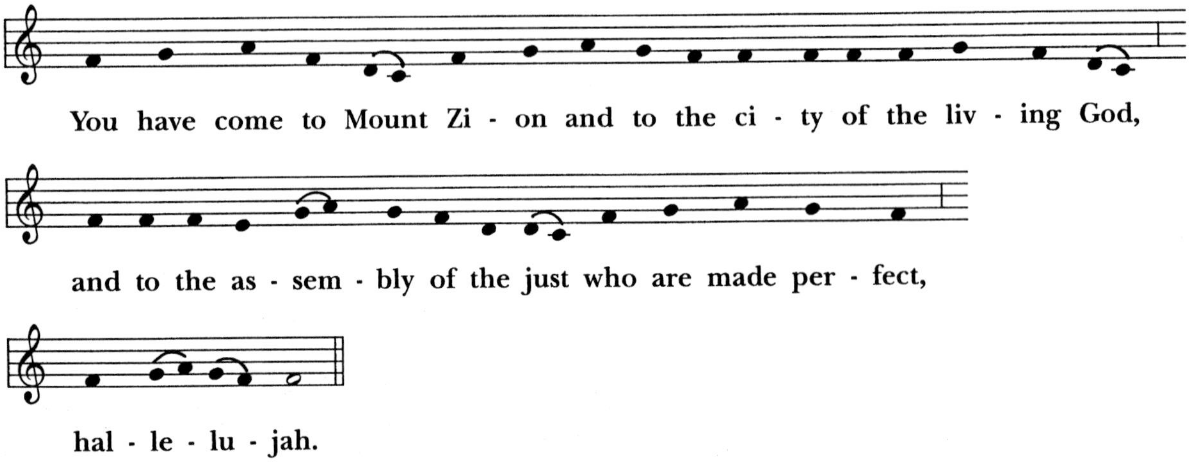
You have come to Mount Zi - on and to the ci - ty of the liv - ing God,
and to the as - sem - bly of the just who are made per - fect,
hal - le - lu - jah.

On other Sundays and Weekdays

Bles - sed are the pure in heart, for they shall see God.

Psalm 15 *Domine, quis habitabit?* *Tone VI*

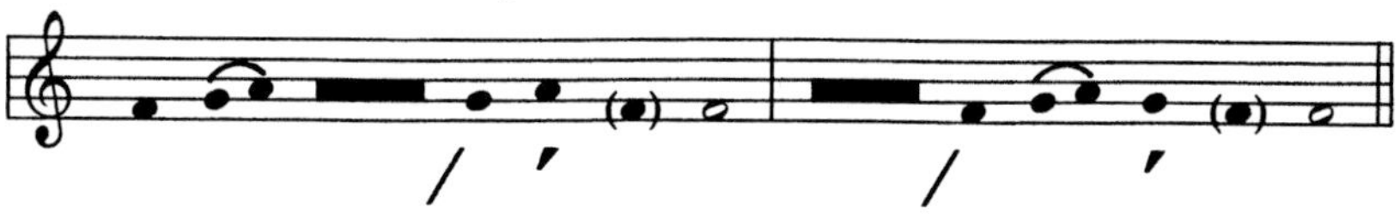

1 *LORD, whö* may dwell in your ta/bernácle? *
who may abide up/on yöur hóly hill?

2 Whoever leads a blameless life and does / what ís right, *
who speaks the / truth fröm hís heart.

3 There is no guile upon his tongue;
he does no e/vil tó his friend; *
he does not heap contempt up/on hïs néighbor.

4 In his sight the wicked is / rejécted, *
but he honors / those whö féar the LORD.

5 He has sworn to / do nó wrong *
and does / not täke báck his word.

6 He does not give his money / in hópe of gain, *
nor does he take a bribe a/gainst thë ínnocent.

7 Whoever / does thése things *
shall ne/ver bë óverthrown. *[Ant.]*

16

In Easter Season

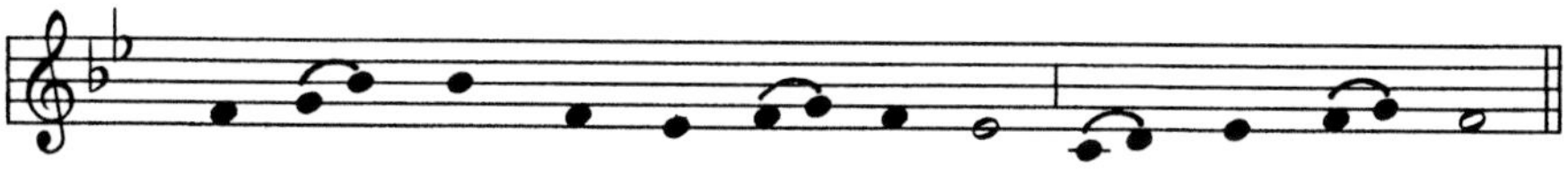

You will show me the path of life, hal - le - lu - jah.

On other Sundays and Weekdays

My bod - y shall rest in hope, for you will not a - ban - don me to

the grave.

Psalm 16 *Conserva me, Domine* *Tone VIII.1*

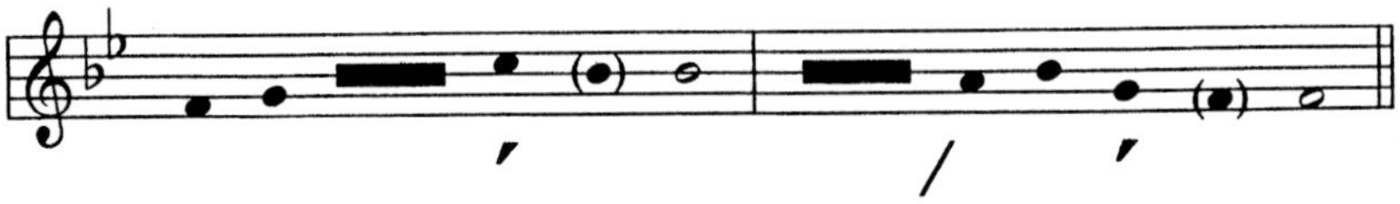

1 *Protect* me, O God, for I take refuge in yóu; *
I have said to the LORD, "You are my Lord,
my good a/bove all óther."

2 All my delight is upon the godly that are in the lánd, *
upon those who are noble a/mong the péople.

3 But those who run after óther gods *
shall have their / troubles múltiplied.

4 Their libations of blood I will not óffer, *
nor take the names of their / gods upón my lips.

5 O LORD, you are my portion and mý cup; *
it is you / who uphóld my lot.

6 My boundaries enclose a pléasant land; *
indeed, I have a / goodly héritage.

7 I will bless the LORD who gives me cóunsel; *
my heart teaches me, / night aftér night.

8 I have set the LORD always befóre me; *
because he is at my right / hand I shá̀ll not fall.

9 My heart, therefore, is glad, and my spirit rejóices; *
my body al/so shall rést in hope.

10 For you will not abandon me to the gráve, *
nor let your ho/ly one sée the Pit.

11 You will show me the páth of life; *
in your presence there is fullness of joy,
and in your right hand are plea/sures for évermore. *[Ant.]*

17

In Easter Season

At my vin - di - ca - tion I shall see your face, hal - le - lu - jah.

On other Sundays and Weekdays

Keep me, O LORD, as the ap - ple of your eye; hide me un - der

the sha - dow of your wings.

Psalm 17 *Exaudi, Domine* *Tone VIII.1*

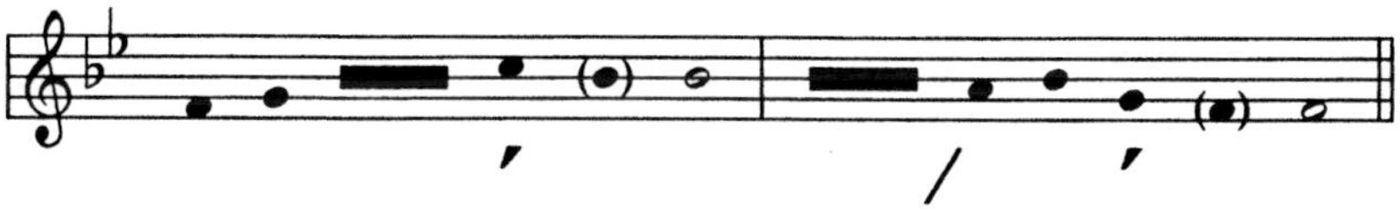

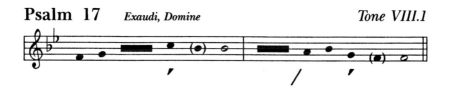

1 *Hear my* plea of innocence, O LORD;
give heed to my crý; *
listen to my prayer, which does not / come from lýing lips.

2 Let my vindication come forth from your présence; *
let your eyes be / fixed on jústice.

3 Weigh my heart, summon me by níght, *
melt me down; you will find no im/puritý in me.

4 I give no offense with my mouth as óthers do; *
I have heeded the / words of yóur lips.

5 My footsteps hold fast to the ways of yóur law; *
in your paths my feet / shall not stúmble.

6 I call upon you, O God, for you will ánswer me; *
incline your ear to / me and héar my words.

7 Show me your marvelous loving-kíndness, *
O Savior of those who take refuge at your right hand
from those who rise / up agáinst them.

8 Keep me as the apple of your eye; *
hide me under the / shadow of your wings,

9 From the wicked who assault me, *
from my deadly enemies / who surround me.

10 They have closed their heart to pity, *
and their / mouth speaks proud things.

11 They press me hard,
now they surround me, *
watching how they may / cast me to the ground,

12 Like a lion, greedy for its prey, *
and like a young lion lurking in / secret places.

13 Arise, O LORD; confront them and bring them down; *
deliver me from the / wicked by your sword.

14 Deliver me, O LORD, by your hand *
from those whose portion in / life is this world;

15 Whose bellies you fill with your treasure, *
who are well supplied with children
and leave their wealth / to their little ones.

16 But at my vindication I shall see your face; *
when I awake, I shall be satisfied, behol/ding your likeness. *[Ant.]*

18:1–20

On the Twelve Days of Christmas

The LORD shows lov - ing - kind - ness to his a - noint - ed, to Da - vid

and his des - cend - ants for ev - er.

In Easter Week

The LORD res - cued me be - cause he de - light - ed in me,

hal - le - lu - jah.

On other Sundays and Weekdays

The LORD has de - liv - ered me from my strong en - e - mies.

Psalm 18 Part 1 *Diligam te, Domine* *Tone VIII.2*

1 *I love* you, O LORD my strength, *
O LORD my stronghold, my crag, / and my haven.

2 My God, my rock in whom I put my trust, *
my shield, the horn of my salvation, and my refuge;
you are / worthy of praise.

3 I will call upon the LORD, *
and so shall I be saved / from my enemies.

4 The breakers of death rolled over me, *
and the torrents of oblivion / made me afraid.

5 The cords of hell entángled me, *
and the snares of / death were sét for me.

6 I called upon the LORD in mý distress *
and cried out / to my Gód for help.

7 He heard my voice from his heavenly dwélling; *
my cry of anguish / came to hís ears.

8 The earth reeled and rócked; *
the roots of the mountains shook;
they reeled because / of his ánger.

9 Smoke rose from his nostrils
and a consuming fire out of his móuth; *
hot burning / coals blazed fórth from him.

10 He parted the heavens and cáme down *
with a storm cloud / under hís feet.

11 He mounted on cherubim and fléw; *
he swooped on the / wings of thé wind.

12 He wrapped darkness abóut him; *
he made dark waters and thick clouds / his pavílion.

13 From the brightness of his presence, thróugh the clouds, *
burst hail/stones and cóals of fire.

14 The LORD thundered out of héaven; *
the Most High / uttered hís voice.

15 He loosed his arrows and scáttered them; *
he hurled thunder/bolts and róuted them.

16 The beds of the seas were uncovered,
and the foundations of the world láid bare, *
at your battle cry, O LORD,
at the blast of the breath / of your nóstrils.

17 He reached down from on high and grásped me; *
he drew me out / of great wáters.

18 He delivered me from my strong enemies
and from those who háted me; *
for they were too / mighty fór me.

19 They confronted me in the day of my disáster; *
but the / LORD was mý support.

20 He brought me out into an ópen place; *
he rescued me because he de/lighted ín me. *[Ant.]*

18:21–50

On the Twelve Days of Christmas

The LORD shows lov - ing - kind - ness to his a - noint - ed, to Da - vid

and his des - cend - ants for ev - er.

In Easter Season

The LORD lives! Ex - alt - ed is the God of my sal - va - tion,

hal - le - lu - jah!

On other Sundays and Weekdays

You, O LORD, are my lamp; my God, you make my dark - ness bright.

Psalm 18 Part 2 *Et retribuet mihi* *Tone V.1*

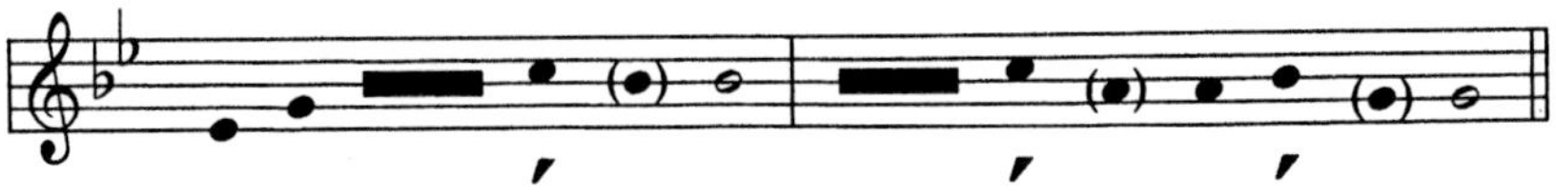

21 *The LORD* rewarded me because of my righteous dealing; *
because my hands were clean he rewarded me;

22 For I have kept the ways of the LORD *
and have not offended against my God;

23 For all his judgments are before my eyes, *
and his decrees I have not put away from me;

24 For I have been blameless with him *
and have kept myself from iniquity;

25 Therefore the LORD rewarded me according to my righteous dealing, *
because of the cleanness of my hands in his sight.

26 With the faithful you show yourself faithful, O God; *
with the forthright you show yourself forthright.

27 With the pure you show yourself pure, *
but with the crooked you are wily.

28 You will save a lowly people, *
but you will humble the haughty eyes.

29 You, O LORD, are my lamp; *
my God, you make my darkness bright.

30 With you I will break down an enclosure; *
with the help of my God I will scale any wall.

31 As for God, his ways are perfect;
the words of the LORD are tried in the fire; *
he is a shield to all who trust in him.

32 For who is God, but the LORD? *
who is the Rock, except our God?

33 It is God who girds me about with strength *
and makes my way secure.

34 He makes me sure-footed like a deer *
and lets me stand firm on the heights.

35 He trains my hands for battle *
and my arms for bending even a bow of bronze.

36 You have given me your shield of victory; *
your right hand also sustains me;
your loving care makes me great.

37 You lengthen my stride beneath me, *
and my ankles do not give way.

38 I pursue my enemies and overtake them; *
I will not turn back till I have destroyed them.

39 I strike them down, and they cannot rise; *
they fall defeated at my feet.

40 You have girded me with strength for the battle; *
you have cast down my adversaries beneath me;
you have put my enemies to flight.

41 I destroy those who hate me;
they cry out, but there is none to help them; *
they cry to the LORD, but he does not answer.

42 I beat them like dust before the wind; *
I trample them like mud in the streets.

43 You deliver me from the strife of the peoples; *
you put me at the head of the nations.

44 A people I have not known shall serve me;
no sooner shall they hear than they shall obey me; *
strangers will cringe before me.

45 The foreign peoples will lose heart; *
they shall come trembling out of their strongholds.

46 The LORD lives! Blessed is my Rock! *
Exalted is the God of my salvation!

47 He is the God who gave me victory *
and cast down the peoples beneath me.

48 You rescued me from the fury of my enemies;
you exalted me above those who rose agáinst me; *
you saved me fróm my déadly foe.

49 Therefore will I extol you among the nations, O LÓRD, *
and sing práises to yóur Name.

50 He multiplies the victories of hís king; *
he shows loving-kindness to his anointed,
to David and his descéndants for éver. *[Ant.]*

19

In Lent

Let the words of my mouth and the med - i - ta - tion of my heart

be ac - cept - a - ble in your sight.

In Easter Season

The glo - ry of God is the light of the cit - y and its lamp is the LORD,

hal - le - lu - jah.

On other Sundays and Weekdays

The heavens de - clare the glo - ry of God, and the fir - ma - ment shows

his hand - i - work. †

Psalm 19 *Coeli enarrant* *Tone VII.3*

1 *The heavens* declare the glory of God, *
and the firmament shows his handiwork.

2 †One day tells its tale to another, *
and one night imparts knowledge to another.

3 Although they have no words or language, *
and their voices are not heard,

4 Their sound has gone out into all lands, *
and their message to the ends of the world.

5 In the deep has he set a pavilion for the sun; *
it comes forth like a bridegroom out of his chamber;
it rejoices like a champion to run its course.

6 It goes forth from the uttermost edge of the heavens
and runs about to the end of it again; *
nothing is hidden from its burning heat.

7 The law of the LORD is perfect and revives the soul; *
the testimony of the LORD is sure and gives wisdom to the innocent.

8 The statutes of the LORD are just and rejoice the heart; *
the commandment of the LORD is clear and gives light to the eyes.

9 The fear of the LORD is clean and endures for ever; *
the judgments of the LORD are true and righteous altogether.

10 More to be desired are they than gold, more than much fine gold, *
sweeter far than honey, than honey in the comb.

11 By them also is your servant enlightened, *
and in keeping them there is great reward.

12 Who can tell how often he offends? *
cleanse me from my secret faults.

13 Above all, keep your servant from presumptuous sins;
let them not get domínion óver me; *
then shall I be whole and sound,
and innocent óf a gréat offense.

14 Let the words of my mouth and the meditation of my
heart be accéptable ín your sight, *
O LORD, my strength and mý redéemer. *[Ant.]*

20

On the Twelve Days of Christmas

We will shout for joy at the vic - tory of our God.

In Easter Season

Now has be - gun the reign of our God, and the pow - er of his

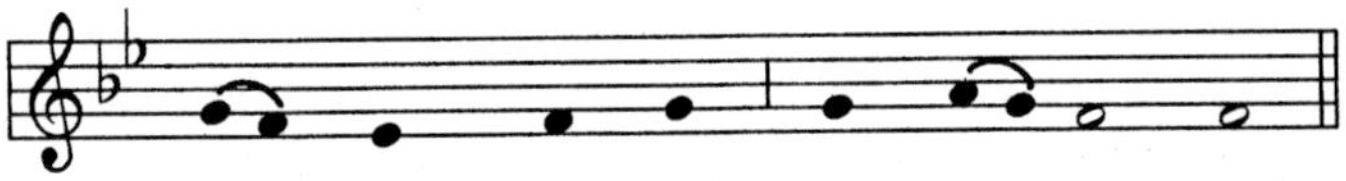

A - noint - ed One, hal - le - lu - jah.

On other Sundays and Weekdays

The LORD has giv - en vic - to - ry to his a - noint - ed.

Psalm 20 *Exaudiat te Dominus* *Tone VIII.2*

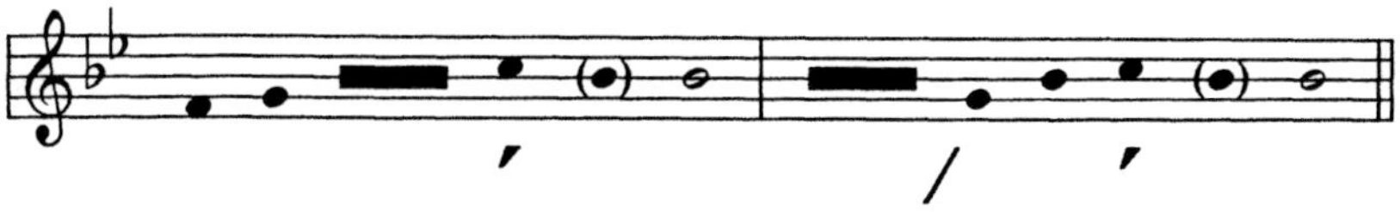

1 *May the* LORD answer you in the day of tróuble, *
  the Name of the God of Ja/cob defénd you;

2 Send you help from his hóly place *
  and strengthen you / out of Zíon;

3 Remember all your óffe rings *
  and accept / your burnt sácrifice;

4 Grant you your héart's desire *
  and / prosper áll your plans.

5 We will shout for joy at your victory
and triumph in the Name of our Gód; *
  may the LORD / grant all yóur requests.

6 Now I know that the LORD gives victory to his anóinted: *
  he will answer him out of his holy heaven,
  with the victorious / strength of hís right hand.

7 Some put their trust in chariots and some in hórses, *
  but we will call upon the Name / of the LÓRD our God.

8 They collapse and fáll down, *
  but we will a/rise and stánd upright.

9 O LORD, give victory to the kíng *
  and an/swer us whén we call. *[Ant.]*

21

On the Twelve Days of Christmas

He asked you for life, and you gave it to him: length of days for ev - er

and ev - er.

In Easter Season

You have ta - ken your great pow - er and be - gun to reign,

hal - le - lu - jah.

On other Sundays and Weekdays

Be ex - alt - ed, O LORD, in your might; we will sing and praise your

pow - er.

Psalm 21 *Domine, in virtute tua* *Tone V.1*

1 *The king* rejoices in your strength, O LORD; *
how greatly he exults in your victory!

2 You have given him his heart's desire; *
you have not denied him the request of his lips.

3 For you meet him with blessings of prosperity, *
and set a crown of fine gold upon his head.

4 He asked you for life, and you gave it to hím: *
length of days, for éver and éver.

5 His honor is great, because of your víctory; *
splendor and majesty have you bestówed upón him.

6 For you will give him everlasting felícity *
and will make him glad with the jóy of your présence.

7 For the king puts his trust in the LÓRD; *
because of the loving-kindness of the Most High, hé will nót fall.

8 Your hand will lay hold upon all your énemies; *
your right hand will seize áll those who háte you.

9 You will make them like a fiery fúrnace *
at the time of your appéaring, Ó LORD;

10 You will swallow them up in yóur wrath, *
and fíre shall consúme them.

11 You will destroy their offspring fróm the land *
and their descendants from among the péoples óf the earth.

12 Though they intend evil against you
and devise wícked schemes, *
yet théy shall nót prevail.

13 For you will put them to flíght *
and aim your árrows át them.

14 Be exalted, O LORD, in yóur might; *
we will sing and práise your pówer. *[Ant.]*

22

In Holy Week

They di - vide my gar - ments a - mong them; they cast lots for my

cloth - ing.

On other Sundays and Weekdays

We be - held him des - pised and re - ject - ed, a man of sor - rows,

and ac - quaint - ed with grief.

Psalm 22 *Deus, Deus meus* *Tone IV.1*

1 *My God,* my God, why have / you forsaken me? *
and are so far from my cry
and from the / words of my distress?

2 O my God, I cry in the daytime, but you / do not answer; *
by night as well, / but I find no rest.

3 Yet you / are the Holy One, *
enthroned upon the / praises of Israel.

4 Our forefathers / put their trust in you; *
they trusted, and / you delivered them.

5 They cried out to you and / were delivered; *
they trusted in you and / were not put to shame.

6 But as for me, I am a / worm and no man, *
scorned by all and / despised by the people.

7 All who see me laugh / me to scórn; *
they curl their lips and / wag their heads, saying,

8 "He trusted in the LORD; let / him delíver him; *
let him rescue him, if / he delights in him."

9 Yet you are he who took me out / of the wómb, *
and kept me safe up/on my mother's breast.

10 I have been entrusted to you ever since / I was bórn; *
you were my God when I was still / in my mother's womb.

11 Be not far from me, for trou/ble is néar, *
and / there is none to help.

12 Many young / bulls encírcle me; *
strong bulls of / Bashan surround me.

13 They open / wide their jáws at me, *
like a ravening / and a roaring lion.

14 I am poured out like water;
all my / bones are óut of joint; *
my heart within my / breast is melting wax.

15 My mouth is dried out like a pot-sherd;
my tongue sticks to the roof / of my móuth; *
and you have laid me / in the dust of the grave.

16 Packs of dogs close me in,
and gangs of evildoers cir/cle aróund me; *
they pierce my hands and my feet;
/ I can count all my bones.

17 They stare / and gloat óver me; *
they divide my garments among them;
they cast / lots for my clothing.

18 Be not / far awáy, O LORD; *
you are my strength; / hasten to help me.

19 Save me / from the swórd, *
my life / from the power of the dog.

20 Save me / from the lion's mouth, *
my wretched body / from the horns of wild bulls.

21 I will declare your Name / to my brethren; *
in the midst of the congrega/tion I will praise you.

22 Praise the LORD, / you that fear him; *
stand in awe of him, O offspring of Israel;
all you of / Jacob's line, give glory.

23 For he does not despise nor abhor the poor in their poverty;
neither does he / hide his face from them; *
but when they / cry to him he hears them.

24 My praise is of him in the / great assembly; *
I will perform my vows in the presence of / those who worship him.

25 The poor shall eat and be satisfied,
and those who seek the / LORD shall praise him: *
"May / your heart live for ever!"

26 All the ends of the earth shall remember and turn / to the LORD, *
and all the families of the na/tions shall bow before him.

27 For kingship belongs / to the LORD; *
he / rules over the nations.

28 To him alone all who sleep in the earth bow / down in worship; *
all who go down to the / dust fall before him.

29 My soul shall live for him;
my descen/dants shall serve him; *
they shall be known / as the LORD's for ever.

30 They shall come and make known to a / people yet unborn *
the saving / deeds that he has done. *[Ant.]*

23

On the Twelve Days of Christmas

He will lead his flock like a shep - herd, he will ga - ther the lambs

in his arms, and gent - ly lead those that are with young.

In Lent

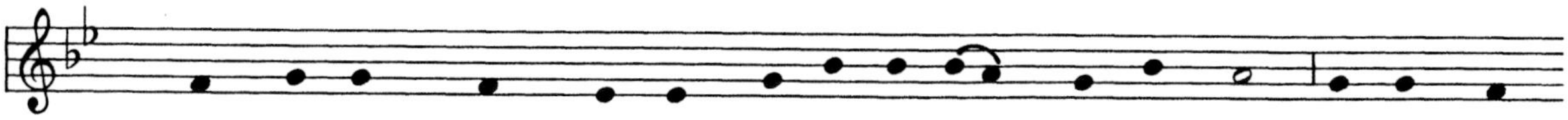

Though I walk through the val - ley of the sha - dow of death, I shall fear

no e - vil; for you are with me.

In Easter Season

I will dwell in the house of the LORD, for ev - er, hal - le - lu - jah.

On other Sundays and Weekdays

We are his peo - ple and the sheep of his pas - ture.

Psalm 23 *Dominus regit me* *Tone VIII.1*

1 *The* LORD is my shépherd; *
  I / shall not bé in want.

2 He makes me lie down in green pástures *
  and leads me be/side still wáters.

3 He revives my sóul *
  and guides me along right pathways / for his Náme's sake.

4a Though I walk through the valley of the shadow of death,
I shall / fear no evil; *

4b for you are with me;
your rod and your / staff, they comfort me.

5 You spread a table before me in the presence of those who trouble me; *
you have anointed my head with oil,
and my cup is / running over.

6 Surely your goodness and mercy shall follow me all
the days of my life, *
and I will dwell in the house of the / LORD for ever. *[Ant.]*

24

In Advent

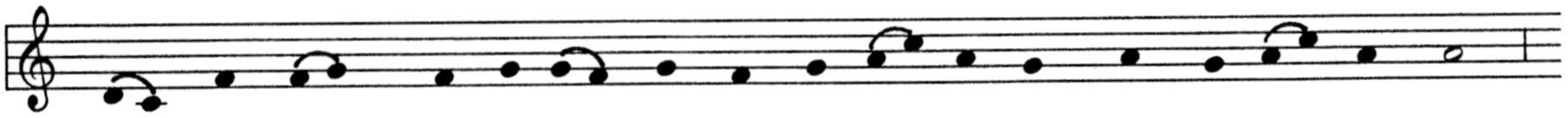

Blow the trum - pet in Zi - on, for the day of the LORD is near at hand.

Be - hold, he comes to save us, hal - le - lu - jah.

In Lent

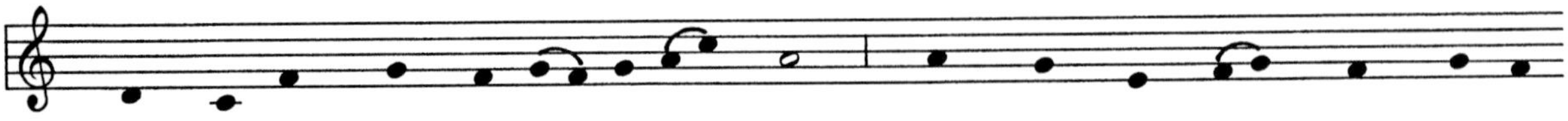

Who can as - cend the hill of the LORD? Those who have clean hands and a

pure heart.

In Easter Season

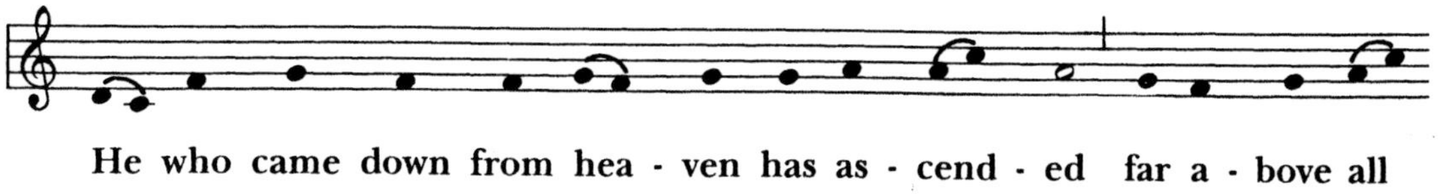
He who came down from hea - ven has as - cend - ed far a - bove all

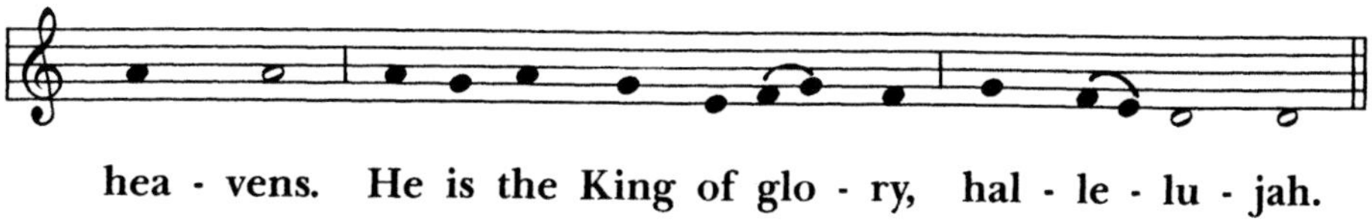
hea - vens. He is the King of glo - ry, hal - le - lu - jah.

On other Sundays and Weekdays

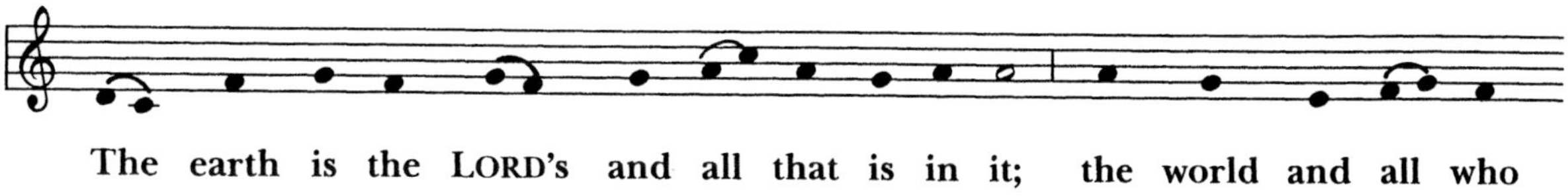
The earth is the LORD's and all that is in it; the world and all who

dwell there - in.†

Psalm 24 *Domini est terra* *Tone I.2*

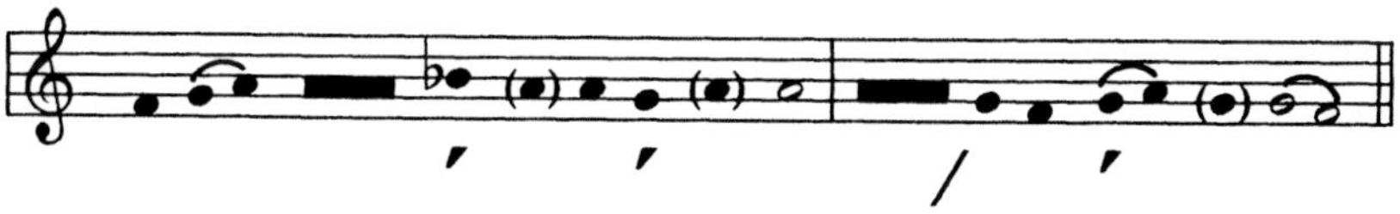

1 *The earth* is the LORD's and all that is in it, *
the world and / all who dwell therein.

2† For it is he who founded it upon the seas *
and made it firm upon the / rivers of the deep.

3 "Who can ascend the hill of the LORD? *
and who can stand / in his holy place?"

4 "Those who have clean hands and a pure heart, *
who have not pledged themselves to falsehood,
nor sworn / by what is a fraud.

5 They shall receive a blessing from the LORD *
and a just reward from the God of / their salvation."

6 Such is the generation of those who seek him, *
of those who seek your face, O / God of Jacob.

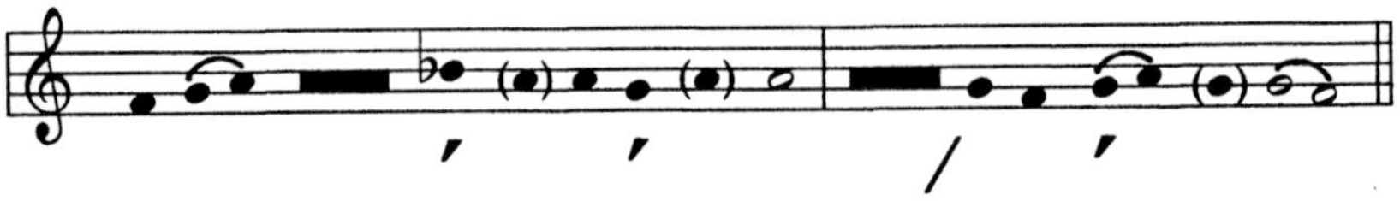

7 Lift up your heads, O gates;
lift them high, O everlasting doors; *
and the King of / glory shall come in.

8 "Who is this King of glory?" *
"The LORD, strong and mighty,
the LORD, migh/ty in battle."

9 Lift up your heads, O gates;
lift them high, O everlasting doors; *
and the King of / glory shall come in.

10 "Who is he, this King of glory?" *
"The LORD of hosts,
he is the / King of glory." *[Ant.]*

25

In Easter Season

The paths of the LORD are love and faith - ful - ness, hal - le - lu - jah.

On other Sundays and Weekdays

Lead me in your truth, O LORD, and teach me.

Psalm 25 *Ad te, Domine, levavi* *Tone I.7*

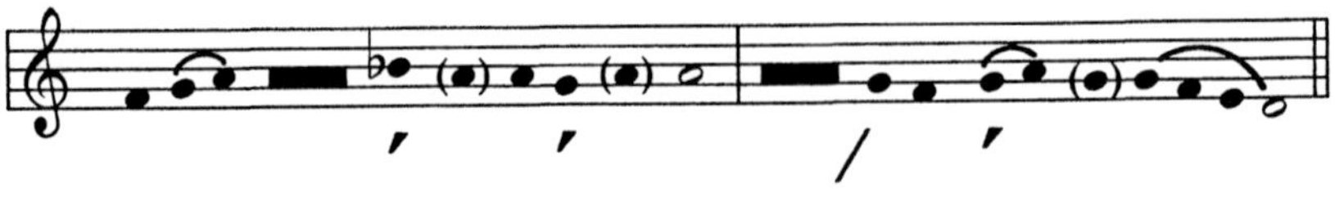

1 *To you,* O LORD, I lift up my soul;
my God, I put my trust in you; *
let me not be humiliated,
nor let my enemies / triumph over me.

2 Let none who look to you be put to shame; *
let the treacherous be disap/pointed in their schemes.

3 Show me your ways, O LORD, *
and / teach me your paths.

4 Lead me in your truth and teach me, *
for you are the God of my salvation;
in you have I trusted / all the day long.

5 Remember, O LORD, your compassion and love, *
for they are from / everlasting.

6 Remember not the sins of my youth and my transgressions; *
remember me according to your love,
and for the sake of your / goodness, O LORD.

7 Gracious and upright is the LORD; *
therefore he teaches / sinners in his way.

8 He guides the humble in doing right *
and teaches his way / to the lowly.

9 All the paths of the LORD are love and faithfulness *
to those who keep his covenant and his / testimonies.

10 For your Name's sake, O LORD, *
forgive my / sin, for it is great.

11 Who are they who fear the LORD? *
he will teach them the / way that they should choose.

12 They shall dwell in prosperity, *
and their offspring shall in/herit the land.

13 The LORD is a friend to those who fear him *
and will show / them his covenant.

14 My eyes are ever looking to the LORD, *
for he shall pluck my / feet out of the net.

15 Turn to me and have pity on me, *
for I am left alone / and in misery.

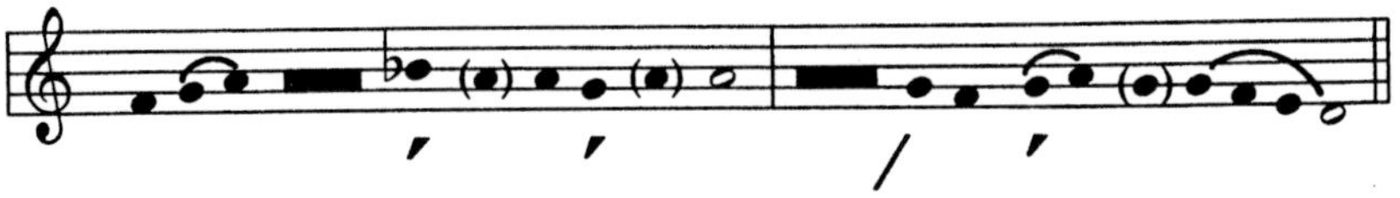

16 The sorrows of my heart have increased; *
bring me / out of my troubles.

17 Look upon my adversity and misery *
and for/give me all my sin.

18 Look upon my enemies, for they are many, *
and they bear a violent / hatred against me.

19 Protect my life and deliver me; *
let me not be put to shame, for I have / trusted in you.

20 Let integrity and uprightness preserve me, *
for my / hope has been in you.

21 Deliver Israel, O God, *
out of / all his troubles. *[Ant.]*

26

In Easter Season

LORD, I love the house in which you dwell, and the place where your

glo - ry a - bides, hal - le - lu - jah.

On other Sundays and Weekdays

I have trust - ed in the LORD and have not fal - tered.

Psalm 26 *Judica me, Domine* *Tone VI*

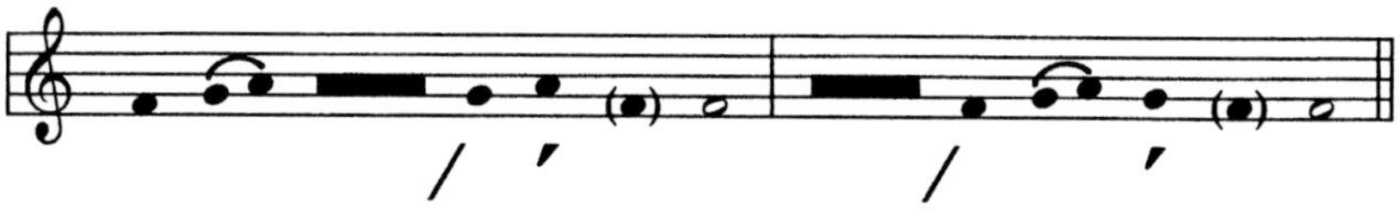

1 *Give judg*ment for me, O LORD,
for I have lived with / integrity; *
I have trusted in the Lord and / have not faltered.

2 Test me, O LORD, / and try me; *
examine / my heart and my mind.

3 For your love is / before my eyes; *
I have walked faith/fully with you.

4 I have not sat with / the worthless, *
nor do I consort with / the deceitful.

5 I have hated the company of e/vildoers; *
I will not sit down / with the wicked.

6 I will wash my hands in inno/cence, O LORD, *
that I may go in procession / round your altar,

7 Singing aloud a song of / thanksgiving *
and recounting all / your wonderful deeds.

8 LORD, I love the house / in which you dwell *
and the place where / your glory abides.

9 Do not sweep me away / with sinners, *
nor my life with / those who thirst for blood,

10 Whose hands are full / of evil plots, *
and their / right hand full of bribes.

11 As for me, I will live with / integrity; *
redeem me, O LORD and have / pity on me.

12 My foot stands / on level ground; *
in the full assembly / I will bless the LORD. *[Ant.]*

27

On the Twelve Days of Christmas

The LORD is my light and my sal - va - tion; whom then shall I fear? †

In Lent

Heark - en to my voice, O LORD; have mer - cy on me and an - swer me.

In Easter Season

I be - lieve that I shall see the good - ness of the LORD in the land of the

liv - ing, hal - le - lu - jah.

On other Sundays and Weekdays

I will of - fer in his dwell - ing an ob - la - tion with sounds of great

glad - ness.

Psalm 27 *Dominus illuminatio* *Tone VIII.1*

1a *The LORD* is my light and my salvátion;
— / whom then sháll I fear? *

† 1b the LORD is the strength of my lífe;
of whom then / shall I bé afraid?

2 When evildoers came upon me to eat up my flésh, *
it was they, my foes and my adversaries, who / stumbled ánd fell.

3 Though an army should encamp agáinst me, *
yet my heart / shall not bé afraid;

4 And though war should rise up agáinst me, *
yet will I / put my trúst in him.

5 One thing have I asked of the LORD;
one thíng I seek; *
that I may dwell in the house of the LORD all the / days of mý life;

6 To behold the fair beauty of the LÓRD *
and to seek him / in his témple.

7 For in the day of trouble he shall keep me safe in his shélter; *
he shall hide me in the secrecy of his dwelling
and set me / high upón a rock.

8 Even now he lifts úp my head *
above my enemies / round abóut me.

9 Therefore I will offer in his dwelling an oblation
with sounds of great gládness; *
I will sing and make / music tó the LORD.

10 Hearken to my voice, O LORD, when I cáll; *
have mercy on / me and ánswer me.

11 You speak in my heart and say, "Séek my face," *
Your / face, LORD, wíll I seek.

12 Hide not your fáce from me, *
nor turn away your servant / in displéasure.

13 You have been my helper;
cast me nót away; *
do not forsake me, O God of / my salvátion.

14 Though my father and my mother forsáke me, *
the LORD / will sustáin me.

15 Show me your way, O LÓRD; *
lead me on a level path, because / of my énemies.

16 Deliver me not into the hand of my adversaries, *
for false witnesses have risen up against me,
and also those / who speak malice.

17 What if I had not believed
that I should see the goodness of the LORD *
in the land / of the living!

18 O tarry and await the LORD's pleasure;
be strong, and he shall comfort your heart; *
wait pa/tiently for the LORD. *[Ant.]*

28

In Easter Season

The LORD is a safe ref - uge for his a - noint - ed, hal - le - lu - jah.

On other Sundays and Weekdays

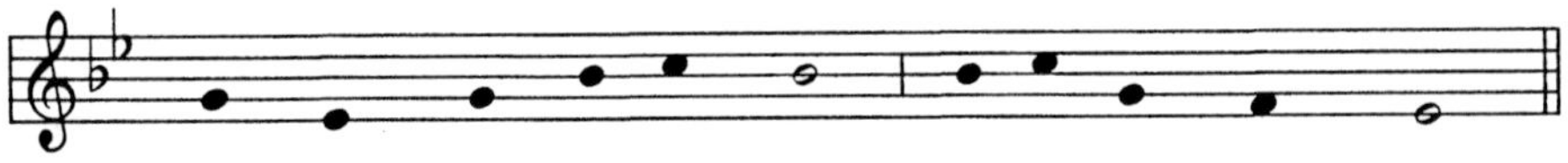

My heart trusts in the LORD; and I have been helped.

Psalm 28 *Ad te, Domine* *Tone V.1*

1 *O LORD,* I call to you;
my Rock, do not be deaf to my cry; *
lest, if you do not hear me,
I become like those who go down to the Pit.

2 Hear the voice of my prayer when I cry out to you, *
when I lift up my hands to your holy of holies.

3 Do not snatch me away with the wicked or with the evildóers, *
who speak peaceably with their neighbors,
while strífe is ín their hearts.

4 Repay them according to théir deeds, *
and according to the wickedness óf their áctions.

5 According to the work of their hands repáy them, *
and gíve them their jút deserts.

6 They have no understanding of the LORD's doings,
nor of the works of hís hands; *
therefore he will break them dówn and not búild them up.

7 Blessed is the LÓRD! *
for he has heard the vóice of mý prayer.

8 The LORD is my strength and mý shield; *
my heart trusts in him, and Í have béen helped;

9 Therefore my heart dances for jóy, *
and in my sóng will I práise him.

10 The LORD is the strength of his péople, *
a safe refuge for hís anóinted.

11 Save your people and bless your inhéritance; *
shepherd them and carry thém for éver. *[Ant.]*

29

In Lent

The LORD shall give strength to his peo - ple.

In Easter Season

The LORD sits en - throned as King for ev - er - more, hal - le - lu - jah.

On other Sundays and Weekdays

Wor - ship the LORD in his ho - ly tem - ple.

Psalm 29 *Afferte Domino* *Tone III.4*

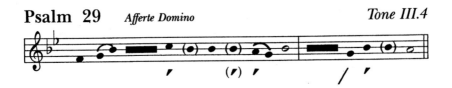

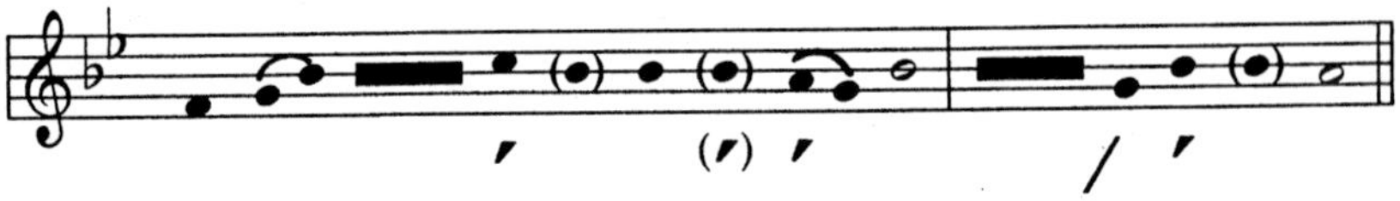

1 *Ascribe*—to the LORD, you gods, *
ascribe to the LORD / glory and strength.

2 Ascribe to the LORD the glory due his Name; *
worship the LORD in the beauty / of holiness.

3 The voice of the LORD is upon the waters;
the God of glory thunders; *
the LORD is upon the migh/ty waters.

4 The voice of the LORD is a powerful voice; *
the voice of the LORD is a voice / of splendor.

5 The voice of the LORD breaks the cedar trees; *
the LORD breaks the cedars / of Lebanon;

6 He makes Lebanon skip like a calf, *
and Mount Hermon like / a young wild ox.

7 The voice of the LORD splits the flames of fire;
the voice of the LORD shakes the wilderness; *
the LORD shakes the wilderness / of Kadesh.

8 The voice of the LORD makes the oak trees writhe *
and strips / the forests bare.

9 And in the temple of the LORD *
all are cry/ing, "Glory!"

10 The LORD sits enthroned above the flood; *
the LORD sits enthroned as King / for evermore.

11 The LORD shall give strength to his people; *
the LORD shall give his people the bless/ing of peace. *[Ant.]*

30

In Easter Season

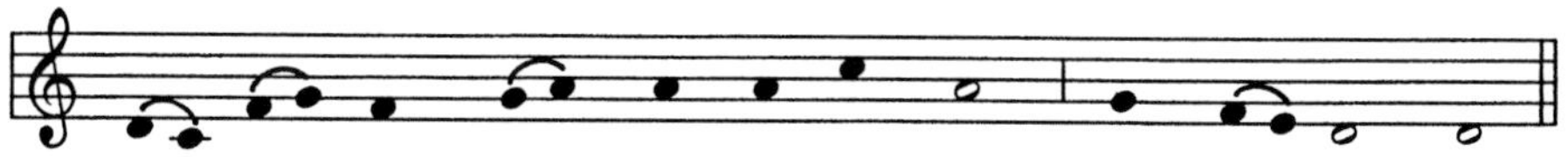

You have re - stored my life, O LORD; hal - le - lu - jah.

On other Sundays and Weekdays

O LORD my God, I cried out to you, and you re - stored me to health.

Psalm 30 *Exaltabo te, Domine* *Tone I.2*

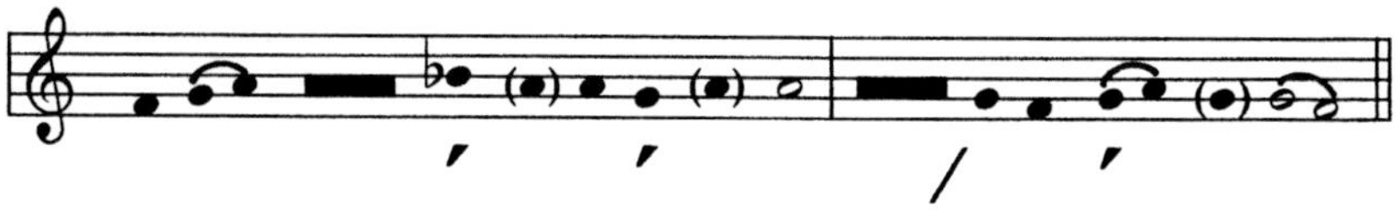

1 *I will* exalt you, O LORD,
because you have lifted me up *
and have not let my enemies / triumph over me.

2 O LORD my God, I cried out to you, *
and you / restored me to health.

3 You brought me up, O LORD, from the dead; *
you restored my life as I was go/ing down to the grave.

4 Sing to the LORD, you servants of his; *
give thanks for the remembrance / of his holiness.

5 For his wrath endures but the twinkling of an eye, *
his favor / for a lifetime.

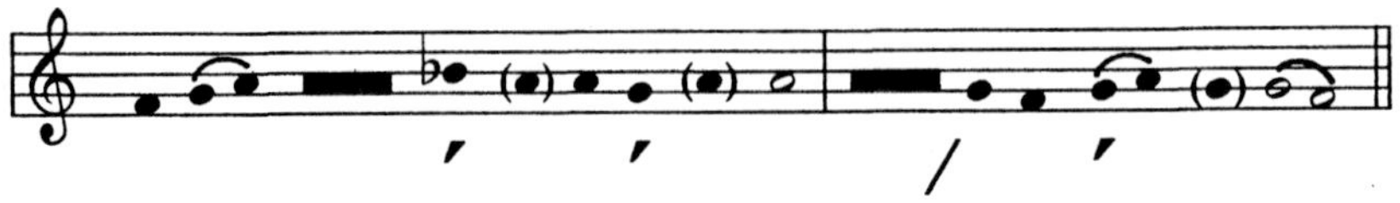

6 —Weeping may spend the night, *
but joy comes / in the morning.

7 While I felt secure, I said,
"I shall never be disturbed. *
You, LORD, with your favor, made me as strong / as the mountains."

8 —Then you hid your face, *
and / I was filled with fear.

9 I cried to you, O LORD; *
I pleaded / with the Lord, saying,

10 "What profit is there in my blood, if I go down to the Pit? *
will the dust praise you or de/clare your faithfulness?

11 Hear, O LORD, and have mercy upon me; *
O LORD, / be my helper."

12 You have turned my wailing into dancing; *
you have put off my sack-cloth and / clothed me with joy.

13 Therefore my heart sings to you without ceasing; *
O LORD my God, I will give you / thanks for ever. *[Ant.]*

31

Antiphon

In - cline your ear to me, O LORD; make haste to de - liv - er me.

Psalm 31 *In te, Domine, speravi* *Tone VII.3*

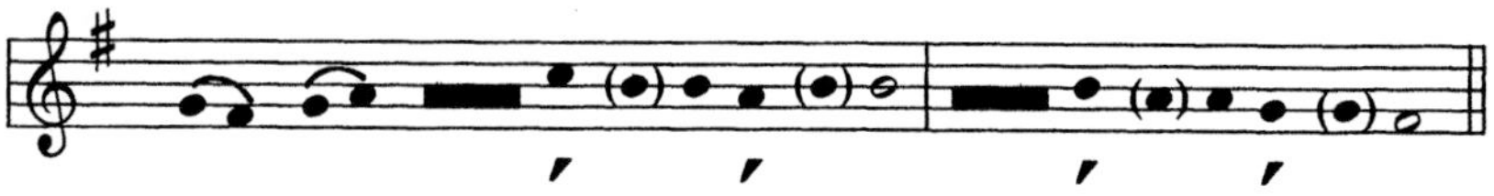

1 *In you,* O Lord, have I taken refuge;
let me never be put to shame; *
deliver me in your righteousness.

2 Incline your ear to me; *
make haste to deliver me.

3 Be my strong rock, a castle to keep me safe,
for you are my crag and my stronghold; *
for the sake of your Name, lead me and guide me.

4 Take me out of the net that they have secretly set for me, *
for you are my tower of strength.

5 Into your hands I commend my spirit, *
for you have redeemed me,
O Lord, O God of truth.

6 I hate those who cling to worthless idols, *
and I put my trust in the Lord.

7 I will rejoice and be glad because of your mercy; *
for you have seen my affliction;
you know my distress.

8 You have not shut me up in the power of the enemy; *
you have set my feet in an open place.

9 Have mercy on me, O Lord, for I am in trouble; *
my eye is consumed with sorrow,
and also my throat and my belly.

10 For my life is wasted with grief,
and my years with sighing; *
my strength fails me because of affliction,
and my bones are consumed.

11 I have become a reproach to all my enemies and even to my neighbors,
a dismay to those of my acquaintance; *
when they see me in the street they avoid me.

12 I am forgotten like a dead man, out of mind; *
I am as useless as a broken pot.

13 For I have heard the whispering of the crowd;
fear is all around; *
they put their heads together against me;
They plot to take my life.

14 But as for me, I have trusted in you, O LORD. *
I have said, "You are my God.

15 My times are in your hand; *
rescue me from the hand of my enemies,
and from those who persecute me.

16 Make your face to shine upon your servant, *
and in your loving-kindness save me."

17 LORD, let me not be ashamed for having called upon you; *
rather, let the wicked be put to shame;
let them be silent in the grave.

18 Let the lying lips be silenced which speak against the righteous, *
haughtily, disdainfully, and with contempt.

19 How great is your goodness, O LORD!
which you have laid up for those who fear you; *
which you have done in the sight of all
for those who put their trust in you.

20 You hide them in the covert of your presence from those who slander them; *
you keep them in your shelter from the strife of tongues.

21 —Blessed be the LORD! *
for he has shown me the wonders of his love in a besieged city.

22 Yet I said in my alarm,
"I have been cut off from the sight of your eyes." *
Nevertheless, you heard the sound of my entreaty when I cried out to you.

23 Love the LORD, all you who worship him; *
the LORD protects the faithful,
but repays to the full those who act haughtily.

24 Be strong and let your heart take courage, *
all you who wait for the LORD. *[Ant.]*

32

In Easter Season

We have been rec - on - ciled to God through the death of his Son,

hal - le - lu - jah.

On other Sundays and Weekdays

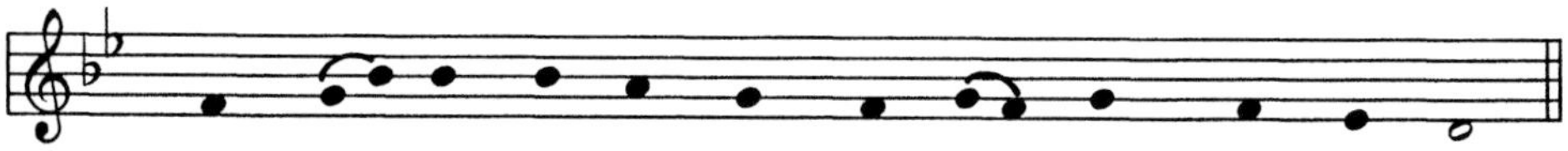

Hap - py are they to whom the LORD im - putes no guilt.

Psalm 32 *Beati quorum* *Tone III.4*

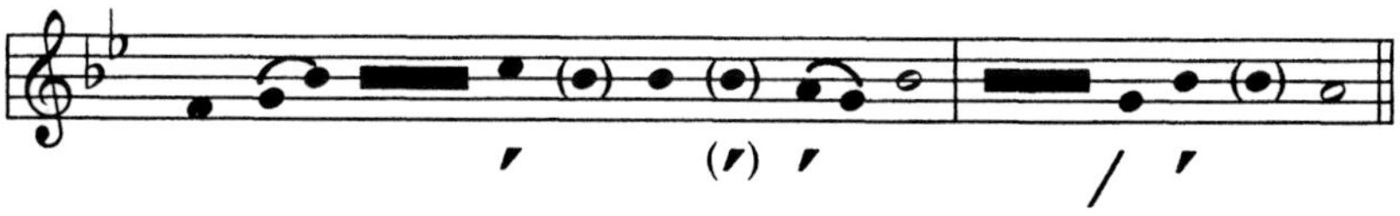

1 *Happy* are they whose transgressions are forgiven, *
and whose sin / is put away!

2 Happy are they to whom the LORD imputes no guilt, *
and in whose spirit there / is no guile!

3 While I held my tongue, my bones withered away, *
because of my groan/ing all day long.

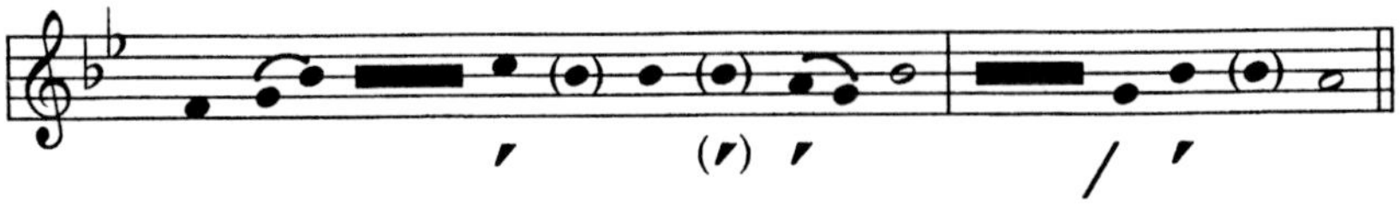

4 For your hand was heavy upon me day and night; *
my moisture was dried up as in the heat / of summer.

5 Then I acknowledged my sin to you, *
and did not / conceal my guilt.

6 I said, "I will confess my transgressions to the LORD." *
Then you forgave me the guilt / of my sin.

7 Therefore all the faithful will make their prayers to you in time of trouble; *
when the great waters overflow, they shall / not reach them.

8 You are my hiding-place;
you preserve me from trouble; *
you surround me with shouts of / deliverance.

9 "I will instruct you and teach you in the way that you should go; *
I will guide / you with my eye.

10 Do not be like horse or mule, which have no understanding; *
who must be fitted with bit and bridle,
or else they will / not stay near you."

11 Great are the tribulations of the wicked; *
but mercy embraces those who trust / in the LORD.

12 Be glad, you righteous, and rejoice in the LORD; *
shout for joy, all who / are true of heart. *[Ant.]*

33

In Lent

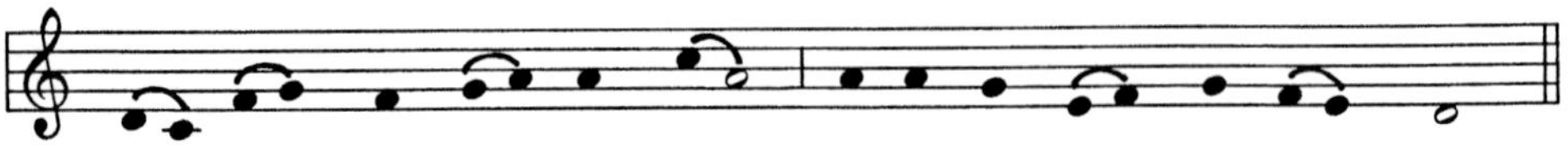

Our soul waits for the LORD; he is our help and our shield.

In Easter Season

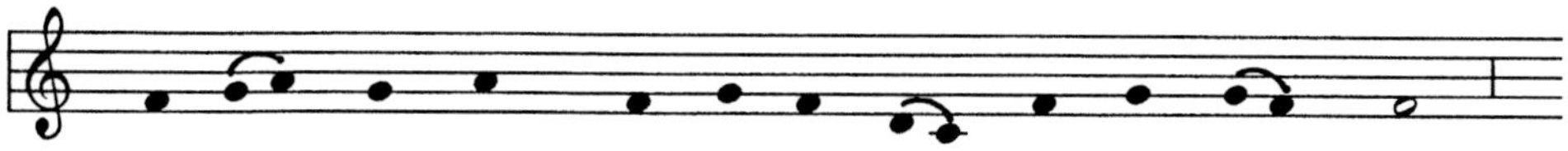

The lov - ing kind - ness of the LORD fills the whole earth,

hal - le - lu - jah.

On other Sundays and Weekdays

By the word of the LORD were the hea - vens made, by the breath of his

mouth all the hea - ven - ly hosts.

Psalm 33 *Exultate, justi* *Tone I.2*

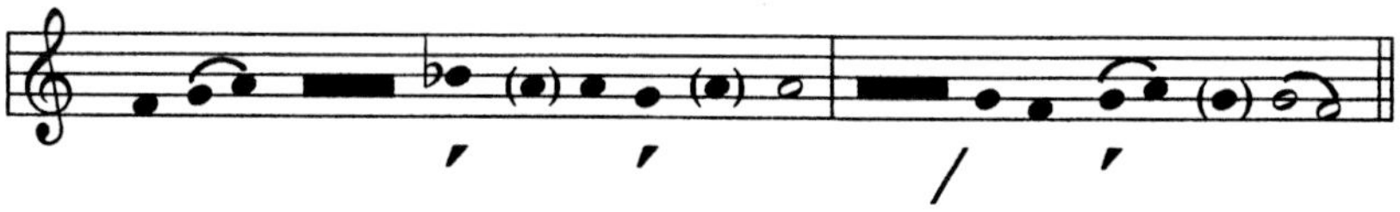

1 *Rejoice* in the LORD, you righteous; *
it is good for the just / to sing praises.

2 Praise the LORD with the harp; *
play to him upon the / psaltery and lyre.

3 Sing for him a new song; *
sound a fanfare with all your skill up/on the trumpet.

4 For the word of the LORD is right, *
and / all his works are sure.

5 He loves righteousness and justice; *
the loving-kindness of the LORD / fills the whole earth.

6 By the word of the LORD were the heavens made, *
by the breath of his mouth / all the heavenly hosts.

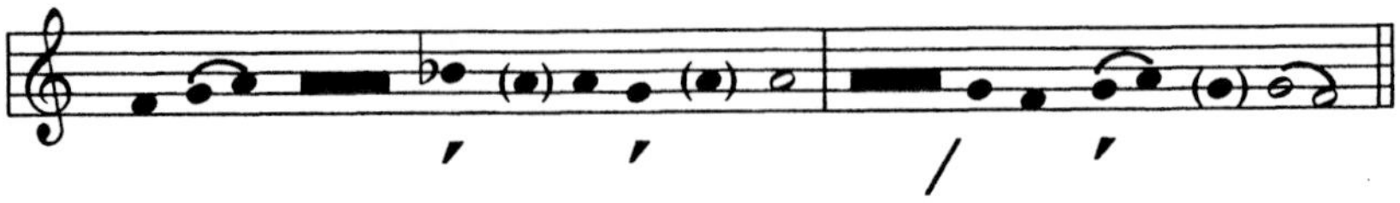

7 He gathers up the waters of the ocean as in a water-skin *
and stores up the / depths of the sea.

8 Let all the earth fear the LORD; *
let all who dwell in the world / stand in awe of him.

9 For he spoke, and it came to pass; *
he commanded, / and it stood fast.

10 The LORD brings the will of the nations to naught; *
he thwarts the designs / of the peoples.

11 But the LORD's will stands fast for ever, *
and the designs of his / heart from age to age.

12 Happy is the nation whose God is the LORD! *
happy the people he has chosen / to be his own!

13 The LORD looks down from heaven, *
and beholds all the / people in the world.

14 From where he sits enthroned he turns his gaze *
on all who / dwell on the earth.

15 He fashions all the hearts of them *
and under/stands all their works.

16 There is no king that can be saved by a mighty army; *
a strong man is not delivered / by his great strength.

17 The horse is a vain hope for deliverance; *
for all its / strength it cannot save.

18 Behold, the eye of the LORD is upon those who fear him, *
on those who / wait upon his love,

19 To pluck their lives from death, *
and to feed them in / time of famine.

20 Our soul waits for the LORD; *
he is our / help and our shield.

21 Indeed, our heart rejóices ín him, *
for in his holy / Name we ṕüt our trüst.

22 Let your loving-kindness, O LÓRD, be upón us, *
as we have / put our tŕüst in yöu. *[Ant.]*

34

On the Twelve Days of Christmas

Look up - on the LORD and be ra - di - ant; hap - py are they who

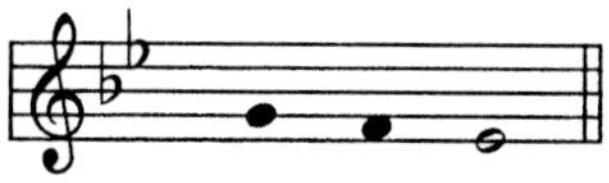

trust in him.

In Lent

Turn from e - vil and do good; seek peace and pur - sue it.

In Easter Season

Taste and see that the LORD is good, hal - le - lu - jah.

On other Sundays and Weekdays

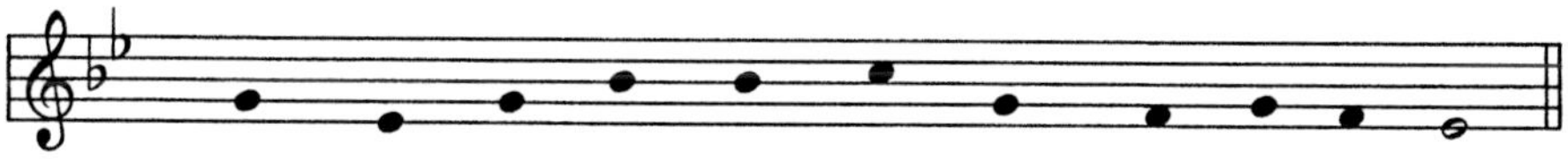

Those who seek the LORD lack noth - ing that is good.

Psalm 34 *Benedicam Dominum* *Tone V.1*

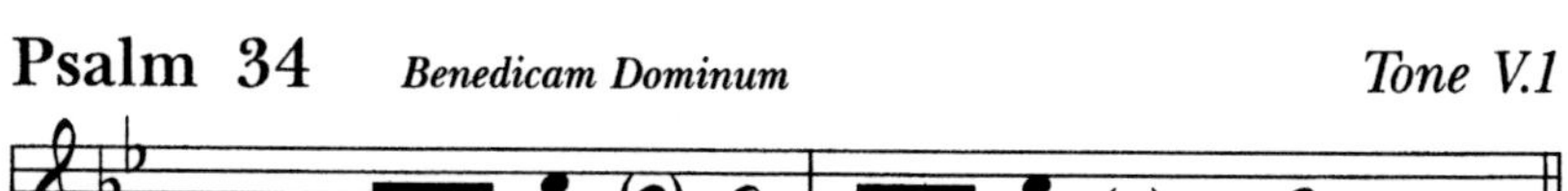

1 *I will* bless the LORD at áll times; *
his praise shall ever bé in mý mouth.

2 I will glory in the LÓRD; *
let the humble héar and réjoice.

3 Proclaim with me the greatness of the LÓRD; *
let us exalt his Náme togéther.

4 I sought the LORD, and he ánswered me *
and delivered me out of áll my térror.

5 Look upon him and be rádiant, *
and let not your fáces bé ashamed.

6 I called in my affliction and the LORD héard me *
and saved me from áll my tróubles.

7 The angel of the LORD encompasses those who féar him, *
and hé will delíver them.

8 Taste and see that the LÓRD is good; *
happy are théy who trúst in him!

9 Fear the LORD, you that are hís saints, *
for those who fear hím lack nóthing.

10 The young lions lack and suffer húnger, *
but those who seek the LORD lack nóthing thát is good.

11 Come, children, and listen to mé; *
I will teach you the féar of thé LORD.

12 Who among you loves lífe *
and desires long life to enjóy prospérity?

13 Keep your tongue from evil-spéaking *
and your líps from lýing words.

14 Turn from evil and dó good; *
seek péace and pursúe it.

15 The eyes of the LORD are upon the ríghteous, *
and his ears are ópen tó their cry.

16 The face of the LORD is against those who do évil, *
to root out the remembrance of thém from thé earth.

17 The righteous cry, and the LORD hears them *
and delivers them from all their troubles.

18 The LORD is near to the brokenhearted *
and will save those whose spirits are crushed.

19 Many are the troubles of the righteous, *
but the LORD will deliver him out of them all.

20 He will keep safe all his bones; *
not one of them shall be broken.

21 Evil shall slay the wicked, *
and those who hate the righteous will be punished.

22 The LORD ransoms the life of his servants, *
and none will be punished who trust in him. *[Ant.]*

35

Antiphon

Be not far from me, O LORD, rise up and help me.

Psalm 35 *Judica, Domine* *Tone VI*

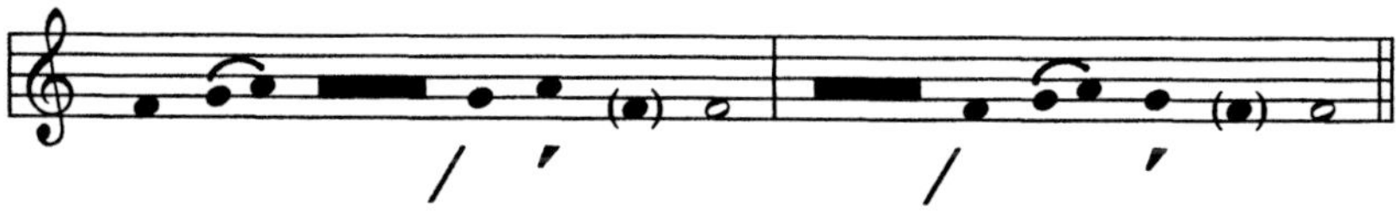

1 *Fight those* who / fight me, O LORD; *
attack those who / are attacking me.

2 Take up shield / and armor *
and rise / up to help me.

3 Draw the sword and bar the way against those who / pursue me; *
say to my soul, "I am / your salvation."

4 Let those who seek after my life be shamed / and humbled; *
let those who plot my ruin fall back / and be dismayed.

5 Let them be like chaff / before the wind, *
and let the angel of the / LORD drive them away.

6 Let their way be dark / and slippery, *
and let the angel of the / LORD pursue them.

7 For they have secretly spread a net for me / without a cause; *
without a cause they have dug a pit / to take me alive.

8 Let ruin come upon / them unawares; *
let them be caught in the net they hid;
let them fall into / the pit they dug.

9 Then I will be joy/ful in the LORD; *
I will glory / in his victory.

10 My very bones will say, "LORD, who / is like you? *
You deliver the poor from those who are too strong for them,
the poor and needy from / those who rob them."

11 Malicious witnesses rise up / against me; *
they charge me with matters I / know nothing about.

12 They pay me evil in / exchange for good; *
my soul / is full of despair.

13 But when they were sick I dressed / in sack-cloth *
and humbled my/self by fasting;

14a I prayed with / my whole heart,*
as one would for a friend / or a brother;

14b I behaved like one who mourns for / his mother, *
bowed / down and grieving.

15 But when I stumbled, they were glad and gathered together;
they gathered / against me; *
strangers whom I did not know tore me to pieces / and would not stop.

16 They put me to the test / and mocked me; *
they gnashed at / me with their teeth.

17 O Lord, how long will / you lóok on? *
rescue me from the roaring beasts,
and my life from / the yöung líons.

18 I will give you thanks in the great con/gregátion; *
I will praise you / in thë míghty throng.

19 Do not let my treacherous foes re/joice óver me, *
nor let those who hate me without a cause wink / at ëach óther.

20 For they do / not plán for peace, *
but invent deceitful schemes against the qui/et ïn thé land.

21 They opened their mouths / at mé and said, *
"Aha! we saw it / with öur ówn eyes."

22 You saw it, O LORD; do not / be sílent; *
O LORD, be / not fär fróm me.

23 Awake, arise / to mý cause! *
to my defense, my / God änd mý Lord!

24 Give me justice, O LORD my God,
according to / your ríghteousness; *
do not let them / trïumph óver me.

25 Do not let them say in their hearts,
"Aha! / just whát we want!" *
Do not let them say, "We / have swällówed him up."

26 Let all who rejoice at my ruin be ashamed / and dísgraced; *
let those who boast against me be clothed with / dismäy ánd shame.

27 Let those who favor my cause sing out with joy / and bé glad; *
let them say always, "Great is the LORD,
who desires the prosperity / of hïs sérvant."

28 And my tongue shall be talking of / your ríghteousness *
and of your praise / all thë dáy long. *[Ant.]*

36

In Easter Season

With you, O LORD, is the well of life, hal - le - lu - jah.

On other Sundays and Weekdays

In your light, O God, we see light.

Psalm 36 *Dixit injustus* *Tone I.1*

1 *There is* a voice of rebellion deep in the heart of the wicked; *
there is no fear of / God before his eyes.

2 He flatters himself in his own eyes *
that his hateful sin will / not be found out.

3 The words of his mouth are wicked and deceitful; *
he has left off acting wise/ly and doing good.

4 He thinks up wickedness upon his bed
and has set himself in no good way; *
he does not abhor that / which is evil.

5 Your love, O LORD, reaches to the heavens, *
and your faith/fulness to the clouds.

6 Your righteousness is like the strong mountains,
your justice like the great deep; *
you save both / man and beast, O LORD.

7 How priceless is your love, O God! *
your people take refuge under the / shadow of your wings.

8 They feast upon the abundance of your house; *
you give them drink from the ri/ver of your delights.

9 For with you is the well of life, *
and in / your light we see light.

10 Continue your loving-kindness to those who know you, *
and your favor to those / who are true of heart.

11 Let not the foot of the proud come near me, *
nor the hand of the wick/ed push me aside.

12 See how they are fallen, those who work wickedness! *
they are cast down and shall not be / able to rise. *[Ant.]*

37:1–18

In Easter Season

The low - ly will de - light in a - bun - dance of peace, hal - le - lu - jah.

On other Sundays and Weekdays

Com - mit your way to the LORD, and put your trust in him.

Psalm 37 Part 1 *Noli oemulari* *Tone III.4*

1 *Do not* fret yourself because of evildoers; *
do not be jealous of those / who do wrong.

2 For they shall soon wither like the grass, *
and like the green / grass fade away.

3 Put your trust in the LORD and do good; *
dwell in the land and feed on / its riches.

4 Take delight in the LORD, *
and he shall give you / your heart's desire.

5 Commit your way to the LORD and put your trust in him, *
and he will bring / it to pass.

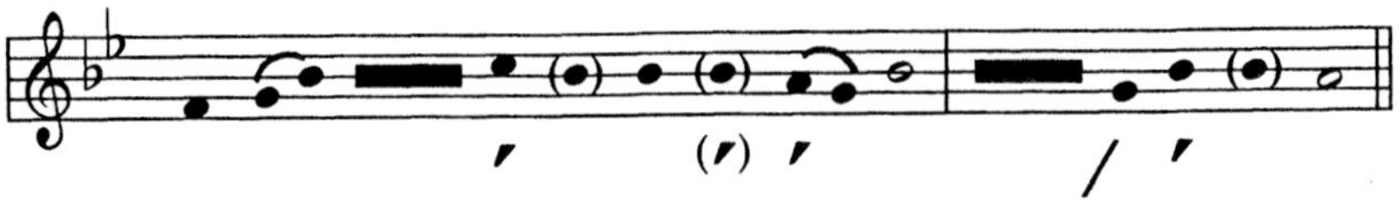

6 He will make your righteousness as clear as the light *
and your just dealing as / the noonday.

7 Be still before the LORD *
and wait pa/tiently for him.

8 Do not fret yourself over the one who prospers, *
the one who succeeds / in evil schemes.

9 Refrain from anger, leave rage alone; *
do not fret yourself; it leads only / to evil.

10 For evildoers shall be cut off, *
but those who wait upon the LORD shall / possess the land.

11 In a little while the wicked shall be no more; *
you shall search out their place, but they / will not be there.

12 But the lowly shall possess the land; *
they will delight in abun/dance of peace.

13 The wicked plot against the righteous *
and gnash at / them with their teeth.

14 The LORD laughs at the wicked, *
because he sees that / their day will come.

15 The wicked draw their sword and bend their bow
to strike down the poor and needy, *
to slaughter those who are up/right in their ways.

16 Their sword shall go through their own heart, *
and their bow shall / be broken.

17 The little that the righteous has *
is better than great riches of / the wicked.

18 For the power of the wicked shall be broken, *
but the LORD upholds / the righteous. *[Ant.]*

37:19–42

In Easter Season

The LORD is a strong - hold in time of trou - ble, hal - le - lu - jah.

On other Sundays and Weekdays

Turn from e - vil and do good, for the LORD up - holds the righ - teous.

Psalm 37 Part 2 *Novit Dominus* *Tone VII.3*

19 *The LORD* cares for the lives of the godly, *
and their inheritance shall last for ever.

20 They shall not be ashamed in bad times, *
and in days of famine they shall have enough.

21 As for the wicked, they shall perish, *
and the enemies of the LORD, like the
glory of the meadows, shall vanish;
they shall vanish like smoke.

22 The wicked borrow and do not repay, *
but the righteous are generous in giving.

23 Those who are blessed by God shall possess the land, *
but those who are cursed by him shall be destroyed.

24 Our steps are directed by the LORD; *
he strengthens those in whose way he delights.

25 If they stumble, they shall not fall headlong, *
for the LORD holds them by the hand.

26 I have been young and now I am old, *
but never have I seen the righteous forsaken,
or their children begging bread.

27 The righteous are always generous in their lending, *
and their children shall be a blessing.

28 Turn from evil, and do good, *
and dwell in the land for ever.

29 For the LORD loves justice; *
he does not forsake his faithful ones.

30 They shall be kept safe for ever, *
but the offspring of the wicked shall be destroyed.

31 The righteous shall possess the land *
and dwell in it for ever.

32 The mouth of the righteous utters wisdom, *
and their tongue speaks what is right.

33 The law of their God is in their heart, *
and their footsteps shall not falter.

34 The wicked spy on the righteous *
and seek occasion to kill them.

35 The LORD will not abandon them to their hand, *
nor let them be found guilty when brought to trial.

36 Wait upon the LORD and keep his way; *
he will raise you up to possess the land,
and when the wicked are cut off, you will see it.

37 I have seen the wicked in their arrogance, *
flourishing like a tree in full leaf.

38 I went by, and behold, they were not there; *
I searched for them, but they could not be found.

39 Mark those who are honest;
observe the upright; *
for there is a future for the peaceable.

40 Transgressors shall be destroyed, one and all; *
the future of the wicked is cut off.

41 But the deliverance of the righteous comes from the LORD; *
he is their stronghold in time of trouble.

42 The LORD will help them and rescue them; *
he will rescue them from the wicked and deliver them,
because they seek refuge in him. *[Ant.]*

38

Antiphon

I will con - fess my in - iq - ui - ty; do not for - sake me, O God of my
sal - va - tion.

Psalm 38 *Domine, ne in furore* *Tone IV.4*

1 *O LORD,* do not rebuke me / in your anger; *
do not / punish me in your wrath.

2 For your arrows have al/ready pierced me, *
and your hand pres/ses hard upon me.

3 There is no health in my flesh,
because of your / indignation; *
there is no soundness in my body, / because of my sin.

4 For my iniquities / overwhelm me; *
like a heavy burden they are / too much for me to bear.

5 My wounds / stink and fester *
by rea/son of my foolishness.

6 I am utterly bowed / down and próstrate; *
I go about in mour/ning all the dáy long.

7 My loins are / filled with séaring pain; *
there is no / health in my bódy.

8 I am utterly / numb and crúshed; *
I wail, because of the / groaning of mý heart.

9 O LORD, you / know all mý desires, *
and my sighing is / not hidden fróm you.

10 My heart is pounding, my / strength has fáiled me; *
and the brightness of / my eyes is góne from me.

11 My friends and companions draw back from / my afflíction; *
my neigh/bors stand afár off.

12 Those who seek after my / life lay snáres for me; *
those who strive to hurt me speak of my ruin
and plot treacher/y all the dáy long.

13 But I am like the / deaf who dó not hear, *
like those who are mute and do / not open théir mouth.

14 I have become like / one who dóes not hear *
and from / whose mouth comes nó defense.

15 For in you, O LORD, have I / fixed my hópe; *
you will an/swer me, O Lórd my God.

16 For I said, "Do not let them re/joice at mý expense, *
those who gloat over / me when my fóot slips."

17 Truly, I am on the / verge of fálling, *
and my pain / is always wíth me.

18 I will confess / my iníquity *
and be / sorry for mý sin.

19 Those who are my enemies without / cause are mighty, *
and many in number are those who / wrongfully hate me.

20 Those who repay evil / for good slander me, *
because I fol/low the course that is right.

21 O LORD, do / not forsake me; *
be not / far from me, O my God.

22 Make / haste to help me, *
O Lord / of my salvation. *[Ant.]*

39

In Easter Season

LORD, you have res - cued my life from death, and my eyes from tears,

hal - le - lu - jah.

On other Sundays and Weekdays

Hear my prayer, O LORD, hold not your peace at my tears.

Psalm 39 *Dixi, Custodiam* *Tone I.2*

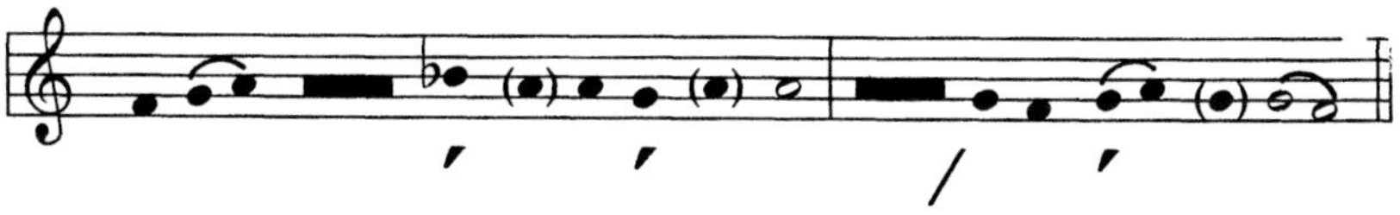

1 *I said,* "I will keep watch upon my ways, *
so that I do not of/fend with my tongue.

2 I will put a muzzle on my mouth *
while the wicked are / in my presence."

3 So I held my tongue and said nothing; *
I refrained from rash words;
but my pain be/came unbearable.

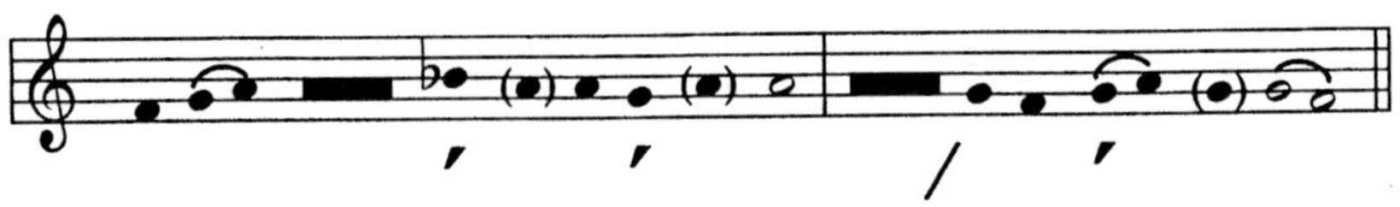

4 My heart was hot within me;
while I pondered, the fire burst into flame; *
I / spoke out with my tongue:

5 LORD, let me know my end and the number of my days, *
so that I may know how / short my life is.

6 You have given me a mere handful of days,
and my lifetime is as nothing in your sight; *
truly, even those who stand erect are / but a puff of wind.

7 We walk about like a shadow,
and in vain we are in turmoil; *
we heap up riches and cannot tell / who will gather them.

8 And now, what is my hope? *
O Lord, / my hope is in you.

9 Deliver me from all my transgressions *
and do not make me the / taunt of the fool.

10 I fell silent and did not open my mouth, *
for surely it was / you that did it.

11 Take your affliction from me; *
I am worn down by the / blows of your hand.

12 With rebukes for sin you punish us;
like a moth you eat away all that is dear to us; *
truly, everyone is / but a puff of wind.

13 Hear my prayer, O LORD,
and give ear to my cry; *
hold not your / peace at my tears.

14 For I am but a sojourner with you, *
a wayfarer, as / all my forebears were.

15 Turn your gaze from me, that I may be glad again, *
before I go my way / and am no more. *[Ant.]*

40

In Holy Week

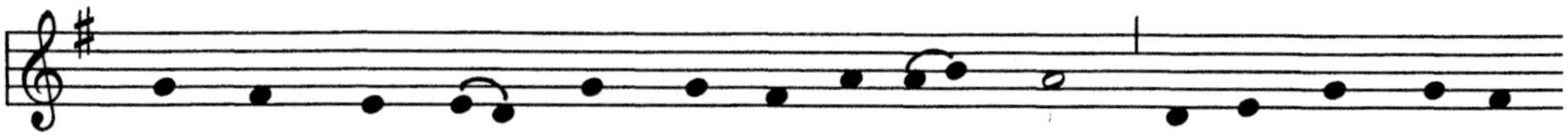

We have been sanc - ti - fied by the of - fering of the bod - y of

Je - sus Christ once for all.

In Easter Season

The LORD has put a new song in my mouth; a song of praise to our God,

hal - le - lu - jah.

On other Sundays and Weekdays

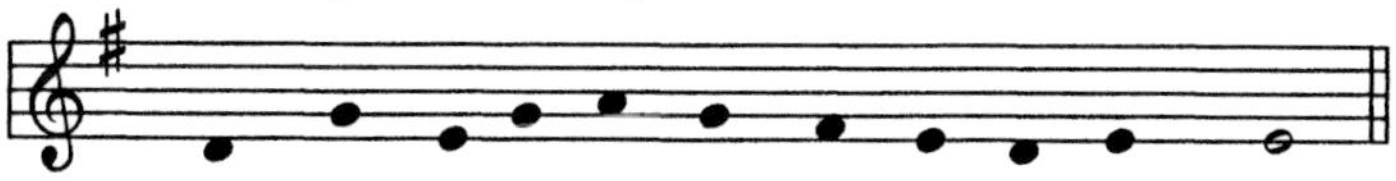

My food is to do the will of my Fa - ther.

Psalm 40 *Expectans, expectavi* *Tone II.1*

1 *I wait*ed patiently upón the LORD; *
he stooped to me / and héard my cry.

2 He lifted me out of the desolate pit, out of the míre and clay; *
he set my feet upon a high cliff and made / my fóoting sure.

3 He put a new song in my mouth,
a song of praise to óur God; *
many shall see, and stand in awe,
and put their / trust ín the LORD.

4 Happy are they who trust in the LÓRD! *
they do not resort to evil spirits or turn / to fálse gods.

5 Great things are they that you have done, O LORD my God!
how great your wonders and your pláns for us! *
there is none who can be / compáred with you.

6 Oh, that I could make them known and téll them! *
but they are more / than Í can count.

7 In a sacrifice and offering you take no pléasure *
(you have given me ears / to héar you);

8 Burnt-offering and sin-offering you have nót required, *
and so I said, "Be/hold, Í come.

9 In the roll of the book it is written concérning me: *
'I love to do your will, O my God;
your law is deep / in mý heart.'"

10 I proclaimed righteousness in the great congregátion; *
behold, I did not restrain my lips;
and that, / O LÓRD, you know.

11 Your righteousness have I not hidden in my heart;
I have spoken of your faithfulness and your delíverance; *
I have not concealed your love and faithfulness from
the great con/gregátion.

12 You are the LORD;
do not withhold your compassion fróm me; *
let your love and your faithfulness keep me safe / for éver,

13 For innumerable troubles have crowded upon me;
my sins have overtaken me, and I cánnot see; *
they are more in number than the hairs of my head,
and my / heart fáils me.

14 Be pleased, O LORD, to delíver me; *
O LORD, make haste / to hélp me.

15 Let them be ashamed and altogether dismayed
who seek after my life to destróy it; *
let them draw back and be disgraced
who take pleasure in my / misfórtune.

16 Let those who say "Aha!" and gloat over me be confóunded, *
because / they áre ashamed.

17 Let all who seek you rejoice in you ánd be glad; *
let those who love your salvation continually say,
"Great / is thé LORD!"

18 Though I am poor and afflícted, *
the Lord will have / regárd for me.

19 You are my helper and my delíverer; *
do not tar/ry, Ó my God. *[Ant.]*

41

In Easter Season

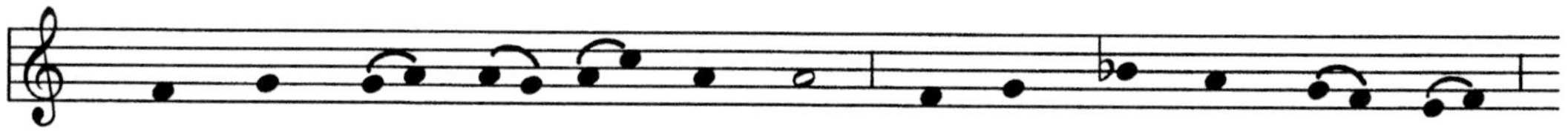

Christ be - came poor for our sake, that we might be - come rich,

hal - le - lu - jah.

On other Sundays and Weekdays

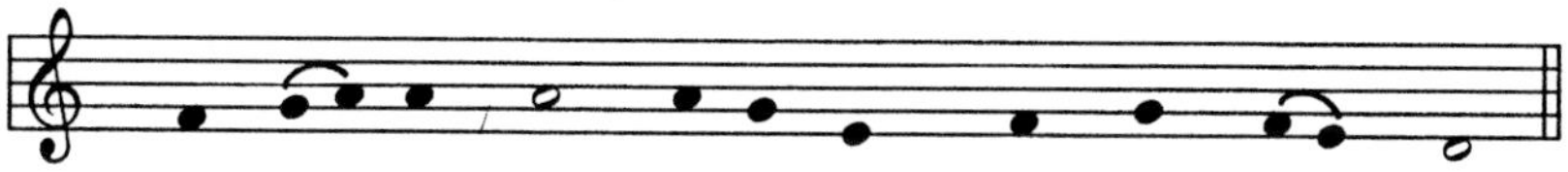

Heal me, O LORD, for I have sinned a - gainst you.

Psalm 41 *Beatus qui intelligit* *Tone I.1*

1 *Happy* are they who consider the poor and needy! *
the LORD will deliver them in the / time of trouble.

2 The LORD preserves them and keeps them alive,
so that they may be happy in the land; *
he does not hand them over to the will / of their enemies.

3 The LORD sustains them on their sickbed *
and ministers to them / in their illness.

4 I said, "LORD, be merciful to me; *
heal me, for I have / sinned against you."

5 My enemies are saying wicked things about me: *
"When will he die, and / his name perish?"

6 Even if they come to see me, they speak empty words; *
their heart collects false rumors;
they go out/side and spread them.

7 All my enemies whisper together about me *
and devise e/vil against me.

8 "A deadly thing," they say, "has fastened on him; *
he has taken to his bed and will ne/ver get up again."

9 Even my best friend, whom I trusted,
who broke bread with me, *
has lifted up his heel and / turned against me.

10 But you, O LORD, be merciful to me and raise me up, *
and I / shall repay them.

11 By this I know you are pleased with me, *
that my enemy does not / triumph over me.

12 In my integrity you hold me fast, *
and shall set me before your / face for ever.

13 Blessed be the LORD God of Israel, *
from age to / age. Amen. Amen. *[Ant.]*

42

In Advent

Let us live righ - teous and god - ly lives, look - ing for that bless - ed

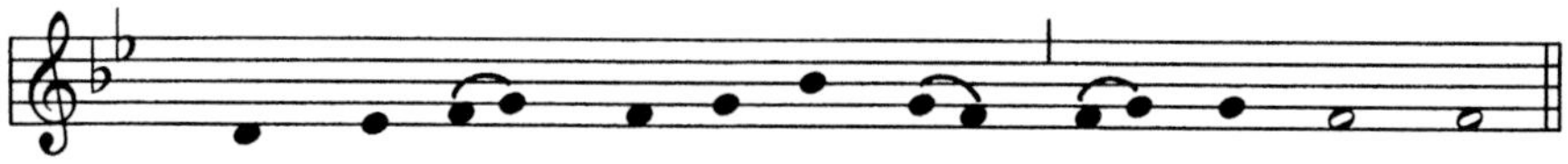

hope, the com - ing of the LORD, hal - le - lu - jah.

In Lent

Why are you so full of heav - i - ness, O my soul?

In Easter Season

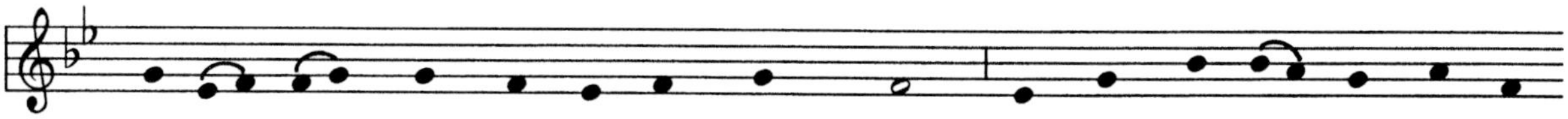

As the deer longs for the wa - ter - brooks, so longs my soul for you, O

God, hal - le - lu - jah. †

On other Sundays and Weekdays

My soul is a - thirst for God, a - thirst for the liv - ing God.

Psalm 42 *Quemadmodum* *Tone VIII.1*

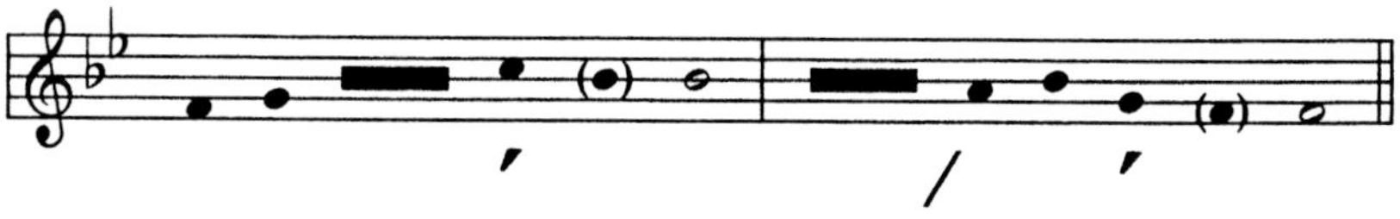

1 *As the* deer longs for the wáter-brooks, *
so longs my / soul for yóu, O God.

2 † My soul is athirst for God, athirst for the líving God; *
when shall I come to appear before the / presence óf God?

3 My tears have been my food dáy and night, *
while all day long they say to me,
/ "Where now ís your God?"

4 I pour out my soul when I think on thése things: *
how I went with the multitude and led them in/to the hóuse of God,

5 With the voice of praise and thanksgíving, *
among those / who keep hóly-day.

6 Why are you so full of heaviness, Ó my soul? *
and why are you so disquiet/ed withín me?

7 Put your trúst in God; *
for I will yet give thanks to him,
who is the help of my counte/nance, and mý God.

8 My soul is heavy withín me; *
therefore I will remember you from the land of Jordan,
and from the peak of Mizar among the / heights of Hérmon.

9 One deep calls to another in the noise of your cátaracts; *
all your rapids and floods / have gone óver me.

10 The LORD grants his loving-kindness in the dáytime; *
in the night season his song is with me,
a prayer to the / God of mý life.

11 I will say to the God of my strength,
"Why have you forgótten me? *
and why do I go so heavily while the ene/my opprésses me?

12 While my bones are being bróken, *
my enemies / mock me tó my face;

13 All day long they móck me *
and say to me, / "Where now ís your God?"

14 Why are you so full of heaviness, Ó my soul? *
and why are you so disquiet/ed withín me?

15 Put your trúst in God; *
for I will yet give thanks to him,
who is the help of my counte/nance, and mý God. *[Ant.]*

43

In Advent

Say to those who are of a fear - ful heart: Be strong, for be - hold, the

Lord our God shall come, hal - le - lu - jah.

In Lent

De - fend my cause a - gainst an un - god - ly peo - ple, O God;

de - liv - er me from the de - ceit - ful and the wick - ed.

In Easter Season

I will go to the al - tar of God, to the God of my joy and

glad - ness, hal - le - lu - jah.

On other Sundays and Weekdays

Send out your light and your truth, that they may lead me.

Psalm 43 *Judica me, Deus* *Tone VII.3*

1 *Gïve jüdg*ment for me, O God,
and defend my cause against an ungódly péople; *
deliver me from the deceitful ánd the wícked.

2 For you are the God of my strength;
why have you pút me fróm you? *
and why do I go so heavily while the enemý opprésses me?

3 Send out your light and your truth, that théy may léad me, *
and bring me to your holy hill
and tó your dwélling;

4 That I may go to the altar of God,
to the God of my jóy and gládness; *
and on the harp I will give thanks to yóu, O Gód my God.

5 Why are you so full of héaviness, Ó my soul? *
and why are you so disquietéd withín me?

6 —Pút your trúst in God; *
for I will yet give thanks to him,
who is the help of my cóuntenance, ánd my God. *[Ant.]*

44

In Easter Season

Save us, O Lord, and we will praise your Name for ev - er,

hal - le - lu - jah.

On other Sundays and Weekdays

Rise up, O Lord, and help us; save us for the sake of your stead · fast love.

Psalm 44 *Deus, auribus* *Tone III.4*

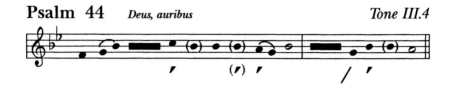

1 *We have* heard with our ears, O God,
our forefathers have told us, *
the deeds you did in their days,
in / the days of old.

2 How with your hand you drove the peoples out
and planted our forefathers in the land; *
how you destroyed nations and made your peo/ple flourish.

3 For they did not take the land by their sword,
nor did their arm win the victory for them; *
but your right hand, your arm, and the light of your countenance,
because / you favored them.

4 You are my King and my God; *
you command victories / for Jacob.

5 Through you we pushed back our adversaries; *
through your Name we trampled on those who rose up / against us.

6 For I do not rely on my bow, *
and my sword does not give me / the victory.

7 Surely, you gave us victory over our adversaries *
and put those who / hate us to shame.

8 Every day we gloried in God, *
and we will praise your Name / for ever.

9 Nevertheless, you have rejected and humbled us *
and do not go forth with / our armies.

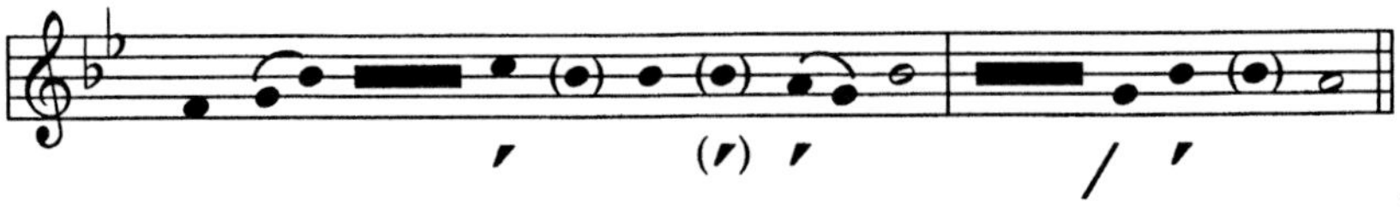

10 You have made us fall back before our adversary, *
and our enemies / have plundered us.

11 You have made us like sheep to be eaten *
and have scattered us among / the nations.

12 You are selling your people for a trifle *
and are making no profit on / the sale of them.

13 You have made us the scorn of our neighbors, *
a mockery and derision to those / around us.

14 You have made us a byword among the nations, *
a laughing-stock among / the peoples.

15 My humiliation is daily before me, *
and shame has co/vered my face;

16 Because of the taunts of the mockers and blasphemers, *
because of the enemy and / avenger.

17 All this has come upon us; *
yet we have not forgotten you,
nor have we betrayed / your covenant.

18 Our heart never turned back, *
nor did our footsteps stray / from your path;

19 Though you thrust us down into a place of misery, *
and covered us over with / deep darkness.

20 If we have forgotten the Name of our God, *
or stretched out our hands to / some strange god,

21 Will not God find it out? *
for he knows the se/crets of the heart.

22 Indeed, for your sake we are killed all the day long; *
we are accounted as sheep for / the slaughter.

23 Awake, O Lord! why are you sleeping? *
Arise! do not reject us / for ever.

24 Why have you hidden your face *
and forgotten our affliction and / oppression?

25 We sink down into the dust; *
our body cleaves / to the ground.

26 Rise up, and help us, *
and save us, for the sake of / your steadfast love. *[Ant.]*

45

In Easter Season

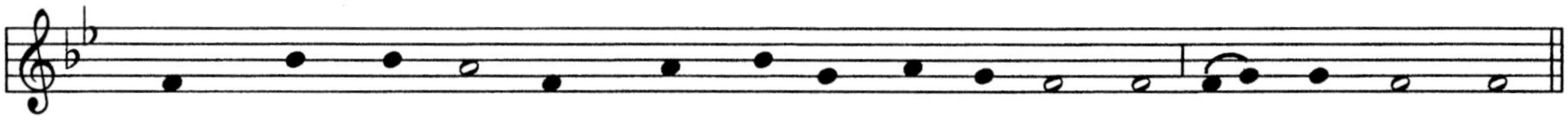

Your throne, O God, en - dures for ev - er and ev - er, hal - le - lu - jah.

On other Sundays and Weekdays

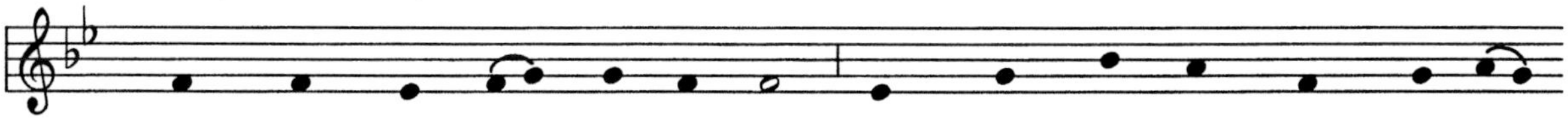

Grace flows from your lips, O king, be - cause God has blessed you for

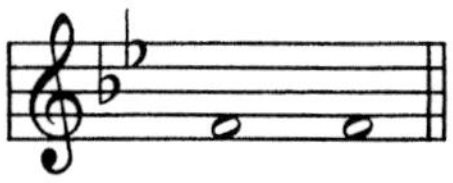

ev - er.

Psalm 45 *Eructavit cor meum* *Tone VIII.1*

1 *My heart* is stirring with a noble song;
let me recite what I have fashioned for the king; *
my tongue shall be the pen of / a skilled writer,

2 You are the fairest of men; *
grace flows from your lips,
because God has blessed / you for ever.

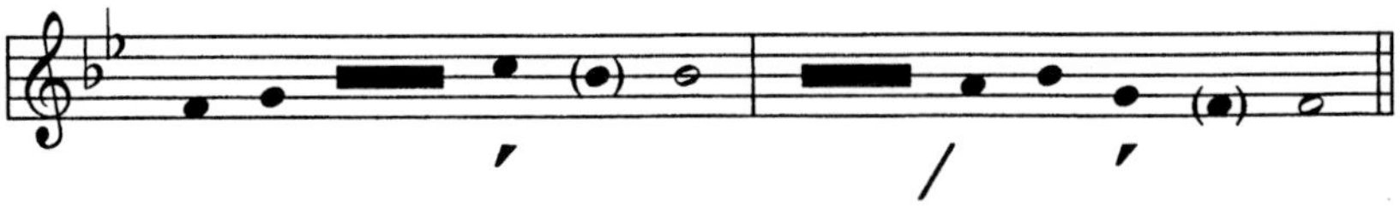

3 Strap your sword upon your thigh, O mighty wárrior, *
in your pride and / in your májesty.

4 Ride out and conquer in the cáuse of truth *
and for the / sake of jústice.

5 Your right hand will show you márvelous things; *
your arrows are very sharp, O / mighty wárrior.

6 The peoples are falling at your féet, *
and the king's ene/mies are lósing heart.

7 Your throne, O God, endures for ever and éver, *
a scepter of righteousness is the scepter of your kingdom;
you love righteousness and / hate iníquity.

8 Therefore God, your God, has anóinted you *
with the oil of gladness a/bove your féllows.

9 All your garments are fragrant with myrrh, aloes, and cássia, *
and the music of strings from ivory pal/aces mákes you glad.

10 Kings' daughters stand among the ladies of the cóurt; *
on your right hand is the queen,
adorned with the / gold of Óphir.

11 "Hear, O daughter; consider and listen clósely; *
forget your people / and your fáther's house.

12 The king will have pleasure in your béauty; *
he is your master; therefore / do him hónor.

13 The people of Tyre are here with a gíft; *
the rich among the people / seek your fávor."

14 All glorious is the princess as she énters; *
her / gown is clóth-of-gold.

15 In embroidered apparel she is brought to the kíng; *
after her the bridesmaids follow / in procéssion.

16 With joy and gladness théy are brought, *
and enter into the / palace óf the king.

17 "In place of fathers, O king, you sháll have sons; *
you shall make them princes / over áll the earth.

18 I will make your name to be remembered
from one generation to anóther; *
therefore nations will praise you for e/ver and éver." *[Ant.]*

46

On the Twelve Days of Christmas

His name shall be called Em - man - u - el: God with us.

In Lent

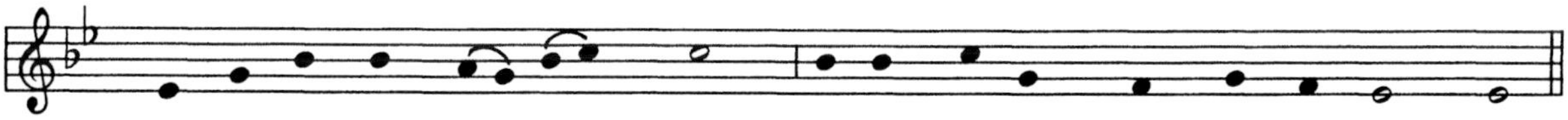

God is our ref - uge and strength, a ver - y pre - sent help in trou - ble. †

In Easter Season

There is a riv - er whose streams make glad the ci - ty of God,

hal - le - lu - jah.

On other Sundays and Weekdays

The LORD of hosts is with us; the God of Ja - cob is our strong - hold.

Psalm 46 *Deus noster refugium* *Tone V.1*

1 *God is* our refuge and strength, *
a very present help in trouble.

2 † Therefore we will not fear, though the earth be moved, *
and though the mountains be toppled into the depths of the sea;

3 Though its waters rage and foam, *
and though the mountains tremble at its tumult.

4 The LORD of hosts is with us; *
the God of Jacob is our stronghold.

5 There is a river whose streams make glad the city of God, *
the holy habitation of the Most High.

6 God is in the midst of her;
she shall not be overthrown; *
God shall help her at the break of day.

7 The nations make much ado, and the kingdoms are shaken; *
God has spoken, and the earth shall melt away.

8 The LORD of hosts is with us; *
the God of Jacob is our stronghold.

9 Come now and look upon the works of the LORD, *
what awesome things he has done on earth.

10 It is he who makes war to cease in all the world; *
he breaks the bow, and shatters the spear,
and burns the shields with fire.

11 "Be still, then, and know that I am God; *
I will be exalted among the nations;
I will be exalted in the earth."

12 The LORD of hosts is with us; *
the God of Jacob is our stronghold. *[Ant.]*

47

In Easter Season

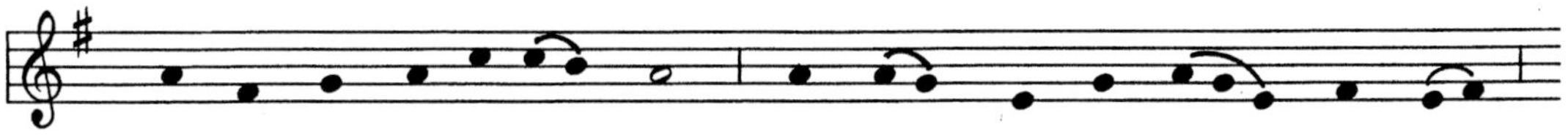
God is King of all the earth; sing prais - es with all your skill,

hal - le - lu - jah.

On other Sundays and Weekdays

Shout to God with a cry of joy.

Psalm 47 *Omnes gentes, plaudite* *Tone VII.3*

1 *Cla̋p yőur* hands, áll you péoples; *
shout to Gód with a crý of joy.

2 For the LORD Most Hígh is tó be feared; *
he is the great King óver áll the earth.

3 He subdues the péoples únder us, *
and the nations únder óur feet.

4 He chooses our inhéritance fór us, *
the pride of Jácob whóm he loves.

5 God has gone úp with á shout, *
the LORD with the sóund of the rám's-horn.

6 Sing praises to Gód, sing práises; *
sing praises to our Kíng, sing práises.

7 For God is Kíng of áll the earth; *
sing práises with áll your skill.

8 God reigns óver the nátions; *
God sits upón his hóly throne.

9 The nobles of the peoples have gáthered tógether *
with the people of the Gód of Ábraham.

10 The rulers of the éarth belóng to God, *
and he is híghly exálted. *[Ant.]*

48

On the Twelve Days of Christmas

Let Mount Zi - on be glad, and let the cit - ies of Ju - dah re - joice,

for the LORD has come.

In Easter Season

This God shall be our guide for ev - er - more, hal - le - lu - jah.

On other Sundays and Weekdays

Great is the LORD, and high - ly to be praised; in the cit - y of our God

is his ho - ly hill. †

Psalm 48 *Magnus Dominus* *Tone VIII.1*

1 *Great is* the LORD, and highly to be práised; *
in the city of our God / is his hóly hill.

2 † Beautiful and lofty, the joy of all the earth, is the hill of Źion, *
the very center of the world and the city / of the gréat King.

3 God is in her ćitadels; *
he is known to be / her sure réfuge.

4 Behold, the kings of the earth assémbled *
and marched for/ward togéther.

5 They looked and were astóunded; *
they retreated and / fled in térror.

6 Trembling seized them thére; *
they writhed like a woman in childbirth,
like ships of the sea when the / east wind shátters them.

7 As we have heard, so have we seen,
in the city of the LORD of hosts, in the city of our Gód; *
God has established / her for éver.

8 We have waited in silence on your loving-kindness, O Gód, *
in the midst / of your témple.

9 Your praise, like your Name, O God, reaches to the wórld's end; *
your right hand is / full of jústice.

10 Let Mount Zion be glad
and the cities of Judah rejóice, *
because / of your júdgments.

11 Make the circuit of Zion;
walk round abóut her; *
count the number / of her tówers.

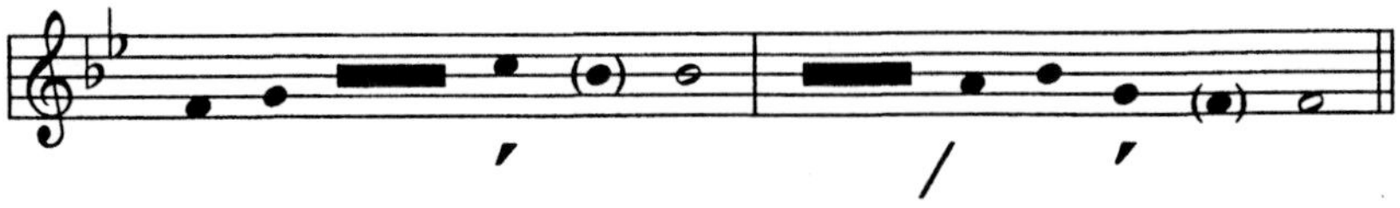

12 Consider well her bulwarks;
examine her strongholds; *
that you may tell those / who come after.

13 This God is our God for ever and ever; *
he shall be our / guide for evermore. *[Ant.]*

49

In Easter Season

From the grasp of death, God has ran - somed my life, hal - le - lu - jah.

On other Sundays and Weekdays

Lay up for your - selves treas - ures in hea - ven, says the Lord.

Psalm 49 *Audite haec, omnes* *Tone II.1*

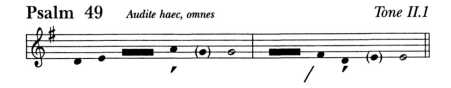

1 *Hear this,* all you peoples;
hearken, all you who dwell in the world, *
you of high degree and low, rich and poor / together.

2 My mouth shall speak of wisdom, *
and my heart shall meditate on un/derstanding.

3 I will incline my ear to a proverb *
and set forth my riddle up/on the harp.

4 Why should I be afraid in evil days, *
when the wickedness of those at my heels / surrounds me,

5 The wickedness of those who put their trust in their goods, *
and boast of their / great riches?

6 We can never ransom ourselves, *
or deliver to God the price / of our life;

7 For the ransom of our life is so great, *
that we should never have enough / to pay it,

8 In order to live for ever and ever, *
and never / see the grave.

9 For we see that the wise die also;
like the dull and stupid they perish *
and leave their wealth to those who / come after them.

10 Their graves shall be their homes for ever,
their dwelling places from generation to generation, *
though they call the lands after / their own names.

11 Even though honored, they cannot live for ever; *
they are like the beasts / that perish.

12 Such is the way of those who foolishly trust in themselves, *
and the end of those who delight in / their own words.

13 Like a flock of sheep they are destined to die;
Death is their shepherd; *
they go down straight/way to the grave.

14 Their form shall waste away, *
and the land of the dead / shall be their home.

15 But God will ransom my life; *
he will snatch me from / the grasp of death.

16 Do not be envious when some become rich, *
or when the grandeur of their house / increases;

17 For they will carry nothing away at their death, *
nor will their gran/deur follow them.

18 Though they thought highly of themselves while they lived, *
and were praised / for their success,

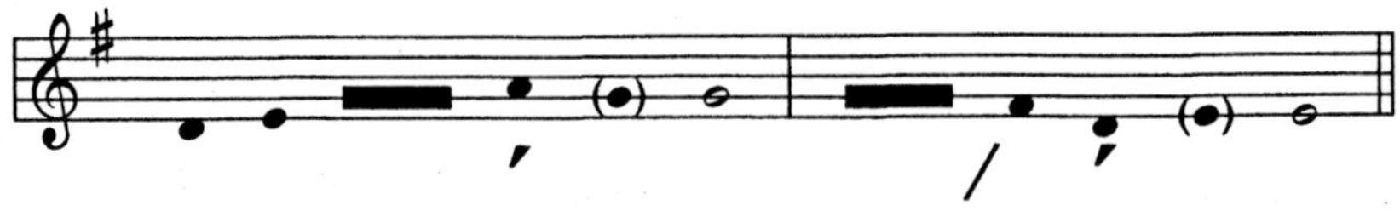

19 They shall join the company of their forebears, *
who will never see / the light again.

20 Those who are honored, but have no understanding, *
are like the beasts / that perish. *[Ant.]*

50

In Easter Season

Of - fer to God a sac - ri - fice of thanks - giv - ing, and make good your

vows to the Most High, hal - le - lu - jah.

On other Sundays and Weekdays

I de - sire mer - cy more than sac - ri - fice, and the know - ledge of God

more than burnt of - ferings.

Psalm 50 *Deus deorum* *Tone I.2*

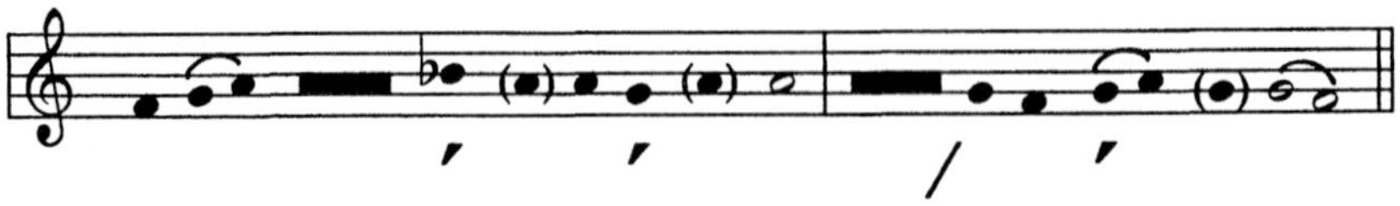

1 *The* LORD, the God of gods, has spoken; *
he has called the earth from the rising of the sun / to its setting.

2 Out of Zion, perfect in its beauty, *
God reveals him/self in glory.

3 Our God will come and will not keep silence; *
before him there is a consuming flame,
and round about / him a raging storm.

4 He calls the heavens and the earth from above *
to witness the judgment / of his people.

5 "Gather before me my loyal followers, *
those who have made a covenant with me and sealed / it with sacrifice."

6 Let the heavens declare the rightness of his cause; *
for / God himself is judge.

7 Hear, O my people, and I will speak:
"O Israel, I will bear witness against you; *
for / I am God, your God.

8 I do not accuse you because of your sacrifices; *
your offerings are al/ways before me.

9 I will take no bull-calf from your stalls, *
nor he-goats / out of your pens;

10 For all the beasts of the forest are mine, *
the herds in their thou/sands upon the hills.

11 I know every bird in the sky, *
and the creatures of the / fields are in my sight.

12 If I were hungry, I would not tell you, *
for the whole world is mine and / all that is in it.

13 Do you think I eat the flesh of bulls, *
or / drink the blood of goats?

14 Offer to God a sacrifice of thanksgiving *
and make good your vows / to the Most High.

15 Call upon me in the day of trouble; *
I will deliver you, and / you shall honor me."

16 But to the wicked God says: *
"Why do you recite my statutes,
and take my cove/nant upon your lips;

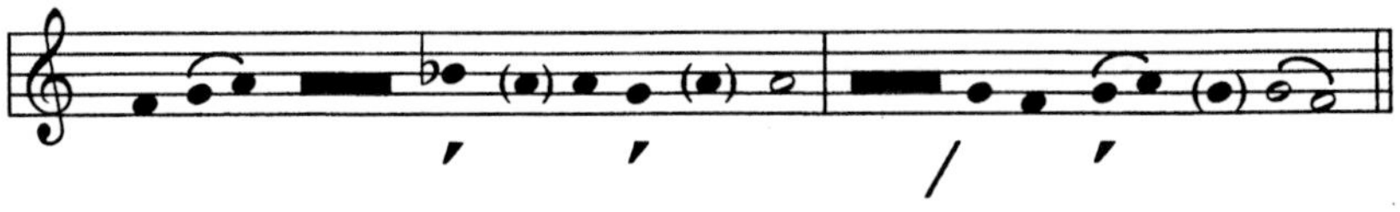

17 Since you refuse discipline, *
and toss my / words behind your back?

18 When you see a thief, you make him your friend, *
and you cast in your lot / with adulterers.

19 You have loosed your lips for evil, *
and harnessed / your tongue to a lie.

20 You are always speaking evil of your brother *
and slandering / your own mother's son.

21 These things you have done, and I kept still, *
and you thought that / I am like you."

22 "I have made my accusation; *
I have put my case in or/der before your eyes.

23 Consider this well, you who forget God, *
lest I rend you and there be none / to deliver you.

24 Whoever offers me the sacrifice of thanksgiving honors me; *
but to those who keep in my way will I show the
sal/vation of God." *[Ant.]*

51

In Holy Week

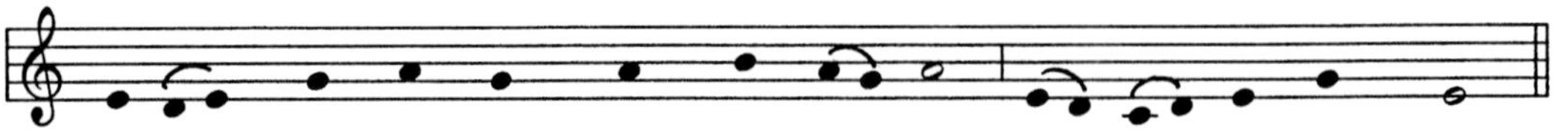

A bro - ken and con - trite heart, O God, you will not des - pise.

In Easter Season

Lord, re - mem - ber me when you come in - to your king - dom,

hal - le - lu - jah.

On other Sundays and Weekdays

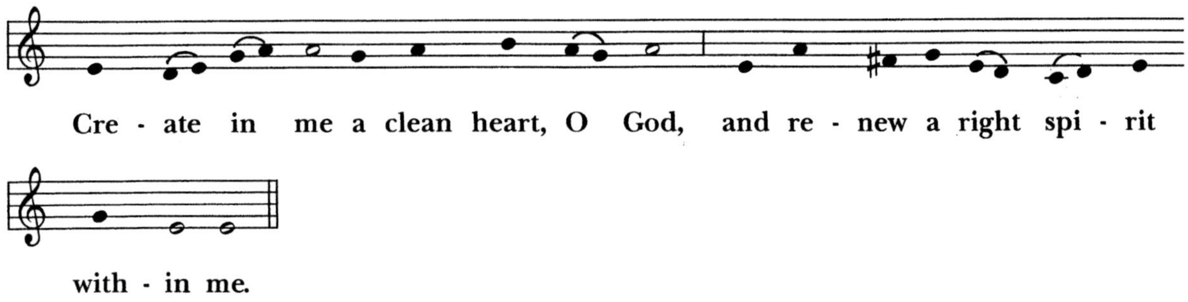
Cre - ate in me a clean heart, O God, and re - new a right spi - rit
with - in me.

Psalm 51 *Miserere mei, Deus* *Tone IV.1*

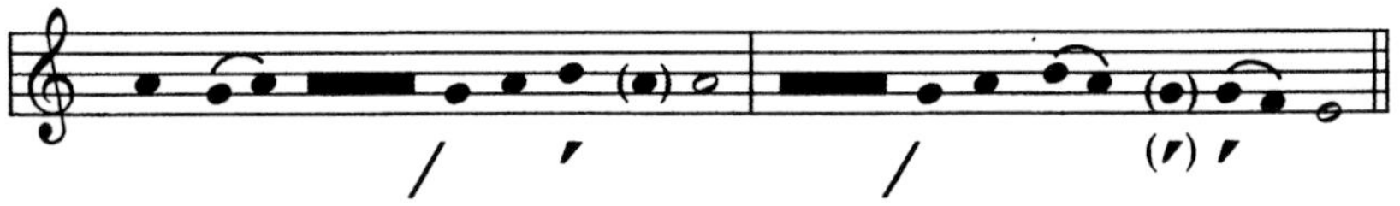

1 *Have mercy* on me, O God, according to your / loving-kindness; *
in your great compassion / blot out my offenses.

2 Wash me through and through / from my wickedness *
and / cleanse me from my sin.

3 For I know / my transgressions, *
and my sin is / ever before me.

4 Against you only / have I sinned *
and done what is / evil in your sight.

5 And so you are justified / when you speak *
and up/right in your judgment.

6 Indeed, I have been wicked / from my birth, *
a sinner / from my mother's womb.

7 For behold, you look for truth / deep within me, *
and will make me understand / wisdom secretly.

8 Purge me from my sin, / and I shall be pure; *
wash me, and I / shall be clean indeed.

9 Make me hear of / joy and gladness, *
that the body you have / broken may rejoice.

10 Hide your face / from my sins *
and blot out / all my iniquities.

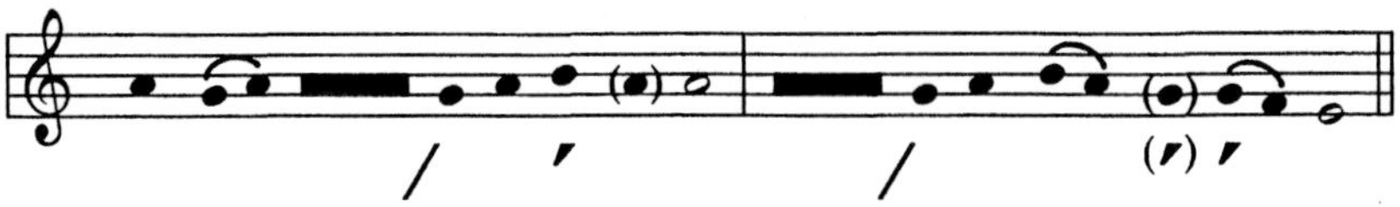

11 Create in me / a clean heart, O God, *
and renew a right / spirit within me.

12 Cast me not away / from your presence *
and take not your / holy Spirit from me.

13 Give me the joy of your / saving help again *
and sustain me with your / bountiful Spirit.

14 I shall teach your ways / to the wicked, *
and sinners / shall return to you.

15 Deliver / me from death, O God, *
and my tongue shall sing of your righteousness,
O / God of my salvation.

16 O/pen my lips, O Lord, *
and my mouth / shall proclaim your praise.

17 Had you desired it, I would have / offered sacrifice, *
but you take no de/light in burnt-offerings.

18 The sacrifice of God is a / troubled spirit; *
a broken and contrite heart, O / God, you will not despise.

19 Be favorable and gra/cious to Zion, *
and rebuild the / walls of Jerusalem.

20 Then you will be pleased with the appointed sacrifices,
with burnt-offerings / and oblations; *
then shall they offer young bul/locks upon your altar. *[Ant.]*

52

In Easter Season

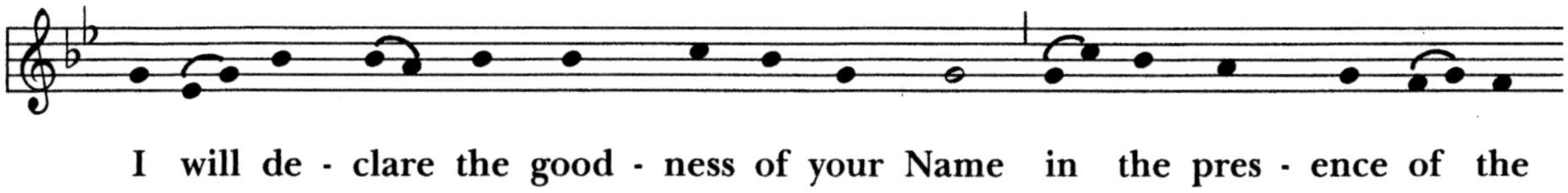
I will de - clare the good - ness of your Name in the pres - ence of the

god - ly, hal - le - lu - jah.

On other Sundays and Weekdays

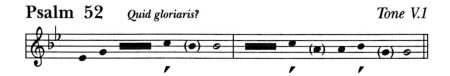

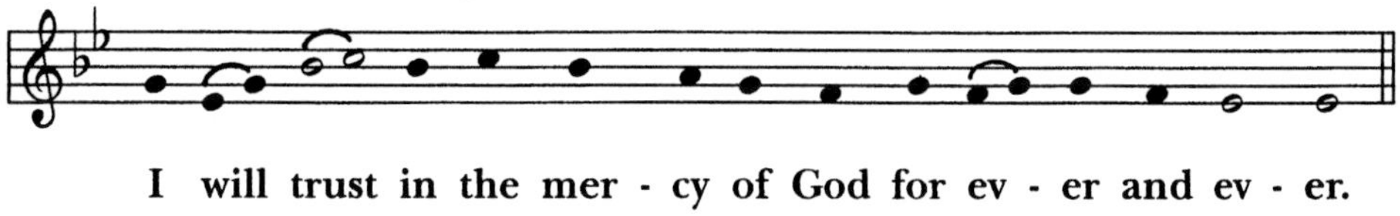
I will trust in the mer - cy of God for ev - er and ev - er.

Psalm 52 *Quid gloriaris?* *Tone V.1*

1 *You ty*rant, why do you boast of wickedness *
  against the godly all day long?

2 You plot ruin;
your tongue is like a sharpened razor, *
  O worker of deception.

3 You love evil more than good *
  and lying more than speaking the truth.

4 You love all words that hurt, *
  O you deceitful tongue.

5 Oh, that God would demolish you utterly, *
  topple you, and snatch you from your dwelling,
  and root you out of the land of the living!

6 The righteous shall see and tremble, *
  and they shall laugh at him, saying,

7 "This is the one who did not take God for a réfuge, *
but trusted in great wealth
and relíed upon wíckedness."

8 But I am like a green olive tree in the hóuse of God; *
I trust in the mercy of God for éver and éver.

9 I will give you thanks for what yóu have done *
and declare the goodness of your Name in the
presence óf the gódly. *[Ant.]*

53

In Easter Season

Our God will re - store the for - tunes of his peo - ple, and we will be

glad, hal - le - lu - jah.

On other Sundays and Weekdays

God looks down from hea - ven up - on us all.

Psalm 53 *Dixit insipiens* *Tone VII.3*

1 *Thë fööl* has said in his heart, "Thére is nó God." *
All are corrupt and commit abominable acts;
there is nóne who does ány good.

2 God looks down from héaven upón us all, *
to see if there is any who is wise,
if there is óne who seeks áfter God.

3 Every one has proved faithless;
all alike_have turned bad; *
there is none who does good; no, not one.

4 Have they no knowledge, those evildoers *
who eat up my people like bread
and do not call upon God?

5 See how greatly they tremble,
such trembling as never was; *
for God has scattered the bones of the enemy;
they are put to shame, because God has rejected them.

6 Oh, that Israel's deliverance would come out of Zion! *
when God restores the fortunes of his people
Jacob will rejoice and Israel be glad. *[Ant.]*

54

In Holy Week

He was led as a lamb to the slaugh - ter, and he o - pened not his mouth.

In Easter Season

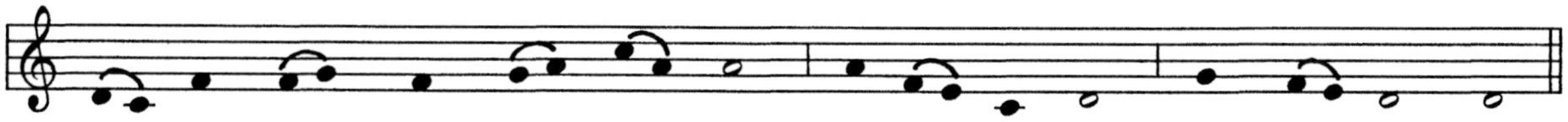

I will praise your Name, O LORD, for it is good, hal - le - lu - jah.

On other Sundays and Weekdays

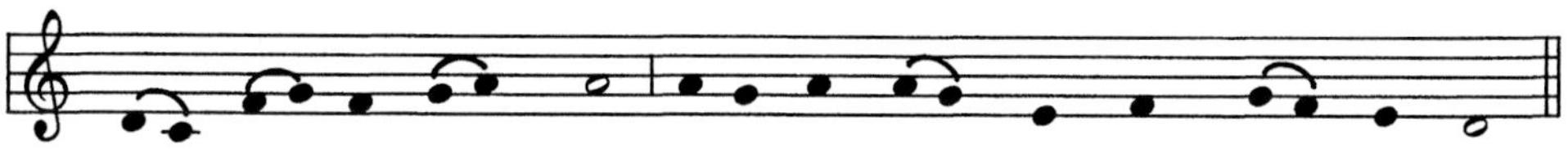

God is my help - er; it is the Lord who sus - tains my life.

Psalm 54 *Deus, in nomine* *Tone I.2*

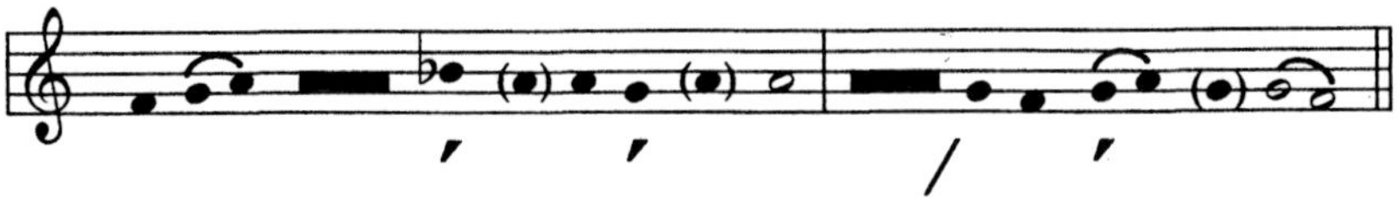

1 *Save me,* O God, by your Name; *
in your / might, defend my cause.

2 —Hear my prayer, O God; *
give ear to the / words of my mouth.

3 For the arrogant have risen up against me,
and the ruthless have sought my life, *
those who have / no regard for God.

4 Behold, God is my helper; *
it is the Lord / who sustains my life.

5 Render evil to those who spy on me; *
in your faithful/ness, destroy them.

6 I will offer you a freewill sacrifice *
and praise your Name, O / LORD, for it is good.

7 For you have rescued me from every trouble, *
and my eye has seen the / ruin of my foes. *[Ant.]*

55

In Holy Week

Had it been an en - e - my who vaunt - ed him - self a - gainst me, then I
could have borne it; but it was you, my com - pan - ion, my own
fa - mil - iar friend.

In Easter Season

Cast your bur - den up - on the LORD, and he will sus - tain you,

hal - le - lu - jah.

On other Sundays and Weekdays

I will call up - on God, and the LORD will de - liv - er me.

Psalm 55 *Exaudi, Deus* *Tone I.1*

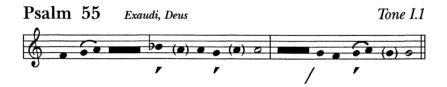

1 *Hear my*—prayer, O God; *
do not hide yourself from / my petition.

2 Listen to me and answer me; *
I have no peace, be/cause of my cares.

3 I am shaken by the noise of the enemy *
and by the pressure / of the wicked;

4 For they have cast an evil spell upon me *
and are set against / me in fury.

5 My heart quakes within me, *
and the terrors of death have / fallen upon me.

6 Fear and trembling have come over me, *
and horror / overwhelms me.

7 And I said, "Oh, that I had wings like a dove! *
I would fly a/way and be at rest.

8 I would flee to a far-off place *
and make my lodging / in the wilderness.

9 I would hasten to escape *
from the stormy / wind and tempest."

10 Swallow them up, O LORD;
confound their speech; *
for I have seen violence and strife / in the city.

11 Day and night the watchmen make their rounds upon her walls, *
but trouble and misery are / in the midst of her.

12 There is corruption at her heart; *
her streets are never free of op/pression and deceit.

13 For had it been an adversary who taunted me,
then I could have borne it; *
or had it been an enemy who vaunted himself against me,
then I could have / hidden from him.

14 But it was you, a man after my own heart, *
my companion, my / own familiar friend.

15 We took sweet counsel together, *
and walked with the throng / in the house of God.

16 Let death come upon them suddenly;
let them go down alive into the grave; *
for wickedness is in their dwellings, / in their very midst.

17 But I will call upon God, *
and the LORD / will deliver me.

18 In the evening, in the morning, and at noonday,
I will complain and lament, *
and / he will hear my voice.

19 He will bring me safely back from the battle waged against me; *
for there are ma/ny who fight me.

20 God, who is enthroned of old, will hear me and bring them down; *
they never change; they / do not fear God.

21 My companion stretched forth his hand against his comrade; *
he has bro/ken his covenant.

22 His speech is softer than butter, *
but / war is in his heart.

23 His words are smoother than oil, *
but / they are drawn swords.

24 Cast your burden upon the LORD,
and he will sustain you; *
he will never let the / righteous stumble.

25 For you will bring the bloodthirsty and deceitful *
down to the pit of des/truction, O God.

26 They shall not live out half their days, *
but I will / put my trust in you. *[Ant.]*

56

In Easter Season

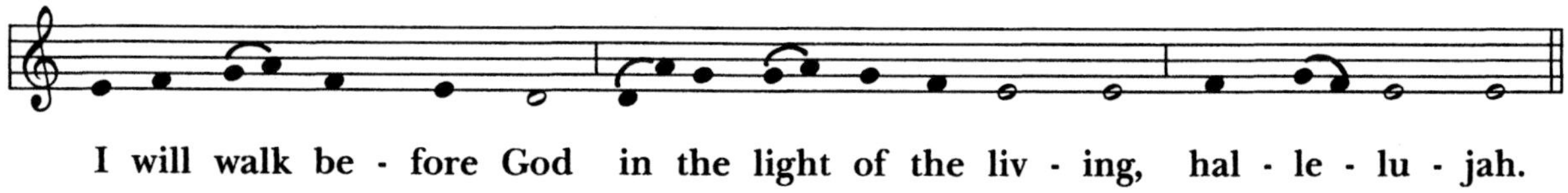
I will walk be - fore God in the light of the liv - ing, hal - le - lu - jah.

On other Sundays and Weekdays

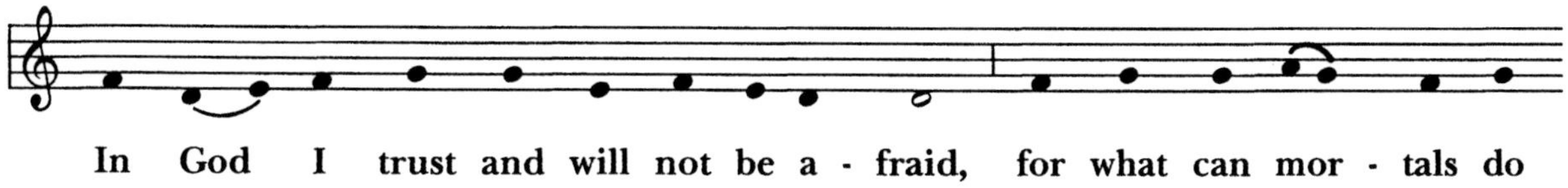
In God I trust and will not be a - fraid, for what can mor - tals do

to me?

Psalm 56 *Miserere mei, Deus* *Tone IV.1*

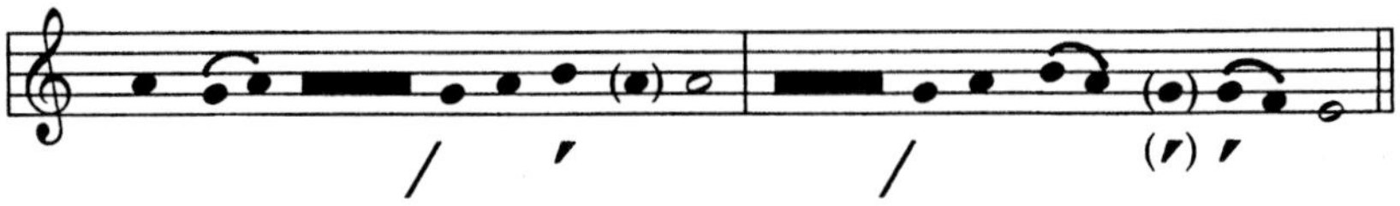

1 *Have mercy* on me, O God,
for my ene/mies are hounding me; *
all day long they as/sault and oppress me.

2 They hound me / all the day long; *
truly there are many who fight a/gainst me, O Most High.

3 Whenever / I am afraid, *
I will / put my trust in you.

4 In God, whose word I praise,
in God I trust and / will not be afraid, *
for / what can flesh do to me?

5 All day long they dam/age my cause; *
their only thought / is to do me evil.

6 They band together; they / lie in wait; *
they spy upon my footsteps;
be/cause they seek my life.

7 Shall they escape de/spite their wickedness? *
O God, in your an/ger, cast down the peoples.

8 You have noted my lamentation;
put my tears in/to your bottle; *
are they not re/corded in your book?

9 Whenever I call upon you, my enemies / will be put to flight; *
this I know, for / God is on my side.

10 In God the LORD, whose word I praise,
in God I trust and / will not be afraid, *
for what can / mortals do to me?

11 I am bound by the vow I / made to you, O God; *
I will pre/sent to you thank-offerings;

12 For you have rescued my soul from death and my / feet from stumbling, *
that I may walk before God in the / light of the living. *[Ant.]*

57

In Easter Season

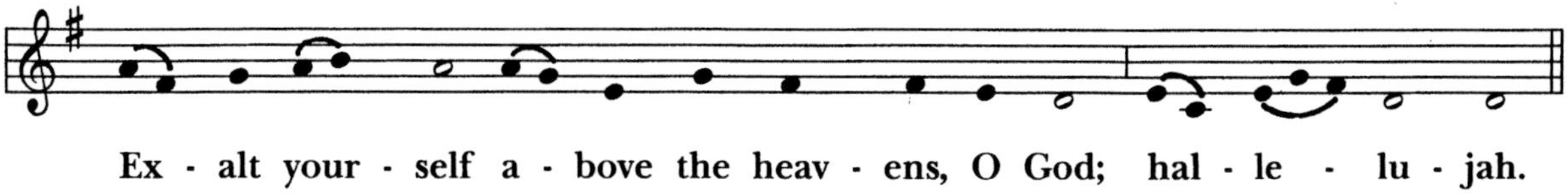
Ex - alt your - self a - bove the heav - ens, O God; hal - le - lu - jah.

On other Sundays and Weekdays

A - wake, lute and harp; I my - self will wak - en the dawn.

Psalm 57 *Miserere mei, Deus* *Tone VII.1*

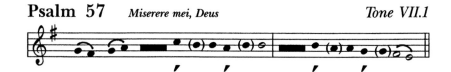

1 *Be mer*ciful to me, O God, be merciful,
for I have taken refuge in you; *
  in the shadow of your wings will I take refuge
  until this time of trouble has gone by.

2 I will call upon the Most High God, *
  the God who maintains my cause.

3 He will send from heaven and save me;
he will confound those who trample upon me; *
  God will send forth his love and his faithfulness.

4 I lie in the midst of lions that devour the people; *
  their teeth are spears and arrows,
  their tongue a sharp sword.

5 They have laid a net for my feet,
and I am bowed low; *
  they have dug a pit before me,
  but have fallen into it themselves.

6 Exalt yourself above the heavens, O God, *
  and your glory over all the earth.

7 My heart is firmly fixed, O God, my heart is fixed; *
  I will sing and make melody.

8 Wake up, my spirit,
awake, lute and harp; *
I myself will waken the dawn.

9 I will confess you among the peoples, O LORD; *
I will sing praise to you among the nations.

10 For your loving-kindness is greater than the heavens, *
and your faithfulness reaches to the clouds.

11 Exalt yourself above the heavens, O God, *
and your glory over all the earth. *[Ant.]*

58

Antiphon

There is a re - ward for the righ - teous; there is a God who rules in

the earth.

Psalm 58 *Si vere utque* *Tone I.2*

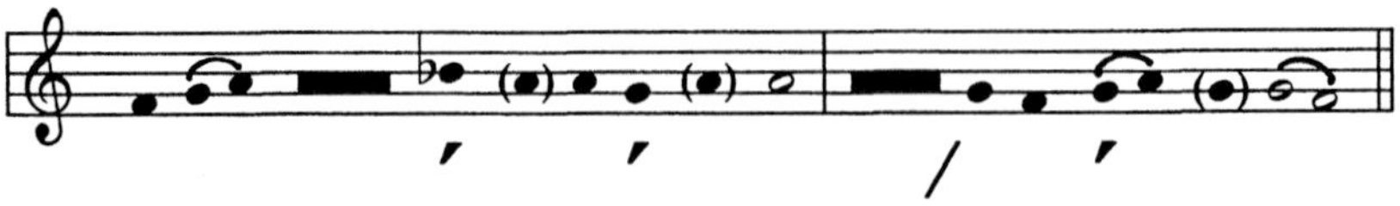

1 *Do you* indeed decree righteousness, you rulers? *
do you judge the peo/ples with equity?

2 No; you devise evil in your hearts, *
and your hands deal out vio/lence in the land.

3 The wicked are perverse from the womb; *
liars go a/stray from their birth.

4 They are as venomous as a serpent, *
they are like the deaf ad/der which stops its ears,

5 Which does not heed the voice of the charmer, *
no matter how skill/ful his charming.

6 O God, break their teeth in their mouths; *
pull the fangs of the young / lions, O LORD.

7 Let them vanish like water that runs off; *
let them wi/ther like trodden grass.

8 Let them be like the snail that melts away, *
like a stillborn child that / never sees the sun.

9 Before they bear fruit, let them be cut down like a brier; *
like thorns and thistles let / them be swept away.

10 The righteous will be glad when they see the vengeance; *
they will bathe their feet in the blood / of the wicked.

11 And they will say,
"Surely, there is a reward for the righteous; *
surely, there is a God who / rules in the earth." *[Ant.]*

59

Antiphon

Pro - tect me, O my God, from those who rise up a - gainst me.

Psalm 59 *Eripe me de inimicis* *Tone IV.1*

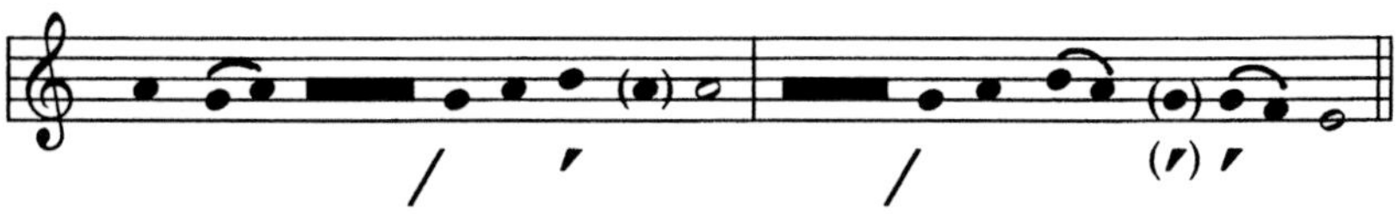

1 *Rescue* me from my en/emies, O God; *
protect me from those who / rise up against me.

2 Rescue me from / evildoers *
and save me from / those who thirst for my blood.

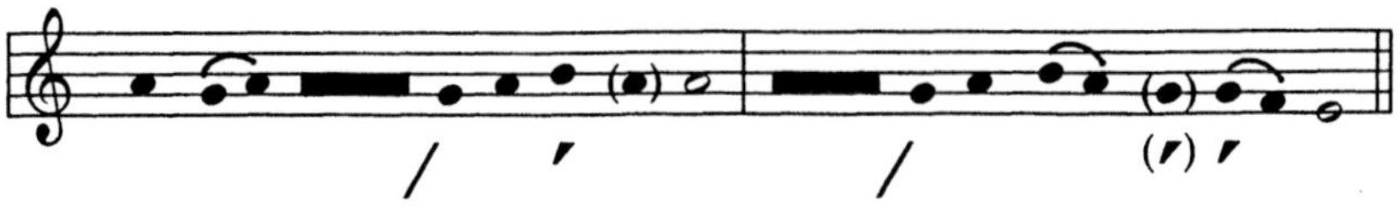

3 See how they lie in wait for my life,
how the mighty gather toge/ther against me; *
not for any offense or / fault of mine, O LORD.

4 Not because of / any guilt of mine *
they run and pre/pare themselves for battle.

5 Rouse yourself, come / to my side, and see; *
for you, LORD God / of hosts, are Israel's God.

6 Awake, and punish all / the ungodly; *
show no mercy to those who are / faithless and evil.

7 They go to and fro / in the evening; *
they snarl like dogs and / run about the city.

8 Behold, they boast with their mouths,
and / taunts are on their lips; *
"For who," / they say, "will hear us?"

9 But you, O / LORD, you laugh at them; *
you laugh all / the ungodly to scorn.

10 My eyes are fixed / on you, O my Strength; *
for you, O / God, are my stronghold.

11 My merciful God / comes to meet me; *
God will let me look in tri/umph on my enemies.

12 Slay them, O God, lest my / people forget; *
send them reeling by your might
and put them / down, O Lord our shield.

13 For the sins of their mouths, for the words of their lips,
for the cursing and lies / that they utter, *
let / them be caught in their pride.

14 Make an end / of them in your wrath; *
make an end of them, / and they shall be no more.

15 Let everyone know that God / rules in Jácob, *
and / to the ënds óf thë earth.

16 They go to and fro / in the évening; *
they snarl like dogs and / run aböut the cíty.

17 They / forage fór food, *
and if they / are not fïlled, théy howl.

18 For my part, I will / sing of yóur strength; *
I will celebrate / your love ïn the mórning;

19 For you have be/come my strónghold, *
a refuge in the / day of mÿ tróuble.

20 To you, O my Strength, / will I síng; *
for you, O God, are my stronghold / and my mërcifül God. *[Ant.]*

60

Antiphon

Save us by your right hand, O God, that those who are dear to you may be

de - liv - ered.

Psalm 60 *Deus, repulisti nos* *Tone VII.3*

1 *Ö Göd,* you have cast us óff and bróken us; *
you have been angry;
oh, take us báck to yóu again.

2 You have shaken the earth and split it ópen; *
repair the cracks in it, fór it tótters.

3 You have made your people know hardship; *
you have given us wine that makes us stagger.

4 You have set up a banner for those who fear you, *
to be a refuge from the power of the bow.

5 Save us by your right hand and answer us, *
that those who are dear to you may be delivered.

6 God spoke from his holy place and said: *
"I will exult and parcel out Shechem;
I will divide the valley of Succoth.

7 Gilead is mine and Manasseh is mine; *
Ephraim is my helmet and Judah my scepter.

8 Moab is my wash-basin,
on Edom I throw down my sandal to claim it, *
and over Philistia will I shout in triumph."

9 Who will lead me into the strong city? *
who will bring me into Edom?

10 Have you not cast us off, O God? *
you no longer go out, O God, with our armies.

11 Grant us your help against the enemy, *
for vain is the help of man.

12 With God we will do valiant deeds, *
and he shall tread our enemies under foot. *[Ant.]*

61

In Easter Season

Let the King sit en - throned be - fore God for ev - er, hal - le - lu - jah.

On other Sundays and Weekdays

You, O Lord, have been my re - fuge, a strong tower a - gainst the

en - e - my.

Psalm 61 *Exaudi, Deus* *Tone I.2*

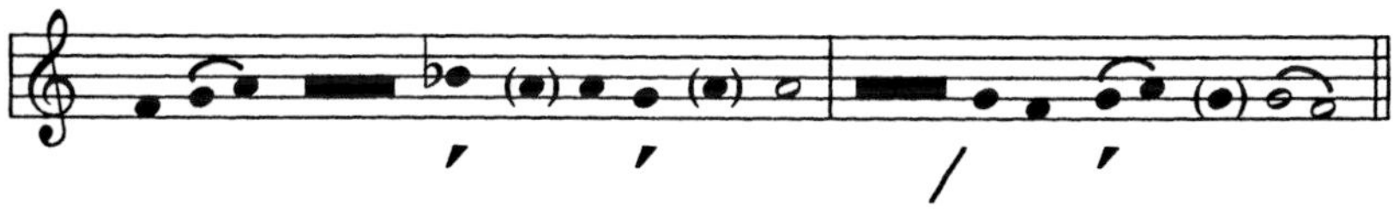

1 *Hear my* cry, O God, * and listen to my prayer.
2 I call upon you from the ends of the earth with heaviness in my heart; *
set me upon the rock / that is higher than I.

3 For you have been my refuge, *
a strong tower a/gainst the enemy.

4 I will dwell in your house for ever; *
I will take refuge under the / cover of your wings.

5 For you, O God, have heard my vows; *
you have granted me the heritage of / those who fear your Name.

6 Add length of days to the king's life; *
let his years extend over many / generations.

7 Let him sit enthroned before God for ever; *
bid love and faithful/ness watch over him.

8 So will I always sing the praise of your Name, *
and day by day I / will fulfill my vows. *[Ant.]*

62

In Easter Season

Let not our hearts be trou - bled; be - lieve in me, hal - le - lu - jah.

On other Sundays and Weekdays

We a - wait our bles - sed hope, the ap - pear - ing of the glo - ry of

our Sav - ior.

Psalm 62 *Nonne Deo?* *Tone VIII.1*

1 *For God* alone my soul in silence waits; *
from him comes / my salvation.

2 He alone is my rock and my salvation, *
my stronghold, so that I shall not be / greatly shaken.

3 How long will you assail me to crush me,
all of you together, *
as if you were a leaning / fence, a toppling wall?

4 They seek only to bring me down from my place of honor; *
lies / are their chief delight.

5 They bless with their lips, *
but / in their hearts they curse.

6 For God alone my soul in silence waits; *
truly, / my hope is in him.

7 He alone is my rock and my salvation, *
my stronghold, so that I shall / not be shaken.

8 In God is my safety and my hónor; *
God is my strong rock / and my réfuge.

9 Put your trust in him always, O péople, *
pour out your hearts before him, for God / is our réfuge.

10 Those of high degree are but a fléeting breath, *
even those of low estate can/not be trústed.

11 On the scales they are lighter than a bréath, *
all of / them togéther.

12 Put no trust in extortion;
in robbery take no émpty pride; *
though wealth increase, set not your / heart upón it.

13 God has spoken once, twice have I héard it, *
that / power belóngs to God.

14 Steadfast love is yóurs, O Lord, *
for you repay everyone ac/cording tó his deeds. *[Ant.]*

63

In Advent

Ho, ev - ery - one who thirsts, come to the wa - ters; seek the Lord while

he wills to be found, hal - le - lu - jah.

In Lent

You have been my help - er, O my God.

In Easter Season

Let who - ev - er thirsts take the wa - ter of life with - out price,

hal - le - lu - jah.

On other Sundays and Weekdays

O God, you are my God; ea - ger - ly I seek you. †

Psalm 63 *Deus, Deus meus* *Tone II.1*

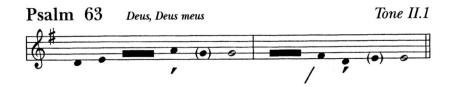

1 *O God,* you are my God; eagerly I seek you; *
*†my soul thirsts for you, my flesh faints for you,
as in a barren and dry land where there is / no water.

2 Therefore I have gazed upon you in your holy place, *
that I might behold your power and / your glory.

3 For your loving-kindness is better than life itself; *
my lips / shall give you praise.

4 So will I bless you as long as I live *
and lift up my hands / in your Name.

5 My soul is content, as with marrow and fatness, *
and my mouth praises you / with joyful lips,

6 When I remember you upon my bed, *
and meditate on you in the / night watches.

7 For you have been my helper, *
and under the shadow of your wings / I will rejoice.

*When the Sundays and Weekdays antiphon is sung, the first verse begins:
my soul thirsts for you, my flesh faints for you.

8 My soul clings to you; *
your right / hand holds me fast.

9 May those who seek my life to destroy it *
go down into the depths / of the earth;

10 Let them fall upon the edge of the sword, *
and let them be food / for jackals.

11 But the king will rejoice in God;
all those who swear by him will be glad; *
for the mouth of those who speak / lies shall be stopped. *[Ant.]*

64

In Easter Season

The righ - teous will re - joice in the LORD, hal - le - lu - jah.

On other Sundays and Weekdays

Pro - tect my life, O God, from fear of the en - e - my.

Psalm 64 *Exaudi, Deus* *Tone I.8*

1 *Hear my* voice, O God, when I complain; *
protect my life from fear / of the enemy.

2 Hide me from the conspiracy of the wicked, *
from the mob of / evildoers.

3 They sharpen their tongue like a sword, *
and aim their bitter / words like arrows,

4 That they may shoot down the blameless from ambush; *
they shoot without warning / and are not afraid.

5 They hold fast to their evil course; *
they plan how / they may hide their snares.

6 They say, "Who will see us?
who will find out our crimes? *
we have thought / out a perfect plot."

7 The human mind and heart are a mystery; *
but God will loose an arrow at them,
and suddenly they / will be wounded.

8 He will make them trip over their tongues, *
and all who see / them will shake their heads.

9 Everyone will stand in awe and declare God's deeds; *
they will / recognize his works.

10 The righteous will rejoice in the LORD and put their trust in him, *
and all who are true of / heart will glory. *[Ant.]*

65

In Easter Season

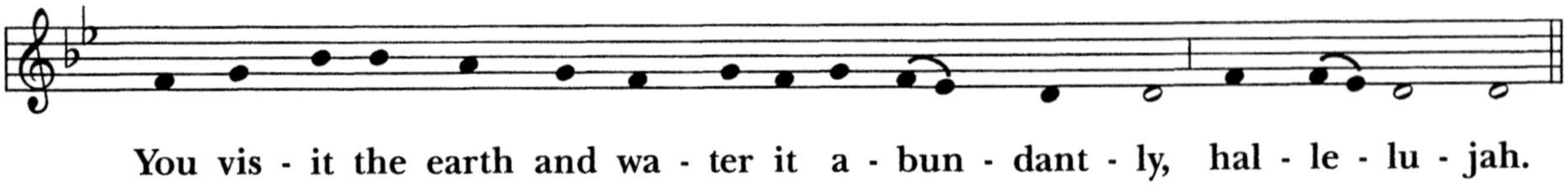
You vis - it the earth and wa - ter it a - bun - dant - ly, hal - le - lu - jah.

On other Sundays and Weekdays

Awe - some things will you show us in your righ - teous - ness, O God of
our sal - va - tion.

Psalm 65 *Te decet hymnus* — *Tone III.4*

1 *You are* to be praised, O God, in Zion; *
to you shall vows be performed in / Jerusalem.

2 To you that hear prayer shall all flesh come, *
because of their / transgressions.

3 Our sins are stronger than we are, *
but you will / blot them out.

4 Happy are they whom you choose
and draw to your courts to dwell there! *
they will be satisfied by the beauty of your house,
by the holiness of / your temple.

5 Awesome things will you show us in your righteousness,
O God of our salvation, *
O Hope of all the ends of the earth
and of the seas that / are far away.

6 You make fast the mountains by your power; *
they are girded a/bout with might.

7 You still the roaring of the seas, *
the roaring of their waves,
and the clamor of / the peoples.

8 Those who dwell at the ends of the earth will tremble at
your marvelous signs; *
you make the dawn and the dusk / to sing for joy.

9 You visit the earth and water it abundantly;
you make it very plenteous; *
the river of God is full / of water.

10 —You prepare the grain, *
for so you provide / for the earth.

11 You drench the furrows and smooth out the ridges; *
with heavy rain you soften the ground and bless / its increase.

12 You crown the year with your goodness, *
and your paths overflow / with plenty.

13 May the fields of the wilderness be rich for grazing, *
and the hills / be clothed with joy.

14 May the meadows cover themselves with flocks,
and the valleys cloak themselves with grain; *
let them shout / for joy and sing. *[Ant.]*

66

On the Twelve Days of Christmas

All the earth bows down be - fore you, sings to you, sings out your name.

In Lent

Come and lis - ten, all you who fear God, and I will tell you what he has

done for me.

In Easter Season

Bless our God, who holds our souls in life, hal - le - lu - jah.

On other Sundays and Weekdays

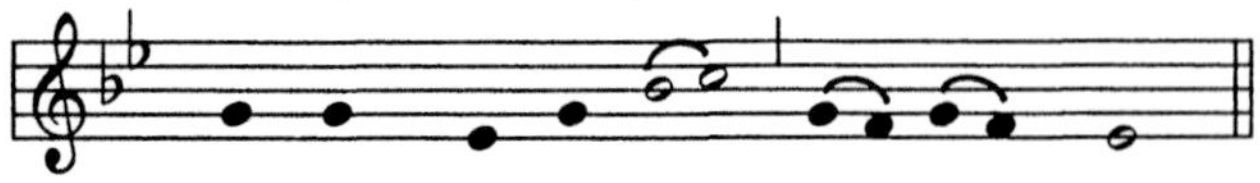

Be joy - ful in God, all you lands. †

Psalm 66 *Jubilate Deo* *Tone V.3*

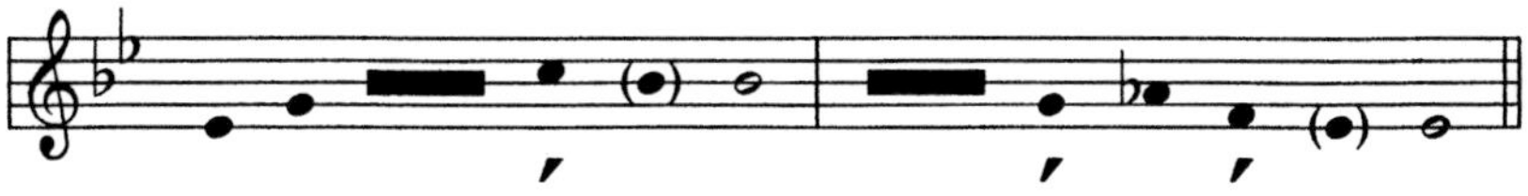

1 *Be joy*ful in God, all you lands; *
*†sing the glory of his Name;
sing the glory of his praise.

2 Say to God, "How awesome are your deeds! *
because of your great strength your enemies cringe before you.

3 All the earth bows down before you, *
sings to you, sings out your Name."

4 Come now and see the works of God, *
how wonderful he is in his doing toward all people.

5 He turned the sea into dry land,
so that they went through the water on foot, *
and there we rejoiced in him.

6 In his might he rules for ever;
his eyes keep watch over the nations; *
let no rebel rise up against him.

7 Bless our God, you peoples; *
make the voice of his praise to be heard;

8 Who holds our souls in life, *
and will not allow our feet to slip.

9 For you, O God, have proved us; *
you have tried us just as silver is tried.

10 You brought us into the snare; *
you laid heavy burdens upon our backs.

11 You let enemies ride over our heads;
we went through fire and water; *
but you brought us out into a place of refreshment.

*When the Sundays and Weekdays antiphon is sung, the first verse begins:
Sing the glory of his Name.

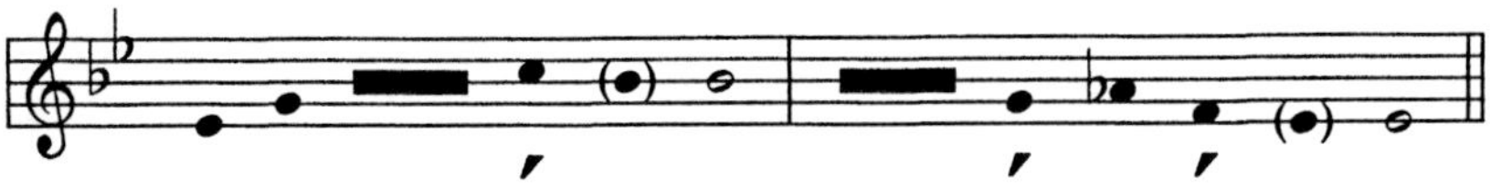

12 I will enter your house with burnt-offerings
and will pay yóu my vows, *
which I promised with my lips
and spoke with my mouth when I wás in tróuble.

13 I will offer you sacrifices of fat beasts
with the smóke of rams; *
I will give you óxen ánd goats.

14 Come and listen, all you who féar God, *
and I will tell you what hé has dóne for me.

15 I called out to him with my móuth, *
and his práise was ón my tongue.

16 If I had found evil in my héart, *
the Lord would nót have héard me;

17 But in truth God has héard me; *
he has attended to the vóice of mý prayer.

18 Blessed be God, who has not rejected my práyer, *
nor withhéld his lóve from me. *[Ant.]*

67

On the Twelve Days of Christmas

Let the peo - ples praise you, O God; let all the peo - ples praise you.

In Lent

Let your ways be known up - on earth, O Lord; your sav - ing health

a - mong all na - tions.

In Easter Season

Let the peo - ples praise you, O God; let all the peo - ples praise you,

hal - le - lu - jah.

On other Sundays and Weekdays

The Lord make his face to shine up - on us, and be gra - cious to us.

Psalm 67 *Deus misereatur* *Tone VIII.1*

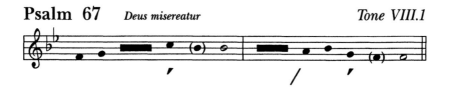

1 *May God* be merciful to us and bléss us, *
show us the light of his counte/nance and cóme to us.

2 Let your ways be known upon éarth, *
your saving health a/mong all nátions.

3 Let the peoples praise you, Ó God; *
let all the / peoples práise you.

4 Let the nations be glad and síng for joy, *
for you judge the peoples with equity
and guide all the na/tions upón earth.

5 Let the peoples praise you, Ó God; *
let all the / peoples práise you.

6 The earth has brought forth her íncrease; *
may God, our own God, give / us his bléssing.

7 May God give us his bléssing, *
and may all the ends of the earth / stand in áwe of him. *[Ant.]*

On the Twelve Days of Christmas

Let the righ - teous be glad and re - joice be - fore God; let them al - so

be mer - ry and joy - ful.

In Easter Season

He is the God of our sal - va - tion, the LORD, by whom we es - cape

death, hal - le - lu - jah.

On other Sundays and Weekdays

Sing to God, O king - doms of the earth; sing prais - es to the LORD.

Psalm 68 *Exsurgat Deus* *Tone VII.3*

1 *Let God* arise, and let his enemies be scattered; *
let those who hate him flee before him.

2 Let them vanish like smoke when the wind drives it away; *
as the wax melts at the fire, so let the wicked perish at the
presence of God.

3 But let the righteous be glad and rejoice before God; *
let them also be merry and joyful.

4 Sing to God, sing praises to his Name;
exalt him who rides upon the heavens; *
YAHWEH is his Name, rejoice before him!

5 Father of orphans, defender of widows, *
God in his holy habitation!

6 God gives the solitary a home and brings forth prisoners into freedom;*
but the rebels shall live in dry places.

7 O God, when you went forth before your people, *
when you marched through the wilderness,

8 The earth shook, and the skies poured down rain,
at the presence of God, the God of Sinai, *
at the presence of God, the God of Israel.

9 You sent a gracious rain, O God, upon your inheritance; *
you refreshed the land when it was weary.

10 Your people found their home in it; *
in your goodness, O God, you have made provision for the poor.

11 The Lord gave the word; *
great was the company of women who bore the tidings:

12 "Kings with their armies are fleeing away; *
the women at home are dividing the spoils."

13 Though you lingered among the sheepfolds, *
you shall be like a dove whose wings are covered with silver,
whose feathers are like green gold.

14 When the Almighty scattered kings, *
it was like snow falling in Zalmon.

15 O mighty mountain, O hill of Bashan! *
O rugged mountain, O hill of Bashan!

16 Why do you look with envy, O rugged mountain,
at the hill which God chose for his resting place? *
truly, the LORD will dwell there for ever.

17 The chariots of God are twenty thousand,
even thousands of thousands; *
the Lord comes in holiness from Sinai.

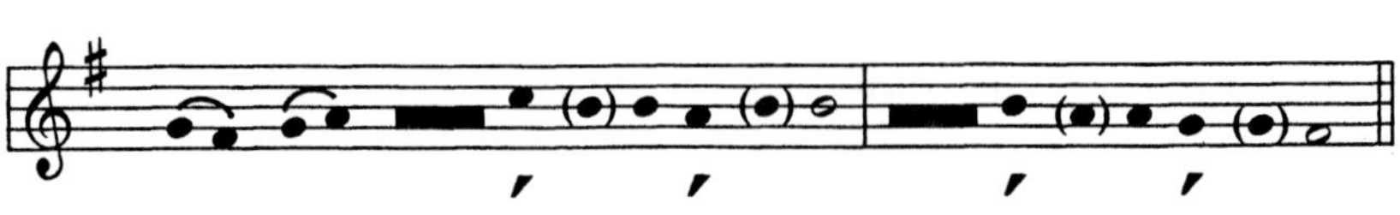

18 You have gone up on high and led captivity captive;
you have received gifts even from your enemies, *
that the LORD God might dwell among them.

19 Blessed be the Lord day by day, *
the God of our salvation, who bears our burdens.

20 He is our God, the God of our salvation; *
God is the LORD, by whom we escape death.

21 God shall crush the heads of his enemies, *
and the hairy scalp of those who go on still in their wickedness.

22 The LORD has said, "I will bring them back from Bashan; *
I will bring them back from the depths of the sea;

23 That your foot may be dipped in blood, *
the tongues of your dogs in the blood of your enemies."

24 They see your procession, O God, *
your procession into the sanctuary, my God and my King.

25 The singers go before, musicians follow after, *
in the midst of maidens playing upon the hand-drums.

26 Bless God in the congregation; *
bless the LORD, you that are of the fountain of Israel.

27 There is Benjamin, least of the tribes, at the head;
the princes of Judah in a company; *
and the princes of Zebulon and Naphtali.

28 Send forth your strength, O God; *
establish, O God, what you have wrought for us.

29 —Kings shall bring gifts to you, *
for your temple's sake at Jerusalem.

30 Rebuke the wild beast of the reeds, *
and the peoples, a herd of wild bulls with its calves.

31 Trample down those who lúst after śilver; *
scatter the peoples thát delíght in war.

32 Let tribute be bróught out of Égypt; *
let Ethiopia stretch óut her hánds to God.

33 Sing to God, O kíngdoms óf the earth; *
sing práises tó the Lord.

34 He rides in the heavens, the áncient héavens; *
he sends forth his vóice, his míghty voice.

35 Ascribe pówer tó God; *
his majesty is over Israel;
his stréngth is ín the skies.

36 How wonderful is God in his hóly pláces! *
the God of Israel giving strength and power to his people!
Bléssèd bé God! *[Ant.]*

69

In Holy Week

They gave me gall to eat; and when I was thirst - y, they gave me

vin - e - gar to drink.

On other Sundays and Weekdays

Zeal for your house has eat - en me up; the scorn of those who scorn you

has fal - len up - on me.

Psalm 69 *Salvum me fac* *Tone III.4*

1 *Save me,* O God,
for the waters have risen up to my neck. *
I am sinking in deep mire,
and there is no firm ground / for my feet.

2 I have come into deep waters, *
and the torrent wash/es over me.

3 I have grown weary with my crying;
my throat is inflamed; *
my eyes have failed from look/ing for my God.

4 Those who hate me without a cause are more than the hairs of my head;
my lying foes who would destroy me are mighty. *
Must I then give back what / I never stole?

5 O God, you know my foolishness, *
and my faults are not hid/den from you.

6 Let not those who hope in you be put to shame through
me, Lord GOD of hosts; *
let not those who seek you be disgraced because of
me, O God / of Israel.

7 Surely, for your sake have I suffered reproach, *
and shame has co/vered my face.

8 I have become a stranger to my own kindred, *
an alien to my mo/ther's children.

9 Zeal for your house has eaten me up; *
the scorn of those who scorn you has fallen / upon me.

10 I humbled myself with fasting, *
but that was turned / to my reproach.

11 I put on sack-cloth also, *
and became a byword / among them.

12 Those who sit at the gate murmur against me, *
and the drunkards make songs a/bout me.

But as for me, this is my prayer to you, *
at the time you / have set, O LORD:

14 "In your great mercy, O God, *
answer me with your / unfailing help.

15 Save me from the mire; do not let me sink; *
let me be rescued from those who hate me
and out of the / deep waters.

16 Let not the torrent of waters wash over me,
neither let the deep swallow me up; *
do not let the Pit shut its mouth / upon me.

17 Answer me, O LORD, for your love is kind; *
in your great compas/sion, turn to me."

18 "Hide not your face from your servant; *
be swift and answer me, for I / am in distress.

19 Draw near to me and redeem me; *
because of my enemies / deliver me.

20 You know my reproach, my shame, and my dishonor; *
my adversaries are all / in your sight."

21 Reproach has broken my heart, and it cannot be healed; *
I looked for sympathy, but there was none,
for comforters, but I could / find no one.

22 They gave me gall to eat, *
and when I was thirsty, they gave me vine/gar to drink.

23 Let the table before them be a trap *
and their sa/cred feasts a snare.

24 Let their eyes be darkened, that they may not see, *
and give them continual trem/bling in their loins.

25 Pour out your indignation upon them, *
and let the fierceness of your anger o/vertake them.

26 Let their camp be desolate, *
and let there be none to dwell / in their tents.

27 For they persecute him whom you have stricken *
and add to the pain of those / whom you have pierced.

28 Lay to their charge guilt upon guilt, *
and let them not receive your vin/dication.

29 Let them be wiped out of the book of the living *
and not be written among / the righteous.

30 As for me, I am afflicted and in pain; *
your help, O God, will lift / me up on high.

31 I will praise the Name of God in song; *
I will proclaim his greatness with / thanksgiving.

32 This will please the LORD more than an offering of oxen, *
more than bullocks / with horns and hoofs.

33 The afflicted shall see and be glad; *
you who seek God, / your heart shall live.

34 For the LORD listens to the needy, *
and his prisoners he / does not despise.

35 Let the heavens and the earth praise him, *
the seas and all / that moves in them;

36 For God will save Zion and rebuild the cities of Judah; *
they shall live there and have it in / possession.

37 The children of his servants will inherit it, *
and those who love his Name / will dwell therein. *[Ant.]*

70

In Easter Season

Let those who love your sal - va - tion say, "Great is the LORD!"

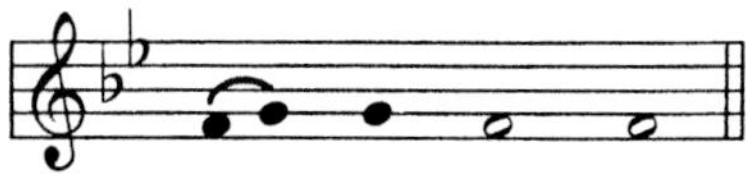

hal - le - lu - jah.

On other Sundays and Weekdays

I am poor and need - y; come to me speed - i - ly, O God.

Psalm 70 *Deus, in adjutorium* *Tone VIII.1*

1 *Be pleased,* O God, to delíver me; *
O LORD, make / haste to hélp me.

2 Let those who seek my life be ashamed
and altogether dismáyed; *
let those who take pleasure in my misfortune
draw / back and bé disgraced.

3 Let those who say to me "Aha!" and gloat over me túrn back, *
be/cause they áre ashamed.

4 Let all who seek you rejoice and be glád in you; *
let those who love your salvation say for ever,
/ "Great is thé LORD!"

5 But as for me, I am poor and néedy; *
come to me speed/ily, Ó God.

6 You are my helper and my delíverer; *
O LORD, / do not tárry. *[Ant.]*

71

In Easter Season

You re - store my life; hal - le - lu - jah.

On other Sundays and Weekdays

You are my hope, O Lord GOD; my con - fi - dence since I was young.

Psalm 71 *In te, Domine, speravi* *Tone VII.3*

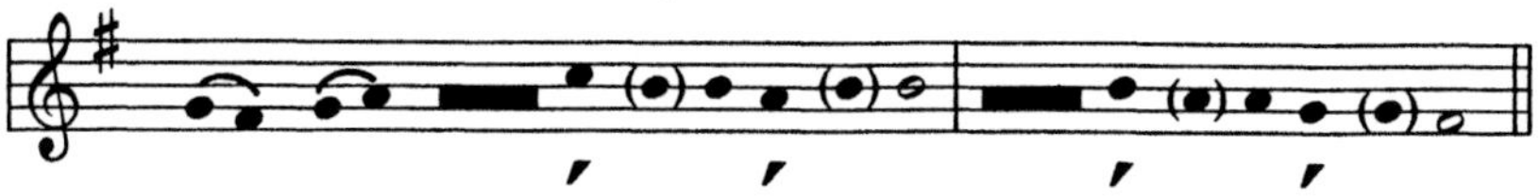

1 *In you,* O LORD, have I taken refuge; *
let me never be ashamed.

2 In your righteousness, deliver me and set me free; *
incline your ear to me and save me.

3 Be my strong rock, a castle to keep me safe; *
you are my crag and my stronghold.

4 Deliver me, my God, from the hand of the wicked, *
from the clutches of the evildoer and the oppressor.

5 For you are my hope, O Lord GOD, *
my confidence since I was young.

6 I have been sustained by you ever since I was born;
from my mother's womb you have been my strength; *
my praise shall be always of you.

7 I have become a portent to many; *
but you are my refuge and my strength.

8 Let my mouth be full of your praise *
and your glory all the day long.

9 Do not cast me off in my old age; *
forsake me not when my strength fails.

10 For my enemies are talking against me, *
and those who lie in wait for my life take counsel together.

11 They say, "God has forsaken him;
go after him and seize him; *
because there is none who will save."

12 O God, be not far from me; *
come quickly to help me, O my God.

13 Let those who set themselves against me be put to
shame and be disgraced; *
let those who seek to do me evil be covered with scorn and reproach.

14 But I shall always wait in patience, *
and shall praise you more and more.

15 My mouth shall recount your mighty acts
and saving deeds all day long; *
though I cannot know the number of them.

16 I will begin with the mighty works of the Lord GOD; *
I will recall your righteousness, yours alone.

17 O God, you have taught me since I was young, *
and to this day I tell of your wonderful works.

18 And now that I am old and gray-headed, O God, do not forsake me, *
till I make known your strength to this generation
and your power to all who are to come.

19 Your righteousness, O God, reaches to the heavens; *
you have done great things;
who is like you, O God?

20 You have showed me great troubles and adversities, *
but you will restore my life
and bring me up again from the deep places of the earth.

21 You strengthen me more and more; *
you enfold and comfort me,

22 Therefore I will praise you upon the lyre for
your faithfulness, O my God; *
I will sing to you with the harp, O Holy One of Israel.

23 My lips will sing with joy when I play to you, *
and so will my soul, which you have redeemed.

24 My tongue will proclaim your righteousness all day long, *
for they are ashamed and disgraced who sought to do me harm. *[Ant.]*

72

On the Twelve Days of Christmas

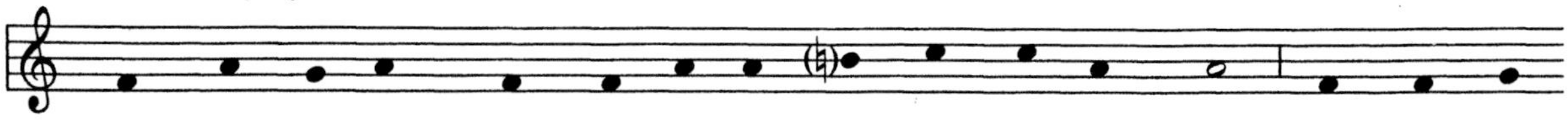

The kings of Tar - shish and of the isles shall pay tri - bute: the kings of

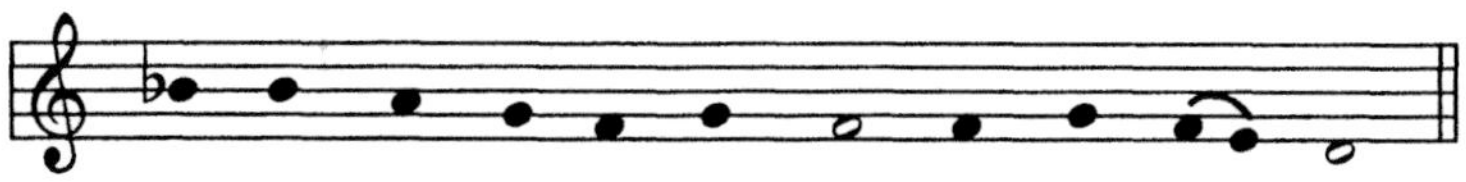

A - ra - bi - a and Sa - ba shall of - fer gifts.

In Easter Season

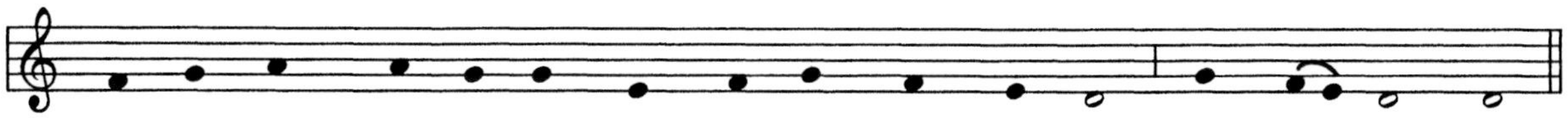

All the peo - ples of the earth will be blessed in him, hal - le - lu - jah.

On other Sundays and Weekdays

He shall have pit - y on the low - ly and poor, and shall re - deem their

lives from op - pres - sion.

Psalm 72 *Deus, judicium* *Tone I.1*

1 *Give the* King your justice, O God, *
and your righteousness / to the King's Son;

2 That he may rule your people righteously *
and the / poor with justice;

3 That the mountains may bring prosperity to the people, *
and the little / hills bring righteousness.

4 He shall defend the needy among the people; *
he shall rescue the poor and crush / the oppressor.

5 He shall live as long as the sun and moon endure, *
from one generation / to another.

6 He shall come down like rain upon the mown field, *
like showers that / water the earth.

7 In his time shall the righteous flourish; *
there shall be abundance of peace till the / moon shall be no more.

8 He shall rule from sea to sea, *
and from the River to the / ends of the earth.

9 His foes shall bow down before him, *
and his en/emies lick the dust.

10 The kings of Tarshish and of the isles shall pay tribute, *
and the kings of Arabia and / Saba offer gifts.

11 All kings shall bow down before him, *
and all the nations / do him service.

12 For he shall deliver the poor who cries out in distress, *
and the oppressed who / has no helper.

13 He shall have pity on the lowly and poor; *
he shall preserve the lives / of the needy.

14 He shall redeem their lives from oppression and violence, *
and dear shall their blood / be in his sight.

15 Long may he live!
and may there be given to him gold from Arabia; *
may prayer be made for him always,
and may they bless him / all the day long.

16 May there be abundance of grain on the earth,
growing thick even on the hilltops; *
may its fruit flourish like Lebanon,
and its grain like / grass upon the earth.

17 May his Name remain for ever,
and be established as long as the sun endures; *
may all the nations bless themselves in him and / call him blessed.

18 Blessed be the Lord GOD, the Gód of Ísrael, *
who a/lone does wóndrous deeds!

19 And blessed be his glorious Náme for éver! *
and may all the earth be filled with his glory.
/ Amen. Ä́men. *[Ant.]*

73

Antiphon

You will guide me by your coun - sel, and af - ter - wards re - ceive me

with glo - ry.

Psalm 73 *Quam bonus Israel!* *Tone II.1*

1 *Truly,* God is good to Ísrael, *
to those who / are púre in heart.

2 But as for me, my feet had néarly slipped; *
I had almost tripped / and fállen;

3 Because I envied the próud *
and saw the prosperity of / the wícked:

4 For they suffer nó pain, *
and their bodies / are sléek and sound;

5 In the misfortunes of others they háve no share; *
they are not afflicted / as óthers are;

6 Therefore they wear their pride like anécklace *
and wrap their violence about / them líke a cloak.

7 Their iniquity comes from gróss minds, *
and their hearts overflow / with wícked thoughts.

8 They scoff and speak maliciously; *
out of their haughtiness they plan / oppression.

9 They set their mouths against the heavens, *
and their evil speech / runs through the world.

10 And so the people turn to them *
and find / in them no fault.

11 They say, "How should God know? *
is there knowledge in / the Most High?"

12 So then, these are the wicked; *
always at ease, they / increase their wealth.

13 In vain have I kept my heart clean, *
and washed my hands / in innocence.

14 I have been afflicted all day long, *
and punished ev/ery morning.

15 Had I gone on speaking this way, *
I should have betrayed the generation of / your children.

16 When I tried to understand these things, *
it was / too hard for me;

17 Until I entered the sanctuary of God *
and discerned the end of / the wicked.

18 Surely, you set them in slippery places; *
you cast them down / in ruin.

19 Oh, how suddenly do they come to destruction, *
come to an end, and perish / from terror!

20 Like a dream when one awakens, O Lord, *
when you arise you will make their im/age vanish.

21 When my mind became embittered, *
I was sorely wound/ed in my heart.

22 I was stupid and had no understánding; *
I was like a brute beast in / your présence.

23 Yet I am always with yóu; *
you hold me by / my ríght hand.

24 You will guide me by your cóunsel, *
and afterwards receive me / with glóry.

25 Whom have I in heaven but yóu? *
and having you I desire nothing / upón earth.

26 Though my flesh and my heart should wáste away, *
God is the strength of my heart and my portion / for éver.

27 Truly, those who forsake you will pérish; *
you destroy all who are / unfáithful.

28 But it is good for me to be near Gód; *
I have made the Lord GOD / my réfuge.

29 I will speak of áll your works *
in the gates of the city / of Zíon. *[Ant.]*

74

In Holy Week

A - rise, O God, main - tain your cause.

In Easter Season

The Lord will re - build Je - ru - sa - lem, hal - le - lu - jah.

On other Sundays and Weekdays

Re - mem - ber your con - gre - ga - tion, O LORD, that you pur - chased

long a - go.

Psalm 74 *Ut quid, Deus?* *Tone IV.4*

1 *O Göd,* why have you ut/terly cást us off? *
why is your wrath so hot against the / sheep of your pásture?

2 Remember your congregation that you / purchased lóng ago, *
the tribe you redeemed to be your inheritance,
and / Mount Zion whére you dwell.

3 Turn your steps toward the / endless rúins; *
the enemy has laid waste everything in / your sanctuáry.

4 Your adversaries roared / in your hóly place; *
they set up their banners as / tokens of víctory.

5 They were like men coming up with axes / to a gróve of trees; *
they broke down all your carved work with / hatchets and hámmers.

6 They set fire / to your hóly place; *
they defiled the dwelling-place of your Name
/ and razed it tó the ground.

7 They said to themselves, "Let us destroy them / altogéther." *
They burned down all the meeting-pla/ces of God ín the land.

8 There are no signs for us to see;
there / is no próphet left; *
there is not one among / us who knows hów long.

9 How long, O God, will the / adversáry scoff? *
will the enemy blaspheme / your Name for éver?

10 Why do / you draw báck your hand? *
why is your right hand hid/den in your bósom?

11 Yet God is my / King from áncient times, *
victorious / in the midst óf the earth.

12 You divided the sea / by your míght *
and shattered the heads of the dragons / upon the wáters;

13 You crushed the heads / of Levíathan *
and gave him to the people of / the desert fór food.

14 You split open / spring and tórrent; *
you dried up ev/er-flowing rívers.

15 Yours is the day, yours al/so the níght; *
you established / the moon and thé sun.

16 You fixed all the / boundaries óf the earth; *
you made both / summer and wínter.

17 Remember, O LORD, how the en/emy scóffed, *
how a foolish / people despísed your Name.

18 Do not hand over the life of your / dove to wíld beasts; *
never forget / the lives of yóur poor.

19 Look up/on your cóvenant; *
the dark places of the earth / are haunts of víolence.

20 Let not the oppressed / turn awáy ashamed; *
let the poor / and needy práise your Name.

21 Arise, O / God, maintáin your cause; *
remember how fools / revile you áll day long.

22 Forget not the clamor of your / adversáries, *
the unending tumult of those who / rise up agáinst you. *[Ant.]*

75

In Easter Season

God does not judge by what the eyes see, but in truth and eq - ui - ty,

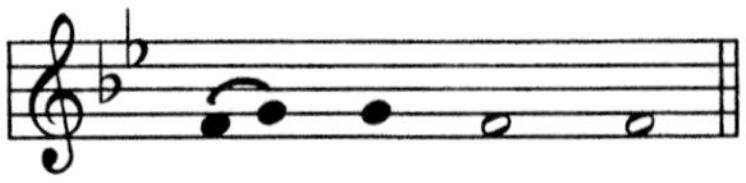

hal - le - lu - jah.

On other Sundays and Weekdays

God does not judge by what the eyes see, but in truth and eq - ui - ty.

Psalm 75 *Confitebimur tibi* *Tone VIII.2*

1 *We give* you thanks, O God, we· gíve you thanks, *
calling upon your Name and declaring all your / wonderfúl deeds.

2 "I will appoint a tíme," says God; *
"I will / judge with équity.

3 Though the earth and all its inhabitants are quáking, *
I will / make its píllars fast.

4 I will say to the boasters, 'Bóast no more,' *
and to the wicked, / 'Do not tóss your horns;

5 Do not toss your hórns so high, *
nor speak / with a próud neck.'"

6 For judgment is neither from the east nor fróm the west, *
nor yet from the wilderness / or the móuntains.

7 It is God who júdges; *
he puts down one and lifts / up anóther.

8 For in the LORD's hand there is a cup,
full of spiced and foaming wine, which hé pours out, *
and all the wicked of the earth shall / drink and dráin the dregs.

9 But I will rejoice for éver; *
I will sing praises to the / God of Jácob.

10 He shall break off all the horns of the wícked; *
but the horns of the righteous shall / be exálted. *[Ant.]*

76

In Easter Season

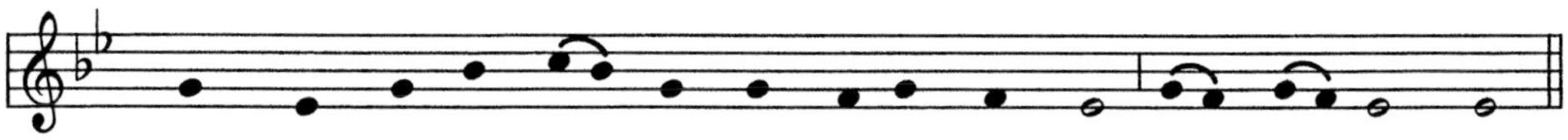

The Name of the LORD is great in Is - ra - el, hal - le - lu - jah.

On other Sundays and Weekdays

The earth was a - fraid and was still, when God rose up to judg - ment.

Psalm 76 *Notus in Judaea* *Tone V.3*

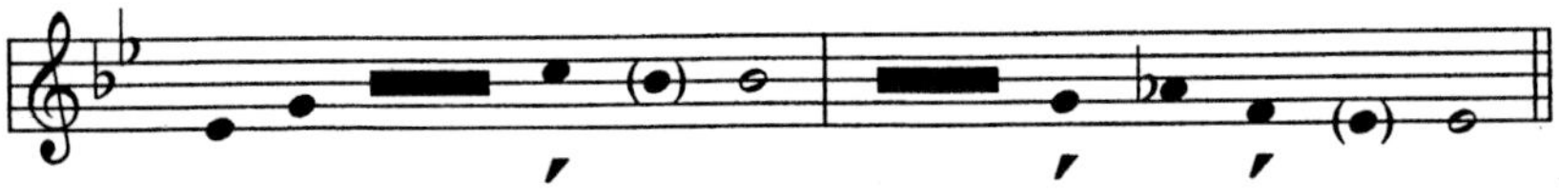

1 *In Ju*dah is God known; *
his Name is great in Israel.

2 At Salem is his tabernacle, *
and his dwelling is in Zion.

3 There he broke the flashing arrows, *
the shield, the sword, and the weapons of battle.

4 How glorious you are! *
more splendid than the everlasting mountains!

5 The strong of heart have been despoiled;
they sink into sleep; *
none of the warriors can lift a hand.

6 At your rebuke, O God of Jacob, *
both horse and rider lie stunned.

7 What terror you inspire! *
who can stand before you when you are angry?

8 From heaven you pronounced judgment; *
the earth was afraid and was still;

9 When God rose up to judgment *
and to save all the oppressed of the earth.

10 Truly, wrathful Edom will give you thanks, *
and the remnant of Hamath will keep your feasts.

11 Make a vow to the LORD your God and keep it; *
let all around him bring gifts to him who is worthy to be feared.

12 He breaks the spirit of princes, *
and strikes terror in the kings of the earth. *[Ant.]*

77

In Easter Season

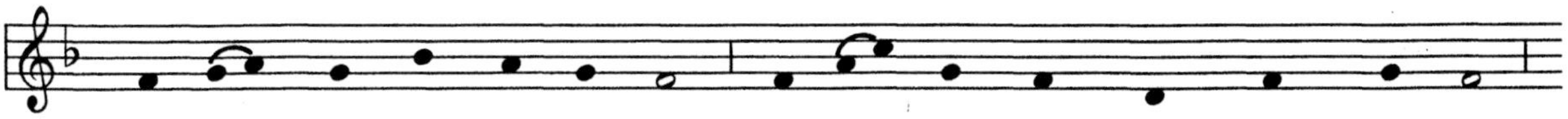

The wa - ters saw you, O God; you led your peo - ple through the sea,

hal - le - lu - jah.

On other Sundays and Weekdays

Your way, O God, is ho - ly; who is so great a god as our God?

Psalm 77 *Voce mea ad Dominum* *Tone VI*

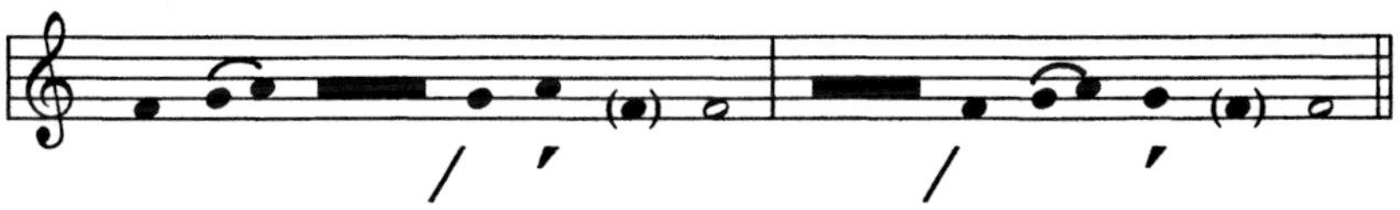

1 *I will* cry / aloud to God; *
I will cry aloud, and / he will hear me.

2 In the day of my trouble / I sought the Lord; *
my hands were stretched out by night and did not tire;
I refused / to be comforted.

3 I think of God, I / am restless, *
I ponder, / and my spirit faints.

4 You will not let / my eyelids close; *
I am troubled / and I cannot speak.

5 I consider / the days of old; *
I remember / the years long past;

6 I commune with my / heart in the night; *
I pon/der and search my mind.

7 Will the Lord cast me off / for ever? *
Will he no more / show his favor?

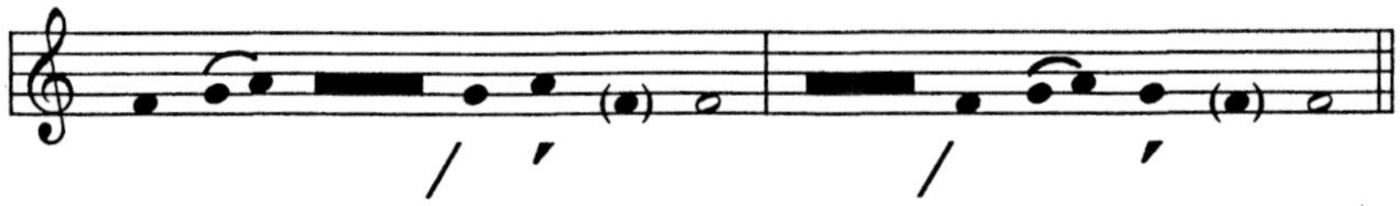

8 Has his loving-kindness come to an end / for éver? *
has his promise / failed för évermore?

9 Has God forgotten to / be grácious? *
has he, in his anger, withheld / his cömpássion?

10 And I said, / "My gríef is this: *
the right hand of the Most High has / lost ïts pówer."

11 I will remember the works / of thé LORD, *
and call to mind your won/ders öf óld time.

12 I will meditate / on áll your acts *
and pon/der yöur míghty deeds.

13 Your way, O God, / is hóly; *
who is so great a / god äs óur God?

14 You are the God who / works wónders *
and have declared your power a/mong thë péoples.

15 By your strength you have redeemed / your péople, *
the children of Ja/cob änd Jóseph.

16 The waters saw you, O God;
the waters saw you / and trémbled; *
the very / depths wëre sháken.

17 The clouds poured out water;
the / skies thúndered; *
your ar/rows fläshed tó and fro;

18 The sound of your thunder was in the whirlwind;
your lightnings / lit úp the world; *
the earth / tremblëd ánd shook.

19 Your way was in the sea,
and your paths in the / great wáters, *
yet your foot/steps wëre nót seen.

20 You led your peo/ple like a flock *
by the hand of Mo/ses and Aaron. *[Ant.]*

78:1–39

In Easter Season

Our fore - fa - thers have told us of the pow - er of the LORD, and the

won - der - ful works he has done, hal - le - lu - jah.

On other Sundays and Weekdays

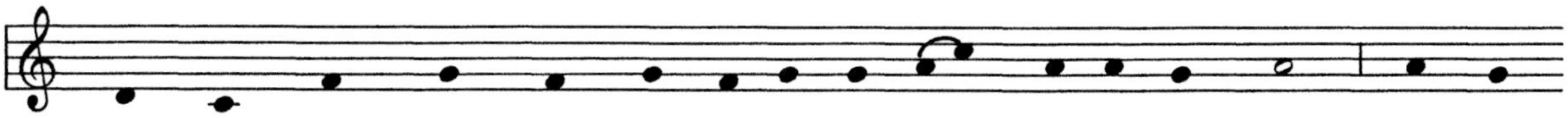
Our fore - fa - thers have told us of the pow - er of the LORD, and the

won - der - ful works he has done.

Psalm 78 Part 1 *Attendite, popule* *Tone I.2*

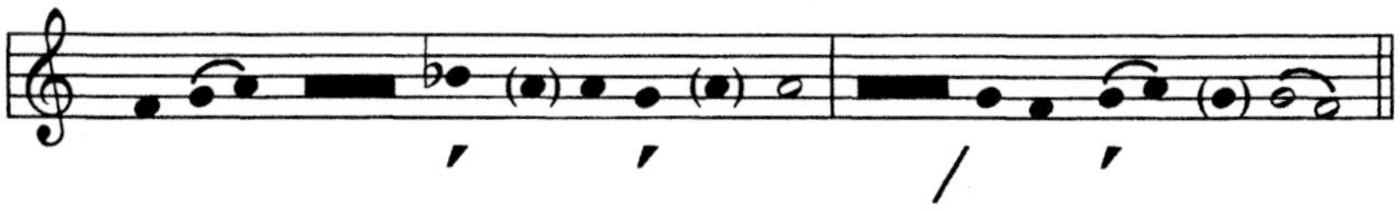

1 *Hear my* teaching, O my people; *
incline your ears to the / words of my mouth.

2 I will open my mouth in a parable; *
I will declare the myster/ies of ancient times.

3 That which we have heard and known,
and what our forefathers have told us, *
we will not / hide from their children.

4 We will recount to generations to come
the praiseworthy deeds and the power of the LORD, *
and the wonderful / works he has done.

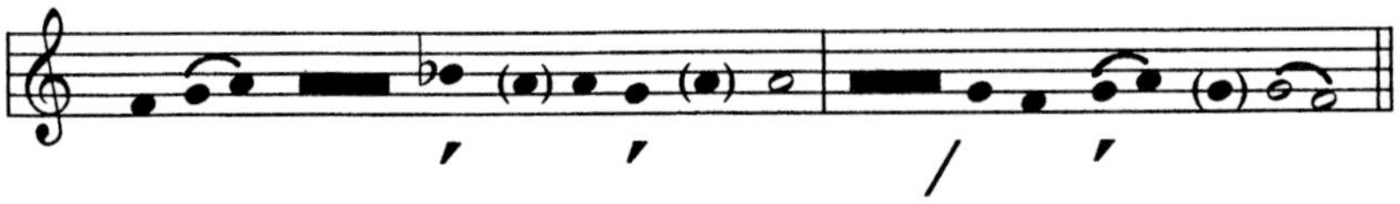

5 He gave his decrees to Jacob
and established a law for Israel, *
which he commanded them to / teach their children;

6 That the generations to come might know,
and the children yet unborn; *
that they in their turn might tell it / to their children;

7 So that they might put their trust in God, *
and not forget the deeds of God,
but keep / his commandments;

8 And not be like their forefathers,
a stubborn and rebellious generation, *
a generation whose heart was not steadfast,
and whose spirit was not / faithful to God.

9 The people of Ephraim, armed with the bow, *
turned back in the / day of battle;

10 They did not keep the covenant of God, *
and refused to / walk in his law;

11 They forgot what he had done, *
and the wonders / he had shown them.

12 He worked marvels in the sight of their forefathers, *
in the land of Egypt, in the / field of Zoan.

13 He split open the sea and let them pass through; *
he made the waters / stand up like walls.

14 He led them with a cloud by day, *
and all the night through / with a glow of fire.

15 He split the hard rocks in the wilderness *
and gave them drink as / from the great deep.

16 He brought streams out of the cliff, *
and the waters gushed / out like rivers.

17 But they went on sinning against him, *
rebelling in the desert a/gainst the Most High.

18 They tested God in their hearts, *
demanding food / for their craving.

19 They railed against God and said, *
"Can God set a table / in the wilderness?

20 True, he struck the rock, the waters gushed out, and the gullies overflowed; *
but is he able to give bread
or to provide meat / for his people?"

21 When the LORD heard this, he was full of wrath; *
a fire was kindled against Jacob,
and his anger mounted / against Israel;

22 For they had no faith in God, *
nor did they put their trust / in his saving power.

23 So he commanded the clouds above *
and opened the / doors of heaven.

24 He rained down manna upon them to eat *
and gave them / grain from heaven.

25 So mortals ate the bread of angels; *
he provided / for them food enough.

26 He caused the east wind to blow in the heavens *
and led out the / south wind by his might.

27 He rained down flesh upon them like dust *
and wingèd birds like the / sand of the sea.

28 He let it fall in the midst of their camp *
and round a/bout their dwellings.

29 So they ate and were well filled, *
for he gave / them what they craved.

30 But they did not stop their craving, *
though the food was / still in their mouths.

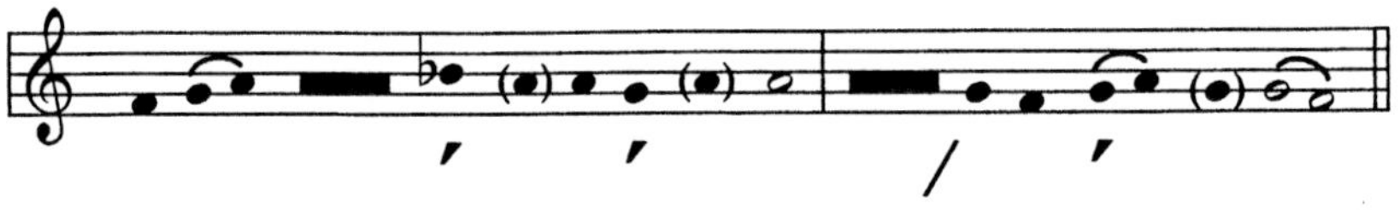

31 So God's anger mounted against them; *
he slew their strongest men
and laid low the / youth of Israel.

32 In spite of all this, they went on sinning *
and had no faith in his / wonderful works.

33 So he brought their days to an end like a breath *
and their years in / sudden terror.

34 Whenever he slew them, they would seek him, *
and repent, and dili/gently search for God.

35 They would remember that God was their rock, *
and the Most High God / their redeemer.

36 But they flattered him with their mouths *
and lied to / him with their tongues.

37 Their heart was not steadfast toward him, *
and they were not faithful / to his covenant.

38 But he was so merciful that he forgave their sins
and did not destroy them; *
many times he held back his anger
and did not permit his / wrath to be roused.

39 For he remembered that they were but flesh, *
a breath that goes forth / and does not return. *[Ant.]*

78:40–72

In Easter Season

The LORD ran - somed his peo - ple from the hand of the en - e - my,

and brought them in - to his ho - ly land, hal - le - lu - jah.

On other Sundays and Weekdays

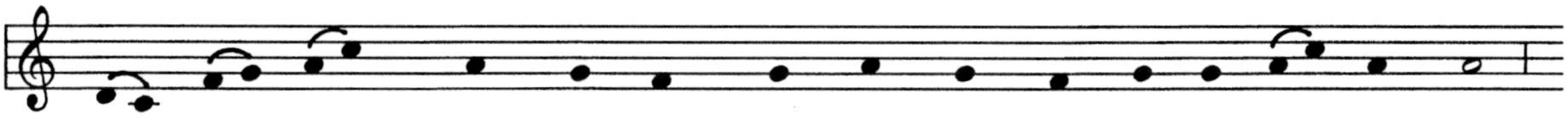

The LORD ran - somed his peo - ple from the hand of the en - e - my,

and brought them in - to his ho - ly land.

Psalm 78 Part 2 *Quoties exacerbaverunt* *Tone I.7*

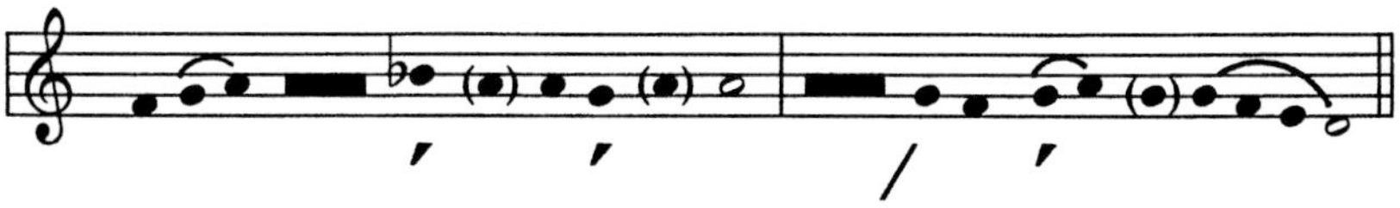

40 *How* often the people disobeyed him in the wilderness *
and offended him / in the desert!

41 Again and again they tempted God *
and provoked the Holy / One of Israel.

42 They did not remember his power *
in the day when he ransomed them / from the enemy;

43 How he wrought his signs in Egypt *
and his omens in the / field of Zoan.

44 He turned their rivers into blood, *
so that they could not / drink of their streams.

45 He sent swarms of flies among them, which ate them up, *
and frogs, / which destroyed them.

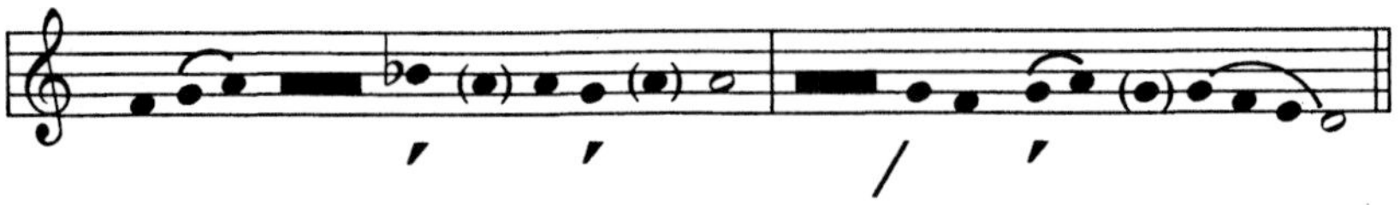

46 He gave their crops to the caterpillar, *
the fruit of their toil / to the locust.

47 He killed their vines with hail *
and their syc/amores with frost.

48 He delivered their cattle to hailstones *
and their livestock / to hot thunderbolts.

49 He poured out upon them his blazing anger: *
fury, indignation, and distress,
a troop of de/stroying angels.

50 He gave full rein to his anger;
he did not spare their souls from death; *
but delivered their / lives to the plague.

51 He struck down all the firstborn of Egypt, *
the flower of manhood in the / dwellings of Ham.

52 He led out his people like sheep *
and guided them in the wil/derness like a flock.

53 He led them to safety, and they were not afraid; *
but the sea over/whelmed their enemies.

54 He brought them to his holy land, *
the mountain his / right hand had won.

55 He drove out the Canaanites before them
and apportioned an inheritance to them by lot; *
he made the tribes of Israel to / dwell in their tents.

56 But they tested the Most High God, and defied him, *
and did not keep / his commandments.

57 They turned away and were disloyal like their fathers; *
they were undependable / like a warped bow.

58 They grieved him with their hill-altars *
and provoked his displeasure / with their idols.

59 When God heard this, he was angry *
and utterly re/jected Israel.

60 He forsook the shrine at Shiloh, *
the tabernacle where he had lived a/mong his people.

61 He delivered the ark into captivity, *
his glory into the / adversary's hand.

62 He gave his people to the sword *
and was angered against / his inheritance.

63 The fire consumed their young men; *
there were no wedding songs / for their maidens.

64 Their priests fell by the sword, *
and their widows made no / lamentation.

65 Then the LORD woke as though from sleep, *
like a war/rior refreshed with wine.

66 He struck his enemies on the backside *
and put them / to perpetual shame.

67 He rejected the tent of Joseph *
and did not choose the / tribe of Ephraim;

68 He chose instead the tribe of Judah *
and Mount / Zion, which he loved.

69 He built his sanctuary like the heights of heaven, *
like the earth which he foun/ded for ever.

70 He chose David his servant, *
and took him away / from the sheepfolds.

71 He brought him from following the ewes, *
to be a shepherd over Jacob his people
and over Israel / his inheritance.

72 So he shepherded them with a faithful and true heart *
and guided them with the skillful/ness of his hands. *[Ant.]*

79

Antiphon

Help us, O God our Sav - ior, and for - give us our sins.

Psalm 79 *Deus, venerunt* *Tone VII.1*

1 *Ö Gö̈d,* the heathen have come into your inheritance;
they have profaned your hóly témple; *
they have made Jerusalem a héap of rúbblë.

2 They have given the bodies of your servants as food for
the bírds of thé air, *
and the flesh of your faithful ones to the béasts of thé fïeld.

3 They have shed their blood like water on every síde of Jerúsalem, *
and there was nó one to búry thëm.

4 We have become a repróach to our néighbors, *
an object of scorn and derision to thóse aróund üs.

5 How long will you be ángry, Ó LORD? *
will your fury blaze like fíre for évër?

6 Pour out your wrath upon the heathen who háve not knówn you *
and upon the kingdoms that have not cálled upon yóur Näme.

7 For they háve devoured Jácob *
and made his dwélling á ruïn.

8 Remember not our past sins;
let your compassion be swíft to méet us; *
for we have been bróught verý löw.

9 Help us, O God our Savior, for the glóry óf your Name; *
deliver us and forgive us our sins, fór your Náme's säke.

10 Why should the heathen say, "Where is their God?" *
Let it be known among the heathen and in our sight
that you avenge the shedding of your servants' blood.

11 Let the sorrowful sighing of the prisoners come before you, *
and by your great might spare those who are condemned to die.

12 May the revilings with which they reviled you, O Lord, *
return seven-fold into their bosoms.

13 For we are your people and the sheep of your pasture; *
we will give you thanks for ever
and show forth your praise from age to age. *[Ant.]*

80

In Easter Season

I am the vine, and you are the branch - es, hal - le - lu - jah.

On other Sundays and Weekdays

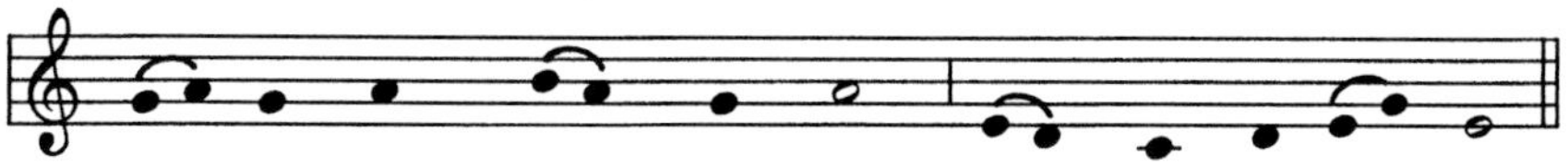
Stir up your strength, O LORD, and come to help us.

Psalm 80 *Qui regis Israel* *Tone IV.4*

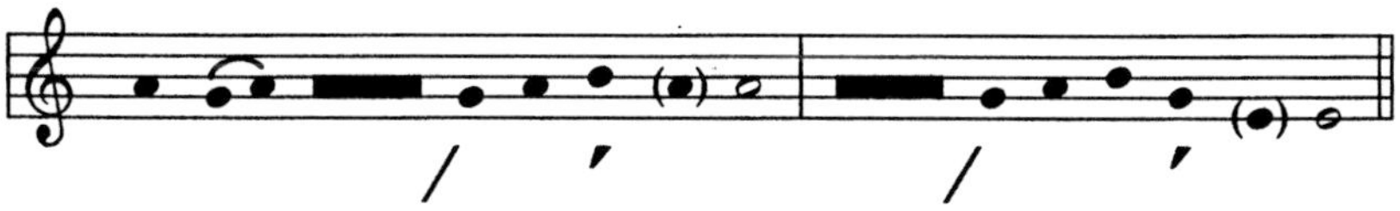

1 *Hear,* O Shepherd of Israel, leading / Joseph like a flock; *
shine forth, you that are enthroned / upon the cherubim.

2 In the presence of Ephraim, Benjamin, / and Manasseh, *
stir up your strength / and come to help us.

3 Restore / us, O God of hosts; *
show the light of your counte/nance, and we shall be saved.

4 —/O LORD Gód of hosts, *
how long will you be angered
despite the / prayers of your péople?

5 You have fed them / with the bréad of tears; *
you have given / them bowls of téars to drink.

6 You have made us the derision / of our néighbors, *
and our en/emies laugh ús to scorn.

7 Restore / us, O Gód of hosts; *
show the light of your counte/nance, and we sháll be saved.

8 You have brought a vine / out of Égypt; *
you cast out the / nations and plánted it.

9 You pre/pared the gróund for it; *
it / took root and fílled the land.

10 The mountains were covered / by its shádow *
and the towering / cedar trees bý its boughs.

11 You stretched out its / tendrils tó the Sea *
and its bran/ches to the Ríver.

12 Why have you / broken dówn its wall, *
so that all who / pass by pluck óff its grapes?

13 The wild boar of the for/est has rávaged it, *
and the beasts of the field / have grazed upón it.

14 Turn now, O God of hosts, look down from heaven;
be/hold and ténd this vine; *
preserve what your / right hand has plánted.

15 They burn it with / fire like rúbbish; *
at the rebuke of your counte/nance let them pérish.

16 Let your hand be upon the man / of your ríght hand, *
the son of man you have / made so strong fór yourself.

17 And so will we never / turn awáy from you; *
give us life, that we may / call upon yóur Name.

18 Restore us, / O LORD Gód of hosts; *
show the light of your counte/nance, and we shál be saved. *[Ant.]*

81

Antiphon

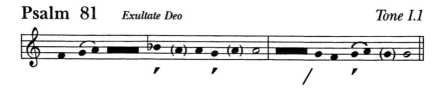

Sing with joy to God our strength, and raise a loud shout to

the God of Ja - cob. †

Psalm 81 *Exultate Deo* *Tone I.1*

1 *Sing with*—jóy to Gód our strength *
and raise a loud shout to the / God of Jácob.

2 †*Raise* ä song and sóund the tímbrel, *
the mer/ry harp, ánd the lyre.

3 Blow the ram's-horn át the néw moon, *
and at the full moon, the / day of óür feast.

4 For this is a státute for Ísrael, *
a law of the / God of Jácob.

5 He laid it as a solemn chárge upon Jóseph, *
when he came out of the / land of Égypt.

6 I heard an unfamíliar voice sáying, *
"I eased his shoulder from the burden;
his hands were set free from / bearing thé load."

7 You called on me in trouble, and I saved you; *
I answered you from the secret place of thunder
and tested you at the wa/ters of Meribah.

8 Hear, O my people, and I will admonish you: *
O Israel, if you would but / listen to me!

9 There shall be no strange god among you; *
you shall not wor/ship a foreign god.

10 I am the LORD your God,
who brought you out of the land of Egypt and said, *
"Open your mouth wide, and / I will fill it."

11 And yet my people did not hear my voice, *
and Israel would / not obey me.

12 So I gave them over to the stubbornness of their hearts, *
to follow their / own devices.

13 Oh, that my people would listen to me! *
that Israel would / walk in my ways!

14 I should soon subdue their enemies *
and turn my / hand against their foes.

15 Those who hate the LORD would cringe before him, *
and their punishment would / last for ever.

16 But Israel would I feed with the finest wheat *
and satisfy him with / honey from the rock. *[Ant.]*

82

Antiphon

A - rise, O God, and rule the earth.

Psalm 82 *Deus stetit* *Tone IV.4*

1 *God takes* his stand in the coun/cil of heaven; *
he gives judgment / in the midst of the gods:

2 "How long will you / judge unjustly, *
and show fa/vor to the wicked?

3 Save the weak / and the orphan; *
defend the / humble and needy;

4 Rescue the / weak and the poor; *
deliver them from the pow/er of the wicked.

5 They do not know, neither do they understand;
they go a/bout in darkness; *
all the foundations of / the earth are shaken.

6 Now I say / to you, 'You are gods, *
and all of you chil/dren of the Most High;

7 Nevertheless, you shall / die like mortals, *
— / and fall like any prince.' "

8 Arise, O / God, and rule the earth, *
for you shall take / all nations for your own. *[Ant.]*

83

Antiphon

They shall know that you, whose Name is YAH - WEH, are the Most High
o - ver all the earth.

Psalm 83 *Deus, quis similis?* *Tone IV.5*

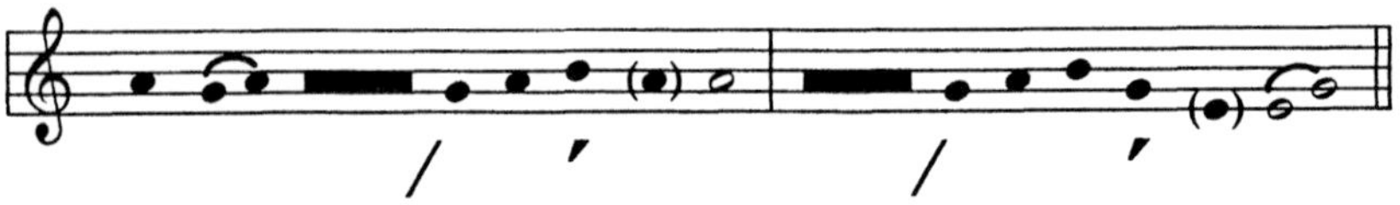

1 *O Göd,* do / not be sílent; *
do not keep still / nor hold your péace, O Göd;

2 For your enemies / are in túmult, *
and those who hate you / have lifted úp their hëads.

3 They take secret counsel a/gainst your péople *
and plot a/gainst those whom yóu protëct.

4 They have said, "Come, let us wipe them out from
a/mong the nátions; *
let the name of Israel be / remembered nó möre."

5 They have con/spired togéther; *
they have made an al/liance agáinst yöu:

6 The tents of Edom / and the Íshmaelites; *
the Moab/ites and the Hágarënes;

7 Gebal, and Am/mon, and Ámalek; *
the Philistines / and those who dwéll in Týre.

8 The Assyrians al/so have jóined them, *
and have come to help / the people óf Löt.

9 Do to them as you / did to Mídian, *
to Sisera, and to Jabin at the / river of Kíshön:

10 They were de/stroyed at Éndor; *
they became / like dung upón the gröund.

11 Make their leaders like Or/eb and Źeëb, *
and all their commanders like Ze/bah and Zalmúnnä,

12 Who said, "Let us / take for óurselves *
the fields of God / as our posséssiön."

13 O my God, make / them like ẃhirling dust *
and like / chaff before thé wïnd;

14 Like fire that burns / down a fórest, *
like the flame / that sets mountáins abläze.

15 Drive them / with your témpest *
and terri/fy them with yóur stör m;

16 Cover their fa/ces with sháme, O LORD, *
that / they may seek yóur Näme.

17 Let them be disgraced and terri/fied for éver; *
let them be put to con/fusion and pérïsh.

18 Let them know that you, whose / Name is YÁHWEH, *
you alone are the Most / High over áll the ëarth. *[Ant.]*

84

In Advent

Be - hold, the De - sire of ev - ery na - tion shall come; and the house of

the LORD shall be filled with glo - ry, hal - le - lu - jah.

In Lent

Be - hold our de - fend - er, O God; and look up - on the face of your

A - noint - ed.

In Easter Season

My heart and my flesh re - joice in the liv - ing God, hal - le - lu - jah.

On other Sundays and Weekdays

How dear to me is your dwel - ling, O LORD of hosts! †

Psalm 84 *Quam dilecta!* *Tone VII.3*

1 *Hŏw dĕar* to me is your dwélling, O LÓRD of hosts! *
†*Mÿ sŏul* has a desire and longing for the cóurts of thé LORD;
my heart and my flesh rejóice in the líving God.

2 The sparrow has found her a house
and the swallow a nest where shé may láy her young; *
by the side of your altars, O LORD of hosts,
my Kíng and mý God.

3 Happy are they who dwell in your house! *
they will always be praising you.

4 Happy are the people whose strength is in you! *
whose hearts are set on the pilgrims' way.

5 Those who go through the desolate valley will find
it a place of springs, *
for the early rains have covered it with pools of water.

6 They will climb from height to height, *
and the God of gods will reveal himself in Zion.

7 LORD God of hosts, hear my prayer; *
hearken, O God of Jacob.

8 Behold our defender, O God; *
and look upon the face of your Anointed.

9 For one day in your courts is better than a thousand in my own room, *
and to stand at the threshold of the house of my God
than to dwell in the tents of the wicked.

10 For the LORD God is both sun and shield; *
he will give grace and glory;

11 No good thing will the LORD withhold *
from those who walk with integrity.

12 —O LORD of hosts, *
happy are they who put their trust in you! *[Ant.]*

†When the antiphon is not sung, the second line of verse 1 is sung to the reciting note of the second half of the psalm tone.

85

On the Twelve Days of Christmas

Truth has sprung up from the earth, and righ - teous - ness has looked down

from heav - en.

In Easter Season

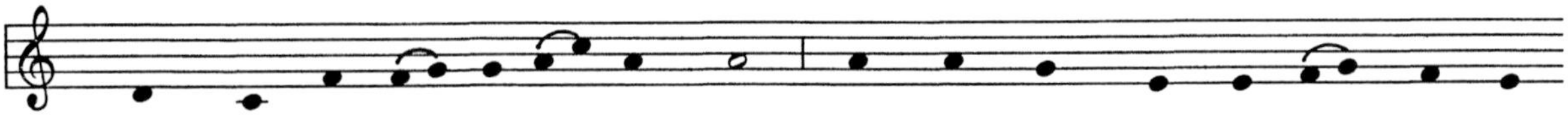

LORD, you will give us life a - gain, that your peo - ple may re - joice in

you, hal - le - lu - jah.

On other Sundays and Weekdays

You have been gra - cious to your land, O LORD; you have for - giv - en the

in - iq - ui - ty of your peo - ple.

Psalm 85 *Benedixisti, Domine* *Tone I.2*

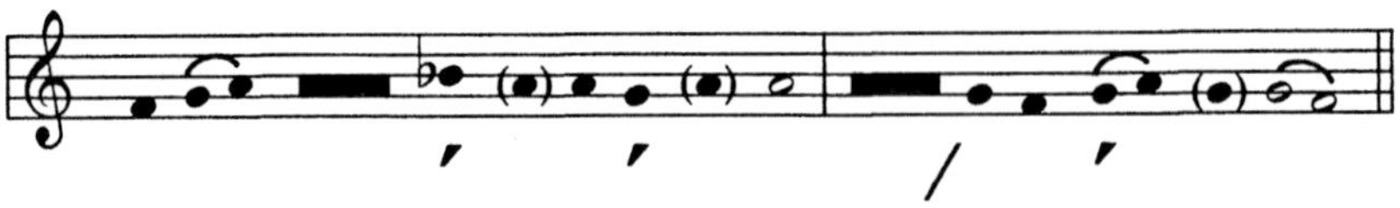

1 *You have* been gracious to your land, O LORD, *
you have restored the good for/tune of Jacob.

2 You have forgiven the iniquity of your people *
and blotted / out all their sins.

3 You have withdrawn all your fury *
and turned yourself from your wrathful / indignation.

4 Restore us then, O God our Savior; *
let your an/ger depart from us.

5 Will you be displeased with us for ever? *
will you prolong your an/ger from age to age?

6 Will you not give us life again, *
that your people / may rejoice in you?

7 Show us your mercy, O LORD, *
and grant us / your salvation.

8 I will listen to what the LORD God is saying, *
for he is speaking peace to his faithful people
and to those who / turn their hearts to him.

9 Truly, his salvation is very near to those who fear him, *
that his glory may / dwell in our land.

10 Mercy and truth have met together; *
righteousness and peace have / kissed each other.

11 Truth shall spring up from the earth, *
and righteousness shall look / down from heaven.

12 The LORD will indeed grant prosperity, *
and our land will / yield its increase.

13 Righteousness shall go before him, *
and peace shall be a / pathway for his feet. *[Ant.]*

86

In Easter Season

All na - tions you have made will come and wor - ship you, O LORD;

hal - le - lu - jah.

On other Sundays and Weekdays

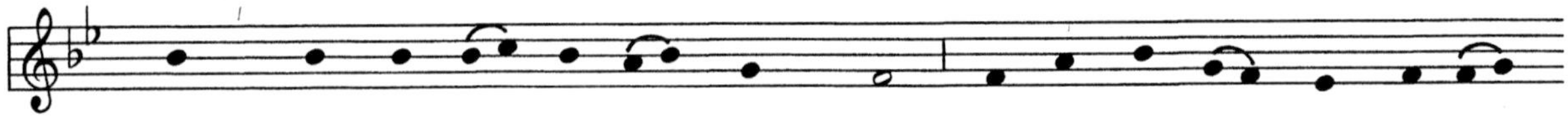
Glad - den the soul of your serv - ant; for to you, O LORD, I lift

up my soul.

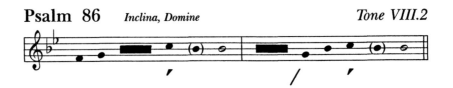

Psalm 86 *Inclina, Domine* *Tone VIII.2*

1 *Bow down* your ear, O LORD, and ánswer me, *
for I am poor / and in mísery.

2 Keep watch over my life, for I am fáithful; *
save your servant who / puts his trúst in you.

3 Be merciful to me, O LORD, for you are mý God; *
I call upon you / all the dáy long.

4 Gladden the soul of your sérvant, *
for to you, O LORD, / I lift úp my soul.

5 For you, O LORD, are good and forgíving, *
and great is your love toward all who / call upón you.

6 Give ear, O LORD, to mý prayer, *
and attend to the voice of my / supplicátions.

7 In the time of my trouble I will call upón you, *
for / you will ánswer me.

8 Among the gods there is none like yóu, O LORD, *
nor any/thing like yóur works.

9 All nations you have made will come and worship yóu, O LORD, *
and / glorifý your Name.

10 For you are great;
you do wóndrous things; *
and / you alóne are God.

11 Teach me your way, O LORD,
and I will walk in yóur truth; *
knit my heart to you that / I may féar your Name.

12 I will thank you, O LORD my God, with áll my heart, *
and glorify your / Name for évermore.

13 For great is your lóve toward me; *
you have delivered me from the / nethermóst Pit.

14 The arrogant rise up against me, O God,
and a band of violent men séeks my life; *
they have not set / you befóre their eyes.

15 But you, O LORD, are gracious and full of compássion, *
slow to anger, and full of / kindness ánd truth.

16 Turn to me and have mercy upón me; *
give your strength to your servant;
and save the child / of your hándmaid.

17 Show me a sign of your favor,
so that those who hate me may see it and bé ashamed; *
because you, O LORD, have helped me and / comfortéd me. *[Ant.]*

87

On the Twelve Days of Christmas

The Most High has found - ed a cit - y, and all peo - ples shall be

en - rolled as her chil - dren.

In Easter Season

The sing - ers and the dan - cers will say: All my fresh springs are in

you, O cit - y of God; hal - le - lu - jah.

On other Sundays and Weekdays

Glo - rious things are spo - ken of you, O cit - y of our God.

Psalm 87 *Fundamenta ejus* *Tone VII.3*

1 *Ŏn thĕ* holy mountain stands the city hé has fóunded; *
the LORD loves the gates of Zion
more than all the dwéllings of Jácob.

2 Glorious things are spóken óf you, *
O cíty óf our God.

3 I count Egypt and Babylon among thóse who knów me; *
behold Philistia, Tyre, and Ethiopia:
in Źion wére they born.

4 Of Zion it shall be said, "Everyóne was bórn in her, *
and the Most High himsélf shall sustáin her."

5 The LORD will record as he enrolls the peoples, *
"These also were born there."

6 The singers and the dancers will say, *
"All my fresh springs are in you." *[Ant.]*

88

In Holy Week

I have be - come like one who has no strength, lost a - mong the dead.

On other Sundays and Weekdays

I cry to you for help, O LORD; do not hide your face from me.

Psalm 88 *Domine, Deus* *Tone I.7*

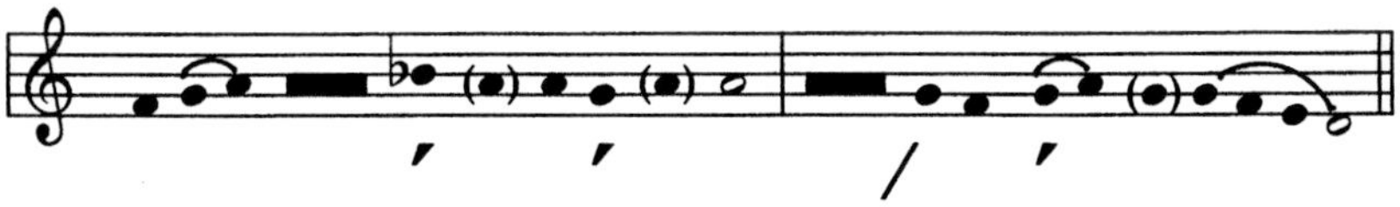

1 *O LORD,* my God, my Savior, *
by day and / night I cry to you.

2 Let my prayer enter into your presence; *
incline your ear to my / lamentation.

3 For I am full of trouble; *
my life is at the / brink of the grave.

4 I am counted among those who go down to the Pit; *
I have become like one / who has no strength;

5 —Lost among the dead, *
like the slain / who lie in the grave,

6 Whom you remember no more, *
for they are / cut off from your hand.

7 You have laid me in the depths of the Pit, *
in dark places, / and in the abyss.

8 Your anger weighs upon me heavily, *
and all your great waves / overwhelm me.

9 You have put my friends far from me;
you have made me to be abhorred by them; *
I am in prison and / cannot get free.

10 My sight has failed me because of trouble; *
LORD, I have called upon you daily;
I have stretched / out my hands to you.

11 Do you work wonders for the dead? *
will those who have died stand / up and give you thanks?

12 Will your loving-kindness be declared in the grave? *
your faithfulness in the land / of destruction?

13 Will your wonders be known in the dark? *
or your righteousness in the country where all / is forgotten?

14 But as for me, O LORD, I cry to you for help; *
in the morning my prayer / comes before you.

15 LORD, why have you rejected me? *
why have you hid/den your face from me?

16 Ever since my youth, I have been wretched and at the point of death; *
I have borne your terrors / with a troubled mind.

17 Your blazing anger has swept over me; *
your terrors / have destroyed me;

18 They surround me all day long like a flood; *
they encompass / me on every side.

19 My friend and my neighbor you have put away from me, *
and darkness is my on/ly companion. *[Ant.]*

89:1–18

On the Twelve Days of Christmas

He will say to me: "You are my Fa - ther"; hal - le - lu - jah.

In Easter Season

The Ho - ly One of Is - ra - el is our King, hal - le - lu - jah.

On other Sundays and Weekdays

Righ - teous - ness and jus - tice, O God, are the foun - da - tions

of your throne.

Psalm 89 Part 1 *Misericordias Domini* *Tone V.1*

1 *Your love,* O LORD, for ever wíll I sing; *
from age to age my mouth will procláim your fáithfulness.

2 For I am persuaded that your love is established for éver; *
you have set your faithfulness firmly ín the héavens.

3 "I have made a covenant with my chósen one; *
I have sworn an oath to Dávid my sérvant:

4 'I will establish your line for éver, *
and preserve your throne for áll generátions.'"

5 The heavens bear witness to your wonders, O LÓRD, *
and to your faithfulness in the assembly óf the hóly ones;

6 For who in the skies can be compared to the LÓRD? *
who is like the LÓRD amóng the gods?

7 God is much to be feared in the council of the holy ones, *
great and terrible to all those round about him.

8 Who is like you, LORD God of hosts? *
O mighty LORD, your faithfulness is all around you.

9 You rule the raging of the sea *
and still the surging of its waves.

10 You have crushed Rahab of the deep with a deadly wound; *
you have scattered your enemies with your mighty arm.

11 Yours are the heavens; the earth also is yours; *
you laid the foundations of the world and all that is in it.

12 You have made the north and the south; *
Tabor and Hermon rejoice in your Name.

13 You have a mighty arm; *
strong is your hand and high is your right hand.

14 Righteousness and justice are the foundations of your throne; *
love and truth go before your face.

15 Happy are the people who know the festal shout! *
they walk, O LORD, in the light of your presence.

16 They rejoice daily in your Name; *
they are jubilant in your righteousness.

17 For you are the glory of their strength, *
and by your favor our might is exalted.

18 Truly, the LORD is our ruler; *
the Holy One of Israel is our King. *[Ant.]*

89:19–52

In Easter Season

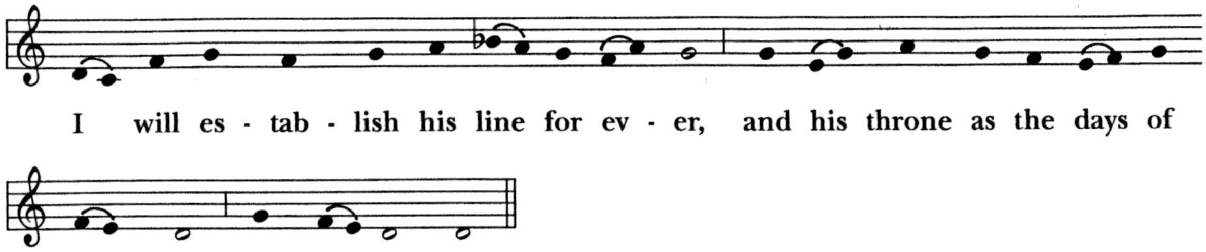
I will es - tab - lish his line for ev - er, and his throne as the days of
hea - ven, hal - le - lu - jah.

On other Sundays and Weekdays

I have sworn an oath to Da - vid my serv - ant; I will es - tab - lish his line
for ev - er.

Psalm 89 Part 2 *Tunc locutus es* *Tone I.1*

19 *You spoke* once in a vision and said to your faithful people: *
"I have set the crown upon a warrior
and have exalted one chosen out / of the people.

20 I have found David my servant; *
with my holy oil have / I anointed him.

21 My hand will hold him fast *
and my / arm will make him strong.

22 No enemy shall deceive him, *
nor any wicked / man bring him down.

23 I will crush his foes before him *
and strike down / those who hate him.

24 My faithfulness and love shall be with him, *
and he shall be vic/torious through my Name.

25 I shall make his dominion extend *
from the Great Sea / to the River.

26 He will say to me, 'You are my Father, *
my God, and the rock of / my salvation.'

27 I will make him my firstborn *
and higher than the / kings of the earth.

28 I will keep my love for him for ever, *
and my covenant will / stand firm for him.

29 I will establish his line for ever *
and his throne as the / days of heaven."

30 "If his children forsake my law, *
and do not walk according / to my judgments;

31 If they break my statutes *
and do not keep / my commandments;

32 I will punish their transgressions with a rod *
and their ini/quities with the lash;

33 But I will not take my love from him, *
nor let my faith/fulness prove false.

34 I will not break my covenant, *
nor change what has gone / out of my lips.

35 Once for all I have sworn by my holiness: *
'I will not / lie to David.

36 His line shall endure for ever *
and his throne as the / sun before me;

37 It shall stand fast for evermore like the moon, *
the abiding / witness in the sky.'"

38 But you have cast off and rejected your anointed; *
you have be/come enraged at him.

39 You have broken your covenant with your servant, *
defiled his crown, and / hurled it to the ground.

40 You have breached all his walls *
and laid his strong/holds in ruins.

41 All who pass by despoil him; *
he has become the scorn / of his neighbors.

42 You have exalted the right hand of his foes *
and made all his / enemies rejoice.

43 You have turned back the edge of his sword *
and have not sustained / him in battle.

44 You have put an end to his splendor *
and cast / his throne to the ground.

45 You have cut short the days of his youth *
and have / covered him with shame.

46 How long will you hide yourself, O LORD?
will you hide yourself for ever? *
how long will your / anger burn like fire?

47 Remember, LORD, how short life is, *
how frail / you have made all flesh.

48 Who can live and not see death? *
who can save himself from the / power of the grave?

49 Where, Lord, are your loving-kindnesses of old, *
which you promised David / in your faithfulness?

50 Remember, Lord, how your servant is mocked, *
how I carry in my bosom the taunts of / many peoples,

51 The taunts your enemies have hurled, O LORD, *
which they hurled at the heels of / your anointed.

52 Blessed be the LORD for evermore! *
Amen, / I say, Amen. *[Ant.]*

90

In Easter Season

May the gra - cious - ness of the LORD our God be up - on us,

hal - le - lu - jah.

On other Sundays and Weekdays

Teach us, O LORD, to num - ber our days, that we may ap - ply our hearts

to wis - dom.

Psalm 90 *Domine, refugium* *Tone VIII.1*

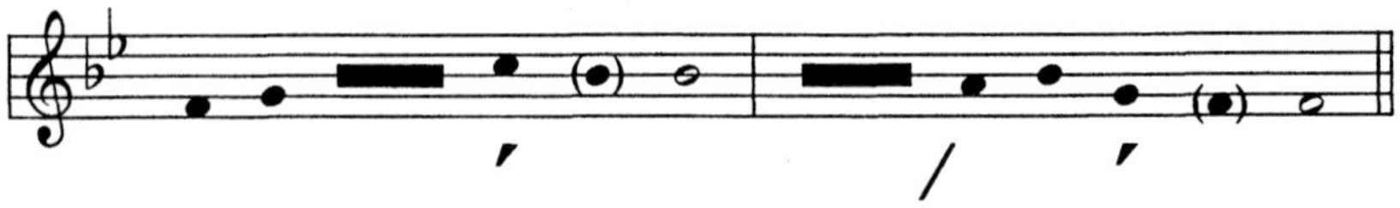

1 *Lord, you* have been our refuge *
from one generation / to another.

2 Before the mountains were brought forth,
or the land and the earth were born, *
from age / to age you are God.

3 You turn us back to the dust and say, *
"Go / back, O child of earth."

4 For a thousand years in your sight are like yesterday when it is past *
and like a / watch in the night.

5 You sweep us away like a dream; *
we fade away sud/denly like the grass.

6 In the morning it is green and flourishes; *
in the evening it is dried / up and withered.

7 For we consume away in your displeasure; *
we are afraid because of your wrathful / indignation.

8 Our iniquities you have set before you, *
and our secret sins in the light / of your countenance.

9 When you are angry, all our days are gone: *
we bring our years to an / end like a sigh.

10 The span of our life is seventy years,
perhaps in strength even eighty; *
yet the sum of them is but labor and sorrow,
for they pass away quick/ly and we are gone.

11 Who regards the power of your wrath? *
who rightly fears your / indignation?

12 So teach us to number our days *
that we may apply our / hearts to wisdom.

13 Return, O LORD; how long will you tarry? *
be gracious / to your servants.

14 Satisfy us by your loving-kindness in the morning; *
so shall we rejoice and be glad all the / days of our life.

15 Make us glad by the measure of the days that you afflicted us *
and the years in which we suf/fered adversity.

16 Show your servants your works *
and your splendor / to their children.

17 May the graciousness of the LORD our God be upon us; *
prosper the work of our hands;
pros/per our handiwork. *[Ant.]*

91

In Easter Season

Be - cause he is bound to me in love, there - fore will I de - liv - er him,

hal - le - lu - jah.

On other Sundays and Weekdays

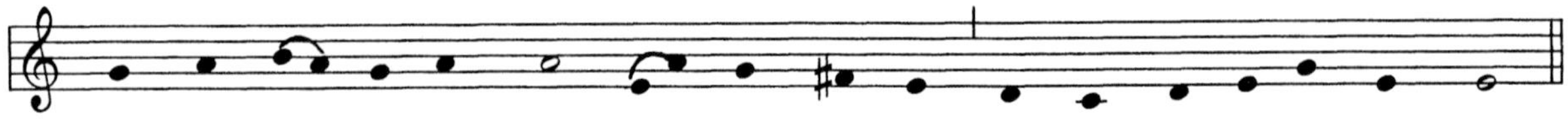
He shall give his an - gels charge o - ver you, to keep you in all your ways.

Psalm 91 *Qui habitat* *Tone IV.4*

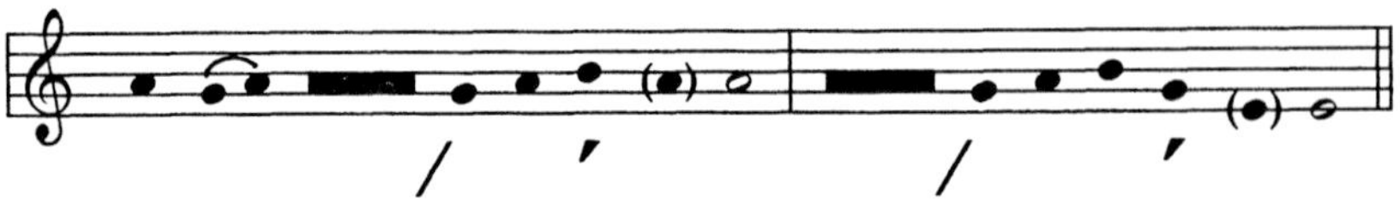

1 *He who* dwells in the shelter / of the Most High, *
abides under the shadow / of the Almighty.

2 He shall say to the LORD,
"You are my refuge / and my stronghold, *
my God / in whom I put my trust."

3 He shall deliver you from the snare / of the hunter *
and from / the deadly pestilence.

4 He shall cover you with his pinions,
and you shall find refuge un/der his wings; *
his faithfulness shall be / a shield and buckler.

5 You shall not be afraid of any / terror by night, *
nor of the / arrow that flies by day;

6 Of the plague that stalks / in the darkness, *
nor of the sickness that / lays waste at mid-day.

7 A thousand shall fall at your side
and ten thousand / at your right hand, *
but it / shall not come near you.

8 Your eyes have / only tó behold *
to see the re/ward of the wícked.

9 Because you have made the / LORD your réfuge, *
and the Most High / your habitátion,

10 There shall no evil hap/pen to yóu, *
neither shall any plague / come near your dwélling.

11 For he shall give his an/gels charge óver you, *
to / keep you in áll your ways.

12 They shall / bear you ín their hands, *
lest you dash / your foot agáinst a stone.

13 You shall tread upon the li/on and ádder; *
you shall trample the young lion and the ser/pent under yóur feet.

14 Because he is bound to me in love,
therefore will / I delíver him; *
I will protect him, / because he knóws my Name.

15 He shall call upon me, and / I will ánswer him; *
I am with him in trouble;
I will rescue him and / bring him to hónor.

16 With long life will I sat/isfy hím, *
and show / him my salvátion. *[Ant.]*

In Easter Season

You have made me glad, O LORD; and I shout for joy be - cause of the

works of your hands, hal - le - lu - jah.

On other Sundays and Weekdays

We will tell of your lov - ing - kind - ness ear - ly in the morn - ing, O

LORD, and of your faith - ful - ness in the night sea - son.

Psalm 92 *Bonum est confiteri* *Tone V.3*

1 *It is* a good thing to give thanks to the LÓRD, *
and to sing praises to your Náme, O Móst High;

2 To tell of your loving-kindness early in the mórning *
and of your faithfulness in thé night séason;

3 On the psaltery, and ón the lyre, *
and to the melódy óf the harp.

4 For you have made me glad by your ácts, O LORD; *
and I shout for joy because of the wórks of yóur hands.

5 LORD, how great are yóur works! *
your thóughts are véry deep.

6 The dullard does not know,
nor does the fool understand, *
that though the wicked grow like weeds,
and all the workers of iniquity flourish,

7 They flourish only to be destroyed for ever; *
but you, O LORD, are exalted for evermore.

8 For lo, your enemies, O LORD,
lo, your enemies shall perish, *
and all the workers of iniquity shall be scattered.

9 But my horn you have exalted like the horns of wild bulls; *
I am anointed with fresh oil.

10 My eyes also gloat over my enemies, *
and my ears rejoice to hear the doom of
the wicked who rise up against me.

11 The righteous shall flourish like a palm tree, *
and shall spread abroad like a cedar of Lebanon.

12 Those who are planted in the house of the LORD *
shall flourish in the courts of our God;

13 They shall still bear fruit in old age; *
they shall be green and succulent;

14 That they may show how upright the LORD is, *
my Rock, in whom there is no fault. *[Ant.]*

93

On the Twelve Days of Christmas

Ev - er since the world be - gan, your throne, O LORD, has been

es - tab - lished.

In Lent

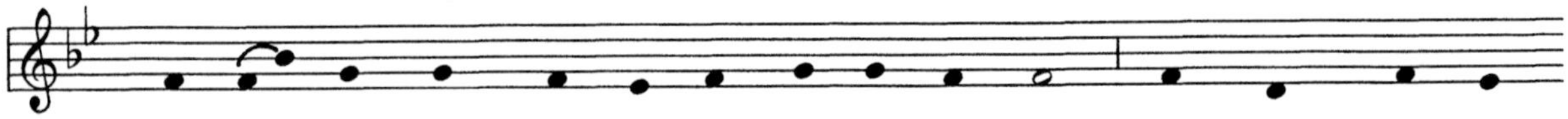

Your tes - ti - mo - nies are ver - y sure, O LORD; and might - ier than

the sound of man - y wa - ters.

In Easter Season

The LORD is King; he has put on splen - did ap - par - el,

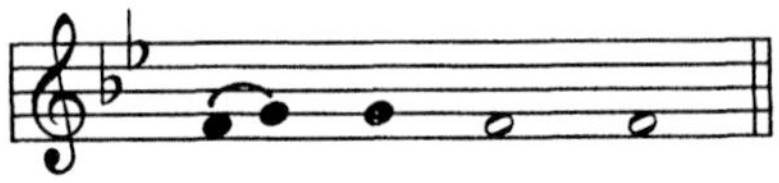

hal - le - lu - jah. †

On other Sundays and Weekdays

Might - y is the LORD who dwells on high.

Psalm 93 *Dominus regnavit* *Tone VIII.1*

1 *The LORD* is King;
he has put on splendid appárel; *
*†the LORD has put on his apparel
and gird/ed himsélf with strength.

2 He has made the whole wórld so sure *
that it / cannot bé moved;

3 Ever since the world began, your throne has been estáblished; *
you are from / everlásting.

4 The waters have lifted up, O LORD,
the waters have lifted úp their voice; *
the waters have lifted / up their póunding waves.

5 Mightier than the sound of many waters,
mightier than the breakers of the séa, *
mightier is the / LORD who dwélls on high.

6 Your testimonies are véry sure, *
and holiness adorns your house, O LORD,
for ever / and for évermore. *[Ant.]*

*When the Easter Season antiphon is sung, the first verse begins: *the LORD* has put on his appárel.

In Holy Week

They con - spire a - gainst the life of the just, and con - demn the

in - no - cent to death.

In Easter Season

The LORD has be - come my strong - hold, and my God the rock of my

trust, hal - le - lu - jah.

On other Sundays and Weekdays

The LORD knows our hu - man thoughts; how like a puff of wind they are.

Psalm 94 *Deus ultionum* *Tone III.5*

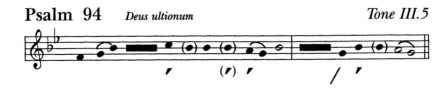

1 *O LORD*—God of vengeance, *
O God of vengeance, / show yourself.

2 Rise up, O Judge of the world; *
give the arrogant / their just deserts.

3 How long shall the wicked, O LORD, *
how long shall the wick/ed triumph?

4 They bluster in their insolence; *
all evildoers are full / of boasting.

5 They crush your people, O LORD, *
and afflict your cho/sen nation.

6 They murder the widow and the stranger *
and put the or/phans to death.

7 Yet they say, "The LORD does not see, *
the God of Jacob takes / no notice."

8 Consider well, you dullards among the people; *
when will you fools / understand?

9 He that planted the ear, does he not hear? *
he that formed the eye, / does he not see?

10 He who admonishes the nations, will he not punish? *
he who teaches all the world, has he / no knowledge?

11 The LORD knows our human thoughts; *
how like a puff / of wind they are.

12 Happy are they whom you instruct, O Lord! *
whom you teach out / of your law;

13 To give them rest in evil days, *
until a pit is dug for / the wicked.

14 For the LORD will not abandon his people, *
nor will he / forsake his own.

15 For judgment will again be just, *
and all the true of heart / will follow it.

16 Who rose up for me against the wicked? *
who took my part against the e/vildoers?

17 If the LORD had not come to my help, *
I should soon have dwelt in the land / of silence.

18 As often as I said, "My foot has slipped," *
your love, O LORD, / upheld me.

19 When many cares fill my mind, *
your consolations / cheer my soul.

20 Can a corrupt tribunal have any part with you, *
one which frames e/vil into law?

21 They conspire against the life of the just *
and condemn the in/nocent to death.

22 But the LORD has become my stronghold, *
and my God the rock / of my trust.

23 He will turn their wickedness back upon them
and destroy them in their own malice; *
the LORD our God will / destroy them. *[Ant.]*

95

In Easter Season

Let us shout for joy to the Rock of our sal - va - tion, hal - le - lu - jah.

On other Sundays and Weekdays

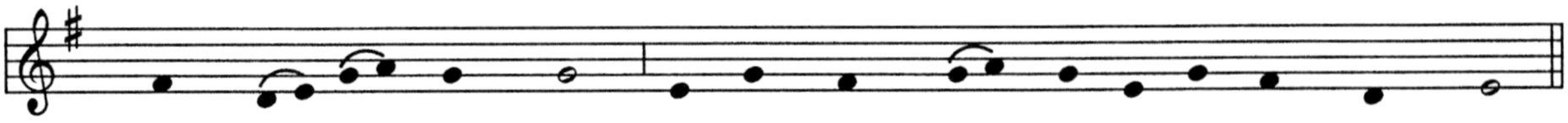
Hard - en not your hearts, as your fore - bears did in the wil - der - ness.

Psalm 95 *Venite, exultemus* *Tone II.1*

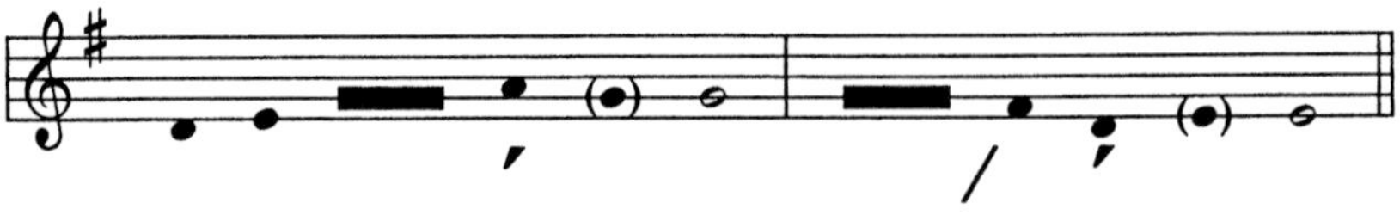

1 *Come, let* us sing to the LORD; *
let us shout for joy to the Rock of our / salvation.

2 Let us come before his presence with thanksgiving *
and raise a loud shout / to him with psalms.

3 For the LORD is a great God, *
and a great King a/bove all gods.

4 In his hand are the caverns of the éarth, *
and the heights of the hills are / his álso.

5 The sea is his, for he máde it, *
and his hands have molded / the drý land.

6 Come, let us bow down, and bénd the knee, *
and kneel before the LORD / our Máker.

7 For he is our God,
and we are the people of his pasture and the sheep of his hánd. *
Oh, that today you would hear/ken tó his voice!

8 Harden not your hearts,
as your forebears did in the ẃilderness, *
at Meribah, and on that day at Massah,
when / they témpted me.

9 They put me to the tést, *
though they / had séen my works.

10 Forty years long I detested that generation and sáid, *
"This people are wayward in their hearts;
they do / not knów my ways."

11 So I swore in my wráth, *
"They shall not enter / intó my rest." *[Ant.]*

96

On the Twelve Days of Christmas

Let the hea - vens re - joice, and let the earth be glad be - fore

the LORD, for he has come.

In Lent

The LORD will judge the world with righ - teous - ness.

In Easter Season

Tell it out a - mong the na - tions; The LORD is King, hal - le - lu - jah.

On other Sundays and Weekdays

Sing to the LORD and bless his Name.

Psalm 96 *Cantate Domino* *Tone V.1*

1 *Sing to* the LORD a néw song; *
sing to the LORD, áll the whóle earth.

2 Sing to the LORD and bléss his Name; *
proclaim the good news of his salvátion from dáy to day.

3 Declare his glory among the nátions *
and his wonders amóng all péoples.

4 For great is the LORD and greatly to be práised; *
he is more to be féared than áll gods.

5 As for all the gods of the nations, they are but idols; *
but it is the LORD who made the heavens.

6 Oh, the majesty and magnificence of his presence! *
Oh, the power and the splendor of his sanctuary!

7 Ascribe to the LORD, you families of the peoples; *
ascribe to the LORD honor and power.

8 Ascribe to the LORD the honor due his Name; *
bring offerings and come into his courts.

9 Worship the LORD in the beauty of holiness; *
let the whole earth tremble before him.

10 Tell it out among the nations: "The LORD is King! *
he has made the world so firm that it cannot be moved;
he will judge the peoples with equity."

11 Let the heavens rejoice, and let the earth be glad;
let the sea thunder and all that is in it; *
let the field be joyful and all that is therein.

12 Then shall all the trees of the wood shout for joy
before the LORD when he comes, *
when he comes to judge the earth.

13 He will judge the world with righteousness *
and the peoples with his truth. *[Ant.]*

97

In Easter Season

Light has sprung up for the righ - teous, and joy - ful glad - ness for those

who are true - heart - ed, hal - le - lu - jah.

On other Sundays and Weekdays

The LORD is King; let the earth re - joice; let the mul - ti - tude of the

isles be glad. †

Psalm 97 *Dominus regnavit* *Tone I.7*

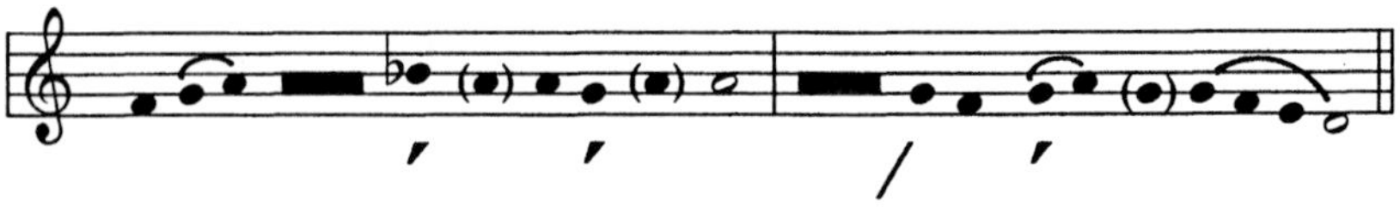

1 *The LORD* is King;
let the earth rejoice; *
let the multitude / of the isles be glad.

2 †*Clouds and* darkness are round about him, *
righteousness and justice are the foun/dations of his throne.

3 A fire goes before him *
and burns up his ene/mies on every side.

4 His lightnings light up the world; *
the earth sees / it and is afraid.

5 The mountains melt like wax at the presence of the LORD, *
at the presence of the Lord / of the whole earth.

6 The heavens declare his righteousness, *
and all the peoples / see his glory.

7 Confounded be all who worship carved images
and delight in false gods! *
Bow down be/fore him, all you gods.

8 Zion hears and is glad, and the cities of Judah rejoice, *
because of your / judgments, O LORD.

9 For you are the LORD,
most high over all the earth; *
you are exalted / far above all gods.

10 The LORD loves those who hate evil; *
he preserves the lives of his saints
and delivers them from the hand / of the wicked.

11 Light has sprung up for the righteous, *
and joyful gladness for those who / are truehearted.

12 Rejoice in the LORD, you righteous, *
and give thanks / to his holy Name. *[Ant.]*

In Advent

Je - ru - sa - lem, re - joice with great re - joic - ing; for your Sav - ior

comes to you, hal - le - lu - jah.

In Lent

The LORD re - mem - bers his mer - cy and faith - ful - ness to the house

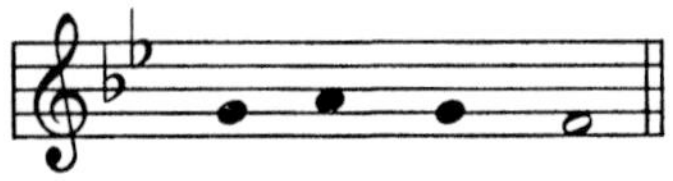

of Is - ra - el.

In Easter Season

All the ends of the earth have seen the vic - to - ry of our God,

hal - le - lu - jah.

On other Sundays and Weekdays

Shout with joy be - fore the King, the LORD.

Psalm 98 *Cantate Domino* *Tone VIII.2*

1 *Sing to* the LORD a néw song, *
for he has done / marvelóus things.

2 With his right hand and his hóly arm *
has he won for him/self the víctory.

3 The LORD has made known his víctory; *
his righteousness has he openly shown in the sight / of the nátions.

4 He remembers his mercy and faithfulness to the house of Ísrael, *
and all the ends of the earth have seen the victo/ry of óur God.

5 Shout with joy to the LORD áll you lands; *
lift up your / voice, rejóice, and sing.

6 Sing to the LORD with the hárp, *
with the harp / and the vóice of song.

7 With trumpets and the sound of the hórn *
shout with joy be/fore the Kíng, the LORD.

8 Let the sea make a noise and all that is ín it, *
the lands and / those who dwéll therein.

9 Let the rivers cláp their hands, *
and let the hills ring out with joy before the LORD,
when he / comes to júdge the earth.

10 In righteousness shall he júdge the world *
and the peo/ples with équity. *[Ant.]*

99

In Easter Season

The LORD is great in Zi - on; he is high a - bove all peo - ples,

hal - le - lu - jah.

On other Sundays and Weekdays

Pro - claim the great - ness of the LORD our God, and wor - ship up - on

his ho - ly hill.

Psalm 99 *Dominus regnavit* *Tone VII.1*

1 *The LORD* is King;
let the people tremble; *
he is enthroned upon the cherubim;
let the earth shake.

2 The LORD is great in Zion; *
he is high above all peoples.

3 Let them confess his Name, which is great and awesome; *
—he is the Holy One.

4 "O mighty King, lover of justice,
you have established equity; *
you have executed justice and righteousness in Jacob."

5 Proclaim the greatness of the LORD our God
and fall down before his footstool; *
—he is the Holy One.

6 Moses and Aaron among his priests,
and Samuel among those who call upon his Name, *
they called upon the LORD, and he answered them.

7 He spoke to them out of the pillar of cloud; *
they kept his testimonies and the decree that he gave them.

8 "O LORD our God, you answered them indeed; *
you were a God who forgave them,
yet punished them for their evil deeds."

9 Proclaim the greatness of the LORD our God
and worship him upon his holy hill; *
for the LORD our God is the Holy One. *[Ant.]*

100

In Easter Season

Serve the LORD with glad - ness, hal - le - lu - jah.

On other Sundays and Weekdays

Come be - fore God's pres - ence with a song.

Psalm 100 *Jubilate Deo* *Tone VIII.1*

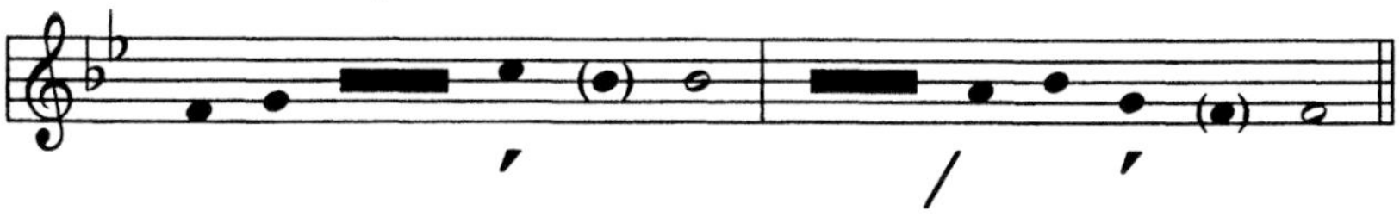

1 *Be joy*ful in the LORD, all you lands; *
serve the LORD with gladness
and come before his / presence with a song.

2 Know this: The LORD himself is God; *
he himself has made us, and we are his;
we are his people and the sheep / of his pasture.

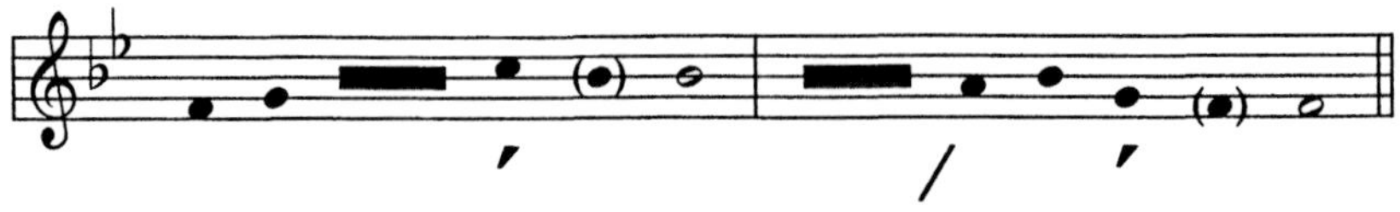

3 Enter his gates with thanksgiving;
go into his cóurts with praise; *
give thanks to him and / call upón his Name.

4 For the LORD is good;
his mercy is everlásting; *
and his faithfulness en/dures from áge to age. *[Ant.]*

101

In Easter Season

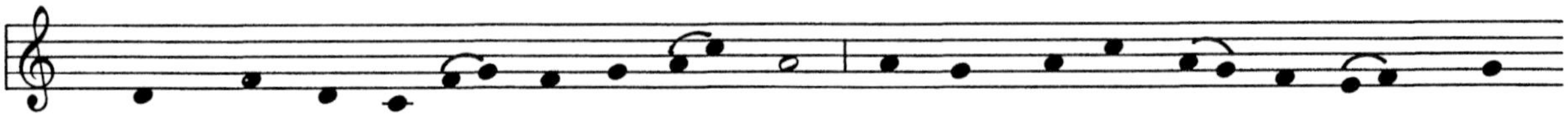

Those who do the will of my Fa - ther will en - ter in - to the king - dom

of heav - en, hal - le - lu - jah.

On other Sundays and Weekdays

To you, O LORD, will I sing prais - es; I will strive to fol - low a

blame - less course.

Psalm 101 *Misericordiam et judicium* *Tone I.2*

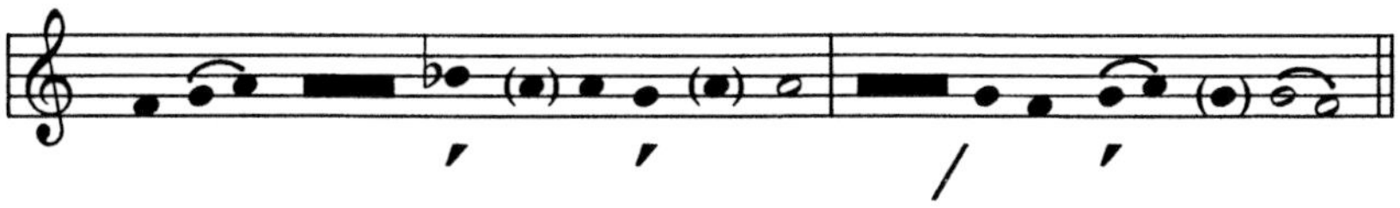

1 *I will* sing of mercy and justice; *
to you, O LORD, will / I sing praises.

2 I will strive to follow a blameless course;
oh, when will you come to me? *
I will walk with sincerity of / heart within my house.

3 I will set no worthless thing before my eyes; *
I hate the doers of evil deeds;
they shall / not remain with me.

4 A crooked heart shall be far from me; *
I / will not know evil.

5 Those who in secret slander their neighbors I will destroy; *
those who have a haughty look and a proud heart / I cannot abide.

6 My eyes are upon the faithful in the land, that they may dwell with me, *
and only those who lead a blameless life shall / be my servants.

7 Those who act deceitfully shall not dwell in my house, *
and those who tell lies shall not con/tinue in my sight.

8 I will soon destroy all the wicked in the land, *
that I may root out all evildoers from the / city of the LORD. *[Ant.]*

102

In Holy Week

I said, O my God, do not take me a - way in the midst of my days.

In Easter Season

You will a - rise, O LORD, and have com - pas - sion on Zi - on,

hal - le - lu - jah.

On other Sundays and Weekdays

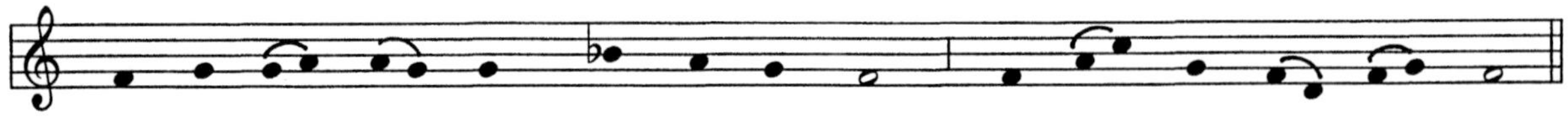

Let my cry come be - fore you, O LORD; hide not your face from me.

Psalm 102 *Domine, exaudi* *Tone VI*

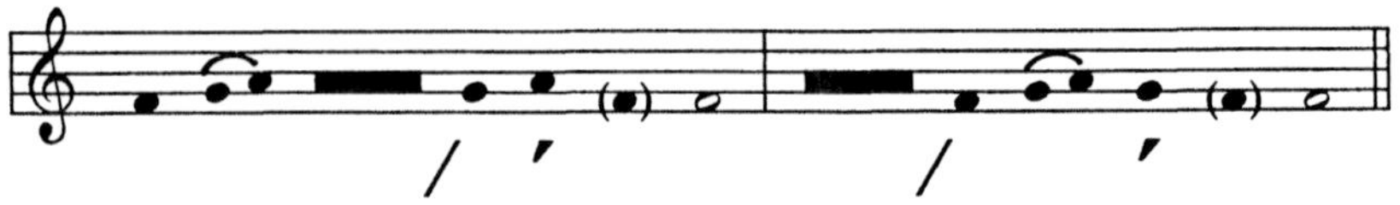

1 *LORD, hëar* my prayer, and let my cry come / befóre you; *
hide not your face from me in the day / of mÿ tróuble.

2 Incline / your éar to me; *
when I call, make / haste tö ánswer me,

3 For my days drift / awáy like smoke, *
and my bones are / hot äs búrning coals.

4 My heart is smitten like grass / and wíthered, *
so that I for/get tö éat my bread.

5 Because of the voice of / my gróaning *
I / am büt skin and bones.

6 I have become like a vulture in / the wílderness, *
like an owl a/mong thë rúins.

7 I lie / awáke and groan; *
I am like a sparrow, lonely / on ä hóuse-top.

8 My enemies revile / me áll day long, *
and those who scoff at me have taken an / oath ägáinst me.

9 For I have eaten ash/es fór bread *
and mingled my / drink wïth wéeping.

10 Because of your indigna/tion ánd wrath *
you have lifted me up / and thröwn mé away.

11 My days pass away like / a shádow, *
and I / withër líke the grass.

12 But you, O LORD, endure / for éver, *
and your / Name fröm áge to age.

13 You will arise and have compassion on Zion,
for it is time to have mercy / upón her; *
indeed, the ap/pointëd tíme has come.

14 For your servants love her ver/y rúbble, *
and are moved to pity / evën fór her dust.

15 The nations shall fear / your Náme, O LORD, *
and all the kings of the / earth yöur glóry.

16 For the LORD will build / up Zíon, *
and his glo/ry wïll áppear.

17 He will look with favor on the prayer of / the hómeless; *
he will / not dëspíse their plea.

18 Let this be written for a future ge/nerátion, *
so that a people yet un/born mäy práise the LORD.

19 For the LORD looked down from his ho/ly pláce on high; *
from the heavens / he bëhéld the earth;

20 That he might hear the groan of / the cáptive *
and set free / those cöndémned to die;

21 That they may declare in Zion the Name / of thé LORD, *
and his praise / in Jërúsalem;

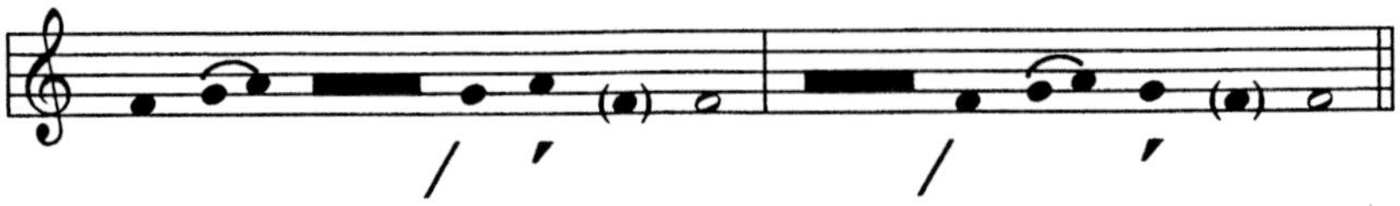

22 When the peoples are gathered / togéther, *
and the kingdoms al/so, tö sérve the LORD.

23 He has brought down my strength / befóre my time; *
he has shortened the num/ber öf mý days;

24 And I said, "O my God,
do not take me away in the midst / of mý days; *
your years endure throughout all / genërátions.

25 In the beginning, O LORD, you laid the founda/tions óf the earth, *
and the heavens are the / work öf yóur hands;

26 They shall perish, but you will endure;
they all shall wear out like / a gárment; *
as clothing you will change them,
and / they shäll bé changed;

27 But you are / alwáys the same, *
and your / years ẅíll néver end.

28 The children of your servants shall / contínue, *
and their offspring shall / stand fäst ín your sight." *[Ant.]*

103

In Advent

Thus says the LORD your God: Re - pent and turn a - gain, be - cause the

king - dom of heaven is at hand, hal - le - lu - jah.

In Lent

The LORD knows where - of we are made; he re - mem - bers that we are

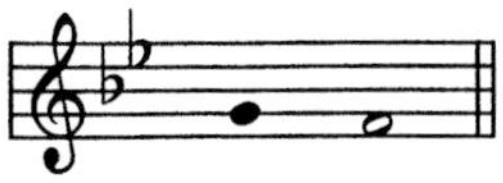

but dust.

In Easter Season

Bless the LORD, O my soul, who re - deems your life from the grave,

hal - le - lu - jah.

On other Sundays and Weekdays

Bless the LORD, O my soul, and for - get not all his ben - e - fits.

Psalm 103 *Benedic, anima mea* *Tone VIII.2*

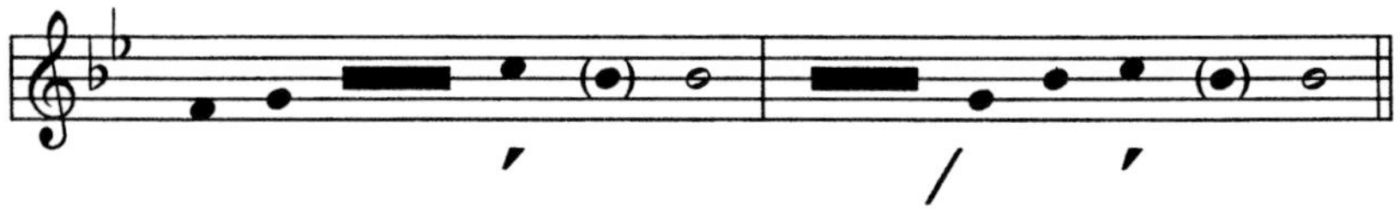

1 *Bless the* LORD, Ó my soul, *
and all that is within me, / bless his hóly Name.

2 Bless the LORD, Ó my soul, *
and forget not / all his bénefits.

3 He forgives áll your sins *
and heals all / your infírmities;

4 He redeems your life from the gráve *
and crowns you with mercy and / loving-kíndness;

5 He satisfies you with góod things, *
and your youth is renewed / like an éagle's.

6 The LORD executes righteousness *
and judgment for / all who are oppressed.

7 He made his ways known to Moses *
and his works to the chil/dren of Israel.

8 The LORD is full of compassion and mercy, *
slow to anger and / of great kindness.

9 He will not always accuse us, *
nor will he keep his an/ger for ever.

10 He has not dealt with us according to our sins, *
nor rewarded us according / to our wickedness.

11 For as the heavens are high above the earth, *
so is his mercy great upon / those who fear him.

12 As far as the east is from the west, *
so far has he re/moved our sins from us.

13 As a father cares for his children, *
so does the LORD care for / those who fear him.

14 For he himself knows whereof we are made; *
he remembers / that we are but dust.

15 Our days are like the grass; *
we flourish like a / flower of the field;

16 When the wind goes over it, it is gone, *
and its place shall / know it no more.

17 But the merciful goodness of the LORD endures for ever on those who fear him, *
and his righteousness on / children's children;

18 On those who keep his covenant *
and remember his command/ments and do them.

19 The LORD has set his throne in héaven, *
and his kingship has do/minion óver all.

20 Bless the LORD, you angels of his,
you mighty ones who do his bídding, *
and hearken to the / voice of hís word.

21 Bless the LORD, all yóu his hosts, *
you ministers of / his who dó his will.

22 Bless the LORD, all you works of his,
in all places of his domínion; *
bless / the LORD, Ó my soul. *[Ant.]*

104

In Advent

Be - hold, the LORD will come, and his saints with him, and on that day

there will be a great light, hal - le - lu - jah.

In Easter Season

Through Christ and in Christ were all things cre - a - ted; he is the

im - age of the in - vis - i - ble God, and the first - born of all

cre - a - tion, hal - le - lu - jah.

On other Sundays and Weekdays

O LORD my God, you are clothed with maj - es - ty and splen - dor;

you wrap your - self with light as with a cloak.

Psalm 104 *Benedic, anima mea* *Tone VIII.1*

1 *Bless the* LORD, Ó my soul; *
O LORD my God, how excellent is your greatness!
you are clothed with majes/ty and spléndor.

2 You wrap yourself with light as wíth a cloak *
and spread out the heavens / like a cúrtain.

3 You lay the beams of your chambers in the waters abóve; *
you make the clouds your chariot;
you ride on the / wings of thé wind.

4 You make the winds your méssengers *
and flames of / fire your sérvants.

5 You have set the earth upon its foundátions, *
so that it never shall / move at ány time.

6 You covered it with the Deep as with a mántle; *
the waters stood higher / than the móuntains.

7 At your rebúke they fled; *
at the voice of your thunder they / hastened áway.

8 They went up into the hills and down to the valleys benéath, *
to the places you had ap/pointed fór them.

9 You set the limits that they shóuld not pass; *
they shall not again / cover thé earth.

10 You send the springs into the válleys; *
they flow be/tween the móuntains.

11 All the beasts of the field drink their fíll from them, *
and the wild / asses quénch their thirst.

12 Beside them the birds of the air máke their nests *
and sing a/mong the bránches.

13 You water the mountains from your dwelling on hígh; *
the earth is fully satisfied by the / fruit of yóur works.

14 You make grass grow for flocks and herds *
and / plants to serve mankind;

15 That they may bring forth food from the earth, *
and wine to / gladden our hearts,

16 Oil to make a cheerful countenance, *
and bread to / strengthen the heart.

17 The trees of the LORD are full of sap, *
the cedars of Lebanon / which he planted,

18 In which the birds build their nests, *
and in whose tops the stork / makes his dwelling.

19 The high hills are a refuge for the mountain goats, *
and the stony cliffs for / the rock badgers.

20 You appointed the moon to mark the seasons, *
and the sun knows the time / of its setting.

21 You make darkness that it may be night, *
in which all the beasts / of the forest prowl.

22 The lions roar after their prey *
and / seek their food from God.

23 The sun rises, and they slip away *
and lay themselves / down in their dens.

24 Man goes forth to his work *
and to his labor un/til the evening.

25 O LORD, how manifold are your works! *
in wisdom you have made them all;
the earth is full / of your creatures.

26 Yonder is the great and wide sea
with its living things too many to number, *
crea/tures both small and great.

27 There move the ships,
and there is that Leviáthan, *
which you have made / for the spórt of it.

28 All of them lóok to you *
to give them their food / in due séason.

29 You give it to them; they gáther it; *
you open your hand, and they are / filled with góod things.

30 You hide your face, and they are térrified; *
you take away their breath,
and they die and re/turn to théir dust.

31 You send forth your Spirit, and they are creáted; *
and so you renew the / face of thé earth.

32 May the glory of the LORD endure for éver; *
may the LORD re/joice in áll his works.

33 He looks at the earth and it trémbles; *
he touches the / mountains ánd they smoke.

34 I will sing to the LORD as long as Í live; *
I will praise my God while I / have my béing.

35 May these words of mine pléase him; *
I will re/joice in thé LORD.

36 Let sinners be consumed out of the éarth, *
and the / wicked bé no more.

37 Bless the LORD, Ó my soul. *
— / Hallelújah! *[Ant.]*

105:1–22

In Easter Season

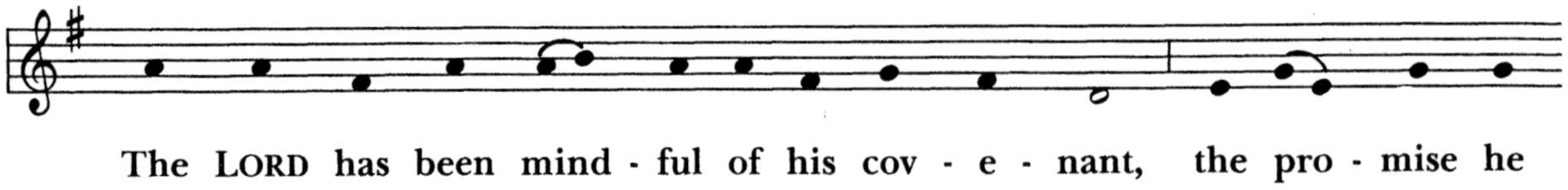
The LORD has been mind - ful of his cov - e - nant, the pro - mise he

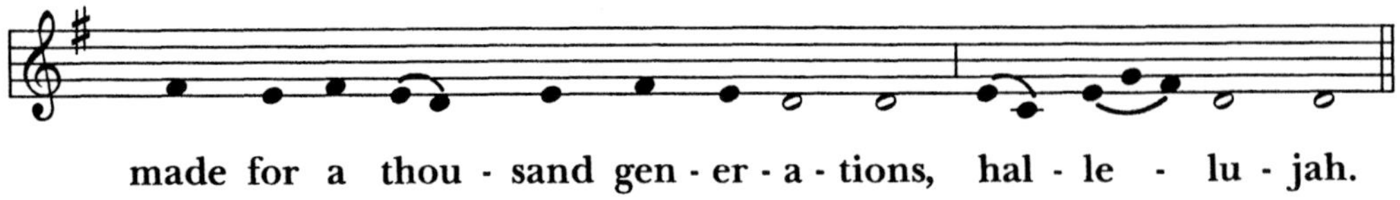
made for a thou - sand gen - er - a - tions, hal - le - lu - jah.

On other Sundays and Weekdays

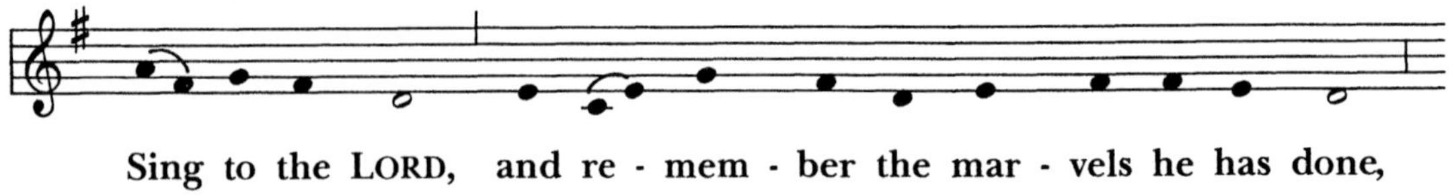
Sing to the LORD, and re - mem - ber the mar - vels he has done,

hal - le - lu - jah.

Psalm 105 Part 1 *Confitemini Domino* *Tone VII.7*

1 *Give thanks* to the LORD and cáll upón his Name; *
make known his deeds amóng the péoples.

2 Sing to him, sing práises tó him, *
and speak of all his márvelóus works.

3 Glory ín his hóly Name; *
let the hearts of those who séek the LÓRD rejoice.

4 Search for the LÓRD and hís strength; *
contínually séek his face.

5 Remember the márvels hé has done, *
his wonders and the júdgments óf his mouth,

6 O offspring of Ábraham hís servant, *
O children of Jácob his chósen.

7 He is the LORD our God; *
his judgments prevail in all the world.

8 He has always been mindful of his covenant, *
the promise he made for a thousand generations:

9 The covenant he made with Abraham, *
the oath that he swore to Isaac,

10 Which he established as a statute for Jacob, *
an everlasting covenant for Israel,

11 Saying, "To you will I give the land of Canaan *
to be your allotted inheritance."

12 When they were few in number, *
of little account, and sojourners in the land,

13 Wandering from nation to nation *
and from one kingdom to another,

14 He let no one oppress them *
and rebuked kings for their sake,

15 Saying, "Do not touch my anointed *
and do my prophets no harm."

16 Then he called for a famine in the land *
and destroyed the supply of bread.

17 He sent a man before them, *
Joseph, who was sold as a slave.

18 They bruised his feet in fetters; *
his neck they put in an iron collar.

19 Until his prediction came to pass, *
the word of the LORD tested him.

20 The king sent and released him; *
the ruler of the peoples set him free.

21 He set him as a master over his household, *
as a ruler over all his possessions,

22 To instruct his princes according to his will *
and to teach his elders wisdom. *[Ant.]*

105:23–45

In Easter Season

God led forth his peo - ple with glad - ness, his cho - sen with shouts of

joy, hal - le - lu - jah.

On other Sundays and Weekdays

God re - mem - bered his ho - ly word, and led forth his peo - ple with

glad - ness, hal - le - lu - jah.

Psalm 105 Part 2 *Et intravit Israel* *Tonus Peregrinus*

23 Ïsrael / came into Égypt, *
and Jacob became a sojourner in / the lánd of Häm.

24 The LORD made his people ex/ceedingly frúitful; *
he made them stronger than / their énemïes;

25 Whose heart he turned, so that they / hated his péople, *
and dealt unjustly with / his sérvänts.

26 He sent / Moses his sérvant, *
and Aaron whom he / had chósën.

27 They worked / his signs amóng them, *
and portents in / the lánd of Häm.

28 He sent / darkness, and it gréw dark; *
but the Egyptians rebelled / agáinst his wörds.

29 He turned / their waters ínto blood *
and caused / their físh to dïe.

30 Their land / was overrún by frogs, *
in the very cham/bers óf their kïngs.

31 He spoke, and there / came swarms of ínsects *
and gnats within all / their bórdërs.

32 He gave them / hailstones instéad of rain, *
and flames of fire through/out théir länd.

33 He blasted their / vines and their fíg trees *
and shattered every tree in / their cóuntrÿ.

34 He / spoke, and the lócust came, *
and young locusts with/out númbër,

35 Which ate up all the / green plants in théir land *
and devoured the fruit / of théir söil.

36 He struck down / the firstborn óf their land, *
the firstfruits of / all théir strength.

37 He led out his people / with silver ánd gold; *
in all their tribes there was not one / that stúmblëd.

38 Egypt was / glad of their góing, *
because they were / afráid of thëm.

39 He spread out a / cloud for a cóvering *
and a fire to give light in / the níght seasön.

40 — / They asked, and quáils appeared, *
and he satisfied them with bread / from héavën.

41 He opened / the rock, and wáter flowed, *
so the river ran in / the drý placës.

42 For God re/membered his hóly word *
and Abraham / his sérvänt.

43 So he led forth his / people with gládness, *
his chosen / with shóuts of jöy.

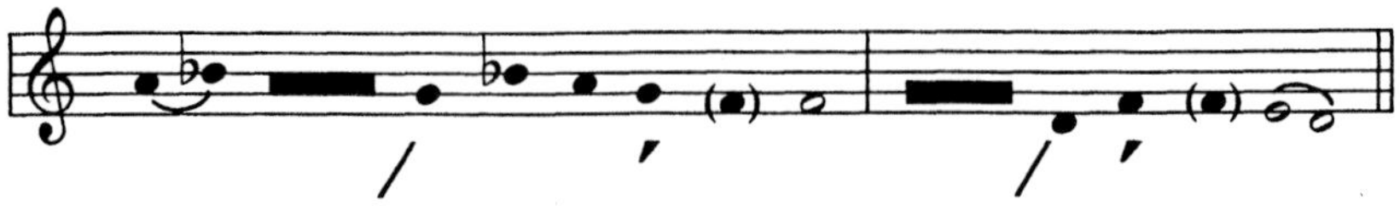

44 He gave his people the / lands of the nátions, *
and they took the fruit / of óthers' töil.

45 That they / might keep his státutes *
and observe his laws. Hal/lelújäh! *[Ant.]*

106:1–18

In Easter Season

Bles - sed be the LORD, the God of Is - ra - el, from ev - er - last - ing

and to ev - er - last - ing, hal - le - lu - jah.

On other Sundays and Weekdays

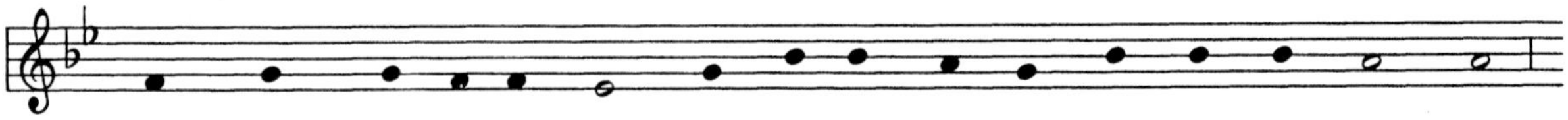

Re - mem - ber us, O LORD, with the fa - vor you have for your peo - ple,

and vis - it us with your sav - ing help, hal - le - lu - jah.

Psalm 106 Part 1 *Confitemini Domino* *Tone VIII.3*

*1 *Hallel*ujah!
Give thanks to the LORD, for hé is good, *
for his mercy en/dures for éver.

**Hallelujah* may be omitted from the first verse of the psalm when the antiphon ends with *hallelujah*; the verse then begins: *Give thanks* to the LORD....

2 Who can declare the mighty acts of the Lord *
or / show forth all his praise?

3 Happy are those who act with justice *
and al/ways do what is right!

4 Remember me, O Lord, with the favor you have for your people, *
and visit me / with your saving help;

5 That I may see the prosperity of your elect
and be glad with the gladness of your people, *
that I may glory with / your inheritance.

6 We have sinned as our forebears did; *
we have done wrong / and dealt wickedly.

7 In Egypt they did not consider your marvelous works,
nor remember the abundance of your love; *
they defied the Most High / at the Red Sea.

8 But he saved them for his Name's sake, *
to / make his power known.

9 He rebuked the Red Sea, and it dried up, *
and he led them through the deep as / through a desert.

10 He saved them from the hand of those who hated them *
and redeemed them from the hand / of the enemy.

11 The waters covered their oppressors; *
not / one of them was left.

12 Then they believed his words *
and / sang him songs of praise.

13 But they soon forgot his deeds *
and did not wait / for his counsel.

14 A craving seized them in the wilderness, *
and they put God to the test / in the desert.

15 He gave them what they asked, *
but sent lean/ness into their soul.

16 They envied Moses in the camp, *
and Aaron, the ho/ly one of the Lord.

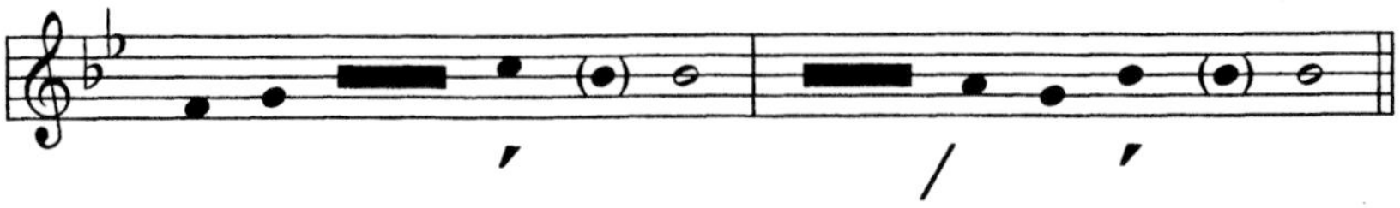

17 The earth opened and swallowed Dáthan *
and covered the company / of Abíram.

18 Fire blazed up against their cómpany, *
and flames de/voured the ẃicked. *[Ant.]*

106:19–48

In Easter Season

Bles - sed be the LORD, the God of Is - ra - el, from ev - er - last - ing and

to ev - er - last - ing, hal - le - lu - jah.

On other Sundays and Weekdays

Save us, O LORD our God, and gath - er us from a - mong the na - tions,

hal - le - lu - jah.

Psalm 106 Part 2 *Et fecerunt vitulum* *Tone IV.2*

19 *Isräel* made a bull-/calf at Hóreb *
and worshiped / a molten ímage;

20 And so they ex/changed their Glóry *
for the image of an / ox that feeds ón grass.

21 They forgot / God their Savior, *
who had done / great things in Egypt,

22 Wonderful deeds / in the land of Ham, *
and fearful / things at the Red Sea.

23 So he would have destroyed them,
had not Moses his chosen stood be/fore him in the breach, *
to turn away his / wrath from consuming them.

24 They re/fused the pleasant land *
and would not / believe his promise.

25 They / grumbled in their tents *
and would not listen to / the voice of the LORD.

26 So he lifted his / hand against them, *
to overthrow / them in the wilderness,

27 To cast out their seed a/mong the nations, *
and to scat/ter them throughout the lands.

28 They joined them/selves to Baal-Peor *
and ate sacrifices / offered to the dead.

29 They provoked him to anger / with their actions, *
and a plague / broke out among them.

30 Then Phinehas stood up and / interceded, *
and the / plague came to an end.

31 This was reckoned to / him as righteousness *
throughout all gene/rations for ever.

32 Again they provoked his anger at the wa/ters of Meribah, *
so that he punished / Moses because of them;

33 For they so embit/tered his spirit *
that he / spoke rash words with his lips.

34 They did not des/troy the peoples *
as the / LORD had commanded them.

35 They intermingled / with the heathen *
— / and learned their pagan ways,

36 So that they wor/shiped their idols, *
which / became a snare to them.

37 They / sacrificed their sons *
and their daughters / to evil spirits.

38 They shed innocent blood,
the blood of their / sons and daughters, *
which they offered to the idols of Canaan,
and the / land was defiled with blood.

39 Thus they were polluted / by their actions *
and went whor/ing in their evil deeds.

40 Therefore the wrath of the Lord was kindled a/gainst his people *
and he ab/horred his inheritance.

41 He gave them over to the hand / of the heathen, *
and those who hat/ed them ruled over them.

42 Their ene/mies oppressed them, *
and they were hum/bled under their hand.

43 Many a time did he deliver them,
but they rebelled through their / own devices, *
and were brought down / in their iniquity.

44 Nevertheless, / he saw their distress, *
when he heard / their lamentation.

45 He remembered his cov/enant with them *
and relented in accordance / with his great mercy.

46 He caused them / to be pitied *
by those / who held them captive.

47 Save us, O Lord our God,
and gather us from a/mong the nations, *
that we may give thanks to your holy Name
/and glory in your praise.

48 Blessed be the LORD, the God of Israel,
from everlasting and to / everlásting; *
and let all the people say, "A/men!"
Hallelújah! *[Ant.]*

107:1–32

In Easter Season

Give thanks to the LORD for his mer - cy, and the won - ders he does for
his chil - dren, hal - le - lu - jah.

On other Sundays and Weekdays

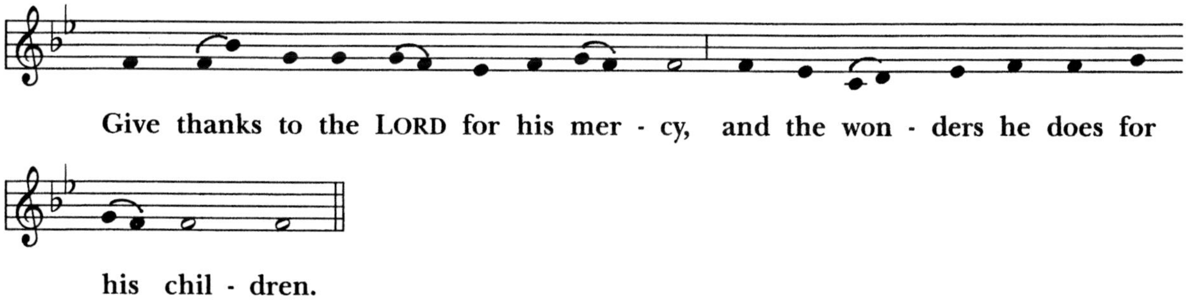
Give thanks to the LORD for his mer - cy, and the won - ders he does for
his chil - dren.

Psalm 107 Part 1 *Confitemini Domino* *Tone V.1*

1 *Give thanks* to the LORD, for hé is good, *
and his mercy endúres for éver.

2 Let all those whom the LORD has redéemed proclaim *
that he redeemed them from the hánd of thé foe.

3 He gathered them out of the lánds; *
from the east and from the west,
from the nórth and fróm the south.

4 Some wandered in désert wastes; *
they found no way to a ćity where théy might dwell.

5 They were hungry and thirsty; *
their spirits languished within them.

6 Then they cried to the LORD in their trouble, *
and he delivered them from their distress.

7 He put their feet on a straight path *
to go to a city where they might dwell.

8 Let them give thanks to the LORD for his mercy *
and the wonders he does for his children.

9 For he satisfies the thirsty *
and fills the hungry with good things.

10 Some sat in darkness and deep gloom, *
bound fast in misery and iron;

11 Because they rebelled against the words of God *
and despised the counsel of the Most High.

12 So he humbled their spirits with hard labor; *
they stumbled, and there was none to help.

13 Then they cried to the LORD in their trouble, *
and he delivered them from their distress.

14 He led them out of darkness and deep gloom *
and broke their bonds asunder.

15 Let them give thanks to the LORD for his mercy *
and the wonders he does for his children.

16 For he shatters the doors of bronze *
and breaks in two the iron bars.

17 Some were fools and took to rebellious ways; *
they were afflicted because of their sins.

18 They abhorred all manner of food *
and drew near to death's door.

19 Then they cried to the LORD in their tróuble, *
and he delivered thém from théir distress.

20 He sent forth his word and héaled them *
and sáved them fróm the grave.

21 Let them give thanks to the LORD for his mércy *
and the wonders he dóes for his chíldren.

22 Let them offer a sacrifice of thanksgíving *
and tell of his ácts with shóuts of joy.

23 Some went down to the sea in shíps *
and plied their tráde in deep wáters;

24 They beheld the works of the LÓRD *
and his wónders ín the deep.

25 Then he spoke, and a stormy wínd arose, *
which tossed high the wáves of thé sea.

26 They mounted up to the heavens and fell back to the dépths; *
their hearts melted becáuse of their péril.

27 They reeled and staggered like drúnkards *
and wére at their wíts' end.

28 Then they cried to the LORD in their tróuble, *
and he delivered thém from théir distress.

29 He stilled the storm to a whísper *
and quieted the wáves of thé sea.

30 Then were they glad because of the cálm, *
and he brought them to the harbor théy were bóund for.

31 Let them give thanks to the LORD for his mércy *
and the wonders he dóes for his chíldren.

32 Let them exalt him in the congregation of the péople *
and praise him in the council óf the élders. *[Ant.]*

107:33–43

In Easter Season

The up - right will see and re - joice, and con - sid - er well the

mer - cies of the LORD, hal - le - lu - jah.

On other Sundays and Weekdays

The up - right will see and re - joice, and con - sid - er well the

mer - cies of the LORD.

Psalm 107 Part 2 *Posuit flumina* *Tone VIII.4*

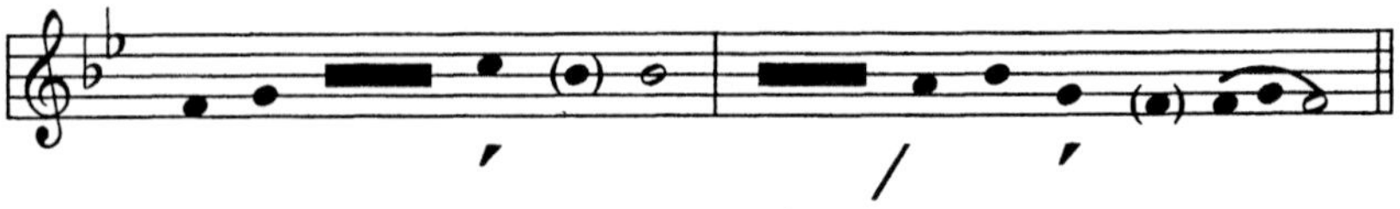

33 *The LORD* changed rivers into deserts, *
and water-springs / into thirsty ground,

34 A fruitful land into salt flats, *
because of the wickedness of / those who dwell there.

35 He changed deserts into pools of water *
and dry land / into water-springs.

36 He settled the hungry there, *
and they founded a / city to dwell in.

37 They sowed fields, and planted vineyards, *
and brought in a / fruitful harvest.

38 He blessed them, so that they increased greatly; *
he did not / let their herds decrease.

39 Yet when they were diminished and brought low, *
through stress of adversi/ty and sorrow,

40 (He pours contempt on princes *
and makes them wan/der in trackless wastes)

41 He lifted up the poor out of misery *
and multiplied their fami/lies like flocks of sheep.

42 The upright will see this and rejoice, *
but all wicked/ness will shut its mouth.

43 Whoever is wise will ponder these things, *
and consider well the / mercies of the LORD. *[Ant.]*

108

In Easter Season

Ex - alt your - self a - bove the heav - ens, O God; hal - le - lu - jah.

On other Sundays and Weekdays

I will con - fess you a - mong the peo - ples, O LORD.

Psalm 108 *Paratum cor meum* *Tone VIII.2*

1 *My heart* is firmly fixed, O God, my heart is fixed; *
I will sing / and make melody.

2 Wake up, my spirit;
awake, lute and harp; *
I myself will / waken the dawn.

3 I will confess you among the peoples, O LORD; *
I will sing praises to you a/mong the nations.

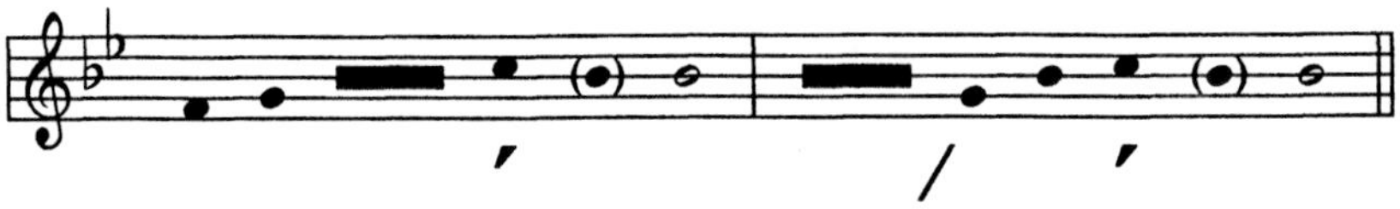

4 For your loving-kindness is greater than the heavens, *
and your faithfulness / reaches to the clouds.

5 Exalt yourself above the heavens, O God, *
and your glory / over all the earth.

6 So that those who are dear to you may be delivered, *
save with your right / hand and answer me.

7 God spoke from his holy place and said, *
"I will exult and parcel out Shechem;
I will divide the val/ley of Succoth.

8 Gilead is mine and Manasseh is mine; *
Ephraim is my helmet and Ju/dah my scepter.

9 Moab is my washbasin,
on Edom I throw down my sandal to claim it, *
and over Philistia will I / shout in triumph."

10 Who will lead me into the strong city? *
who will bring me / into Edom?

11 Have you not cast us off, O God? *
you no longer go out, O God, / with our armies.

12 Grant us your help against the enemy, *
for vain / is the help of man.

13 With God we will do valiant deeds, *
and he shall tread our e/nemies under foot. *[Ant.]*

109

Antiphon

For your ten - der mer - cy's sake, de - liv - er me, O LORD.

Psalm 109 *Deus, lauden* *Tone II.1*

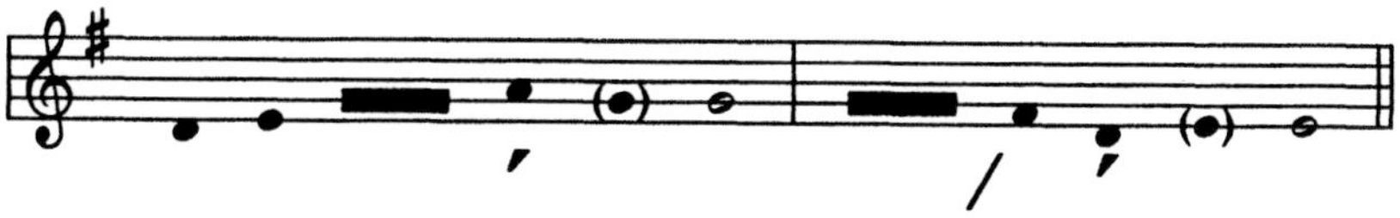

1 *Hold not* your tongue, O God of my praise; *
for the mouth of the wicked,
the mouth of the deceitful, is opened / against me.

2 They speak to me with a lying tongue; *
they encompass me with hateful words
and fight against me / without a cause.

3 Despite my love, they accuse me; *
but as for me, / I pray for them.

4 They repay evil for good, *
and ha/tred for my love.

5 Set a wicked man against him, *
and let an accuser stand / at his right hand.

6 When he is judged, let him be found guilty, *
and let his appeal / be in vain.

7 Let his days be few, *
and let another take / his office.

8 Let his children be fatherless, *
and his wife become / a widow.

9 Let his children be waifs and beggars; *
let them be driven from the ru/ins of their homes.

10 Let the creditor seize everything he has; *
let strangers plun/der his gains.

11 Let there be no one to show him kindness, *
and none to pity his father/less children.

12 Let his descendants be destroyed, *
and his name be blotted out in the next ge/neration.

13 Let the wickedness of his fathers be remembered before the LORD, *
and his mother's sin not / be blotted out;

14 Let their sin be always before the LORD; *
but let him root out their names / from the earth;

15 Because he did not remember to show mercy, *
but persecuted the poor and needy
and sought to kill the bro/kenhearted.

16 He loved cursing,
let it come upon him; *
he took no delight in blessing,
let it / depart from him.

17 He put on cursing like a garment, *
let it soak into his body like water
and into / his bones like oil;

18 Let it be to him like the cloak which he wraps around himself, *
and like the belt that he wears / continually.

19 Let this be the recompense from the LORD to my accusers, *
and to those who speak evil / against me.

20 But you, O Lord my GOD,
oh, deal with me according to your Name; *
for your tender mercy's sake, / deliver me.

21 For I am poor and needy, *
and my heart is wounded / within me.

22 I have faded away like a shadow when it lengthens; *
I am shaken off like / a locust.

23 My knees are weak through fásting, *
and my flesh is was/ted ánd gaunt.

24 I have become a repróach to them; *
they see / and sháke their heads.

25 Help me, O LÓRD my God; *
save me for / your mércy's sake.

26 Let them know that this is yóur hand, *
that you, O LORD, / have dóne it.

27 They may curse, but yóu will bless; *
let those who rise up against me be put to shame,
and your ser/vant wíll rejoice.

28 Let my accusers be clothed with disgráce *
and wrap themselves in their shame / as ín a cloak.

29 I will give great thanks to the LORD wíth my mouth; *
in the midst of the multitude will / I práise him;

30 Because he stands at the right hand of the néedy, *
to save his life from those who would / condémn him. *[Ant.]*

110

In Advent

Be - hold, the LORD shall ap - pear in the clouds of heav - en

with pow - er and great glo - ry, hal - le - lu - jah.

On the Twelve Days of Christmas

Prince - ly state has been yours from the day of your birth; in the

beau - ty of ho - li - ness have I be - got - ten you, like dew from

the womb of the morn - ing.

In Easter Season

The LORD has ris - en from the dead, and is seat - ed at the right hand

of God, hal - le - lu - jah.

On other Sundays and Weekdays

Christ the LORD is a priest for ev - er aft - er the or - der of

Mel - chiz - e - dek.

Psalm 110 *Dixit Dominus* *Tone III.4*

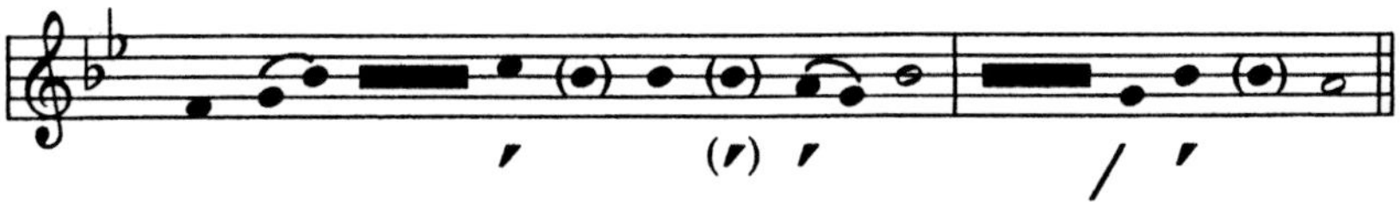

1 *The* L*ORD* said to my Lord, "Sit at my right hand, *
until I make your enemies / your footstool."

2 The LORD will send the scepter of your power out of Zion, *
saying, "Rule over your enemies round / about you.

3 Princely state has been yours from the day of your birth; *
in the beauty of holiness have I begotten you,
like dew from the womb of / the morning."

4 The LORD has sworn and he will not recant: *
"You are a priest for ever after the order of / Melchizedek."

5 The Lord who is at your right hand
will smite kings in the day of his wrath; *
he will rule over / the nations.

6 He will heap high the corpses; *
he will smash heads over / the wide earth.

7 He will drink from the brook beside the road; *
therefore he will / lift high his head. *[Ant.]*

111

In Advent

Be joy - ful, O daugh - ter of Zi - on; shout for joy, O daugh - ter of

Je - ru - sa - lem, hal - le - lu - jah.

In Easter Season

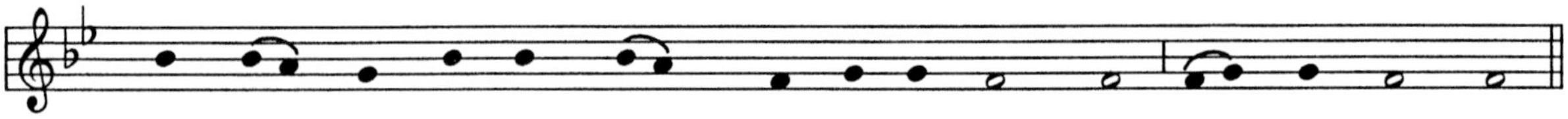

The LORD has sent re - demp - tion to his peo - ple, hal - le - lu - jah.

On other Sundays and Weekdays

The grac - ious LORD makes his mar - vel - ous works to be

re - mem - bered, hal - le - lu - jah.

Psalm 111 *Confitebor tibi* *Tone VIII.5*

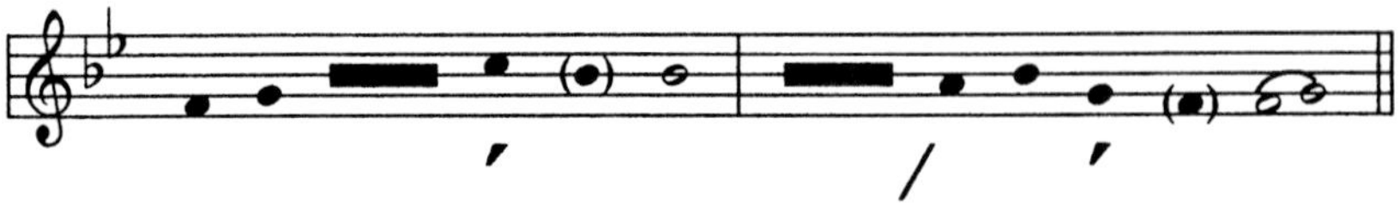

*1 *Halle*lujah!
I will give thanks to the LORD with my whole heart, *
in the assembly of the upright, in the / congregation.

2 Great are the deeds of the LORD! *
they are studied by all / who delight in them.

3 His work is full of majesty and splendor, *
and his righteousness en/dures for ever.

**Hallelujah* may be omitted from the first verse of the psalm when the antiphon ends with *Hallelujah*; the verse then begins: *I will* give thanks....

4 He makes his marvelous works to be remembered; *
the LORD is gracious and full / of compassion.

5 He gives food to those who fear him; *
he is ever mindful / of his covenant.

6 He has shown his people the power of his works *
in giving them the lands / of the nations.

7 The works of his hands are faithfulness and justice; *
all his com/mandments are sure.

8 They stand fast for ever and ever, *
because they are done in / truth and equity.

9 He sent redemption to his people;
he commanded his covenant for ever; *
holy and / awesome is his Name.

10 The fear of the LORD is the beginning of wisdom; *
those who act accordingly have a good understanding;
his praise en/dures for ever. *[Ant.]*

112

In Advent

Let the moun - tains break forth in - to sing - ing, and the hills with

righ - teous - ness; for the LORD, the light of the world, is com - ing

with pow - er, hal - le - lu - jah.

In Easter Season

Light shines in the dark - ness for the up - right, hal - le - lu - jah.

On other Sundays and Weekdays

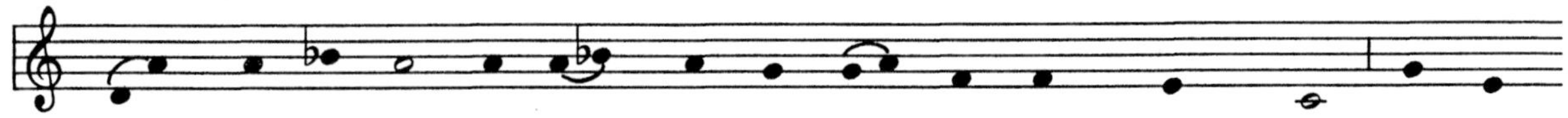

Bless - ed are they who hun - ger and thirst for righ - teous - ness, for they

shall be sat - is - fied, hal - le - lu - jah.

Psalm 112 *Beatus vir* *Tone I.7*

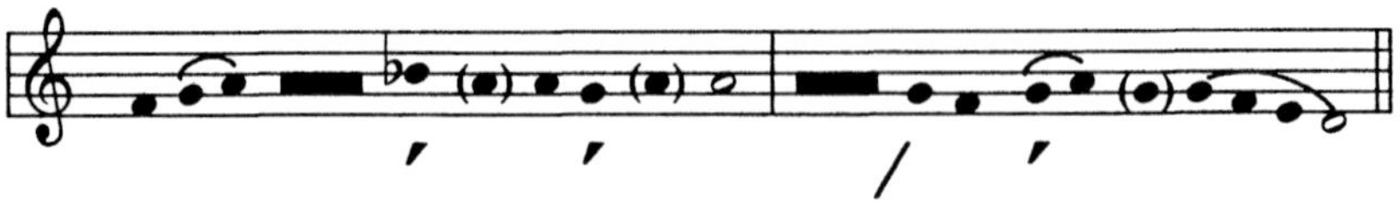

1 *Hallelujah!*
Happy are they who fear the LORD *
and have great delight in / his commandments!

2 Their descendants will be mighty in the land; *
the generation of the / upright will be blessed.

3 Wealth and riches will be in their house, *
and their righteousness will / last for ever.

4 Light shines in the darkness for the upright; *
the righteous are merciful and full / of compassion.

5 It is good for them to be generous in lending *
and to manage their af/fairs with justice.

6 For they will never be shaken; *
the righteous will be kept in everlast/ing remembrance.

7 They will not be afraid of any evil rumors; *
their heart is right;
they put their / trust in the Lord.

8 Their heart is established and will not shrink, *
until they see their desire up/on their enemies.

9 They have given freely to the poor, *
and their righteousness stands fast for ever;
they will hold up their / head with honor.

10 The wicked will see it and be angry;
they will gnash their teeth and pine away; *
the desires of the wick/ed will perish. *[Ant.]*

113

In Advent

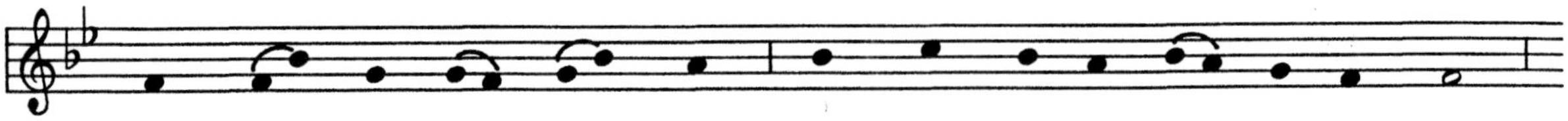

Be - hold, the LORD shall come, the Prince of the kings of the earth;

Bless - ed are they who are pre - pared to meet him,

hal - le - lu - jah.

In Easter Season

The LORD, who is high a - bove all na - tions, has raised us up with

Christ Je - sus, hal - le - lu - jah.

On other Sundays and Weekdays

From the ris - ing of the sun to its go - ing down, let the Name of the

LORD be praised, hal - le - lu - jah.

Psalm 113 *Laudate, pueri* — *Tone III.4*

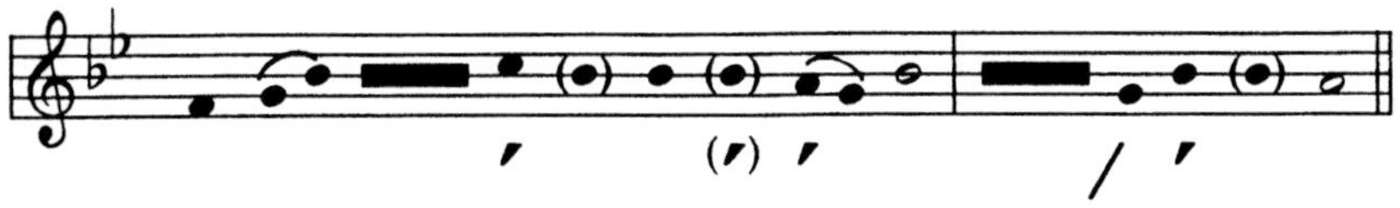

*1 *Hallelujah!*
Give praise, you servants of the LORD; *
praise the Name / of the LORD.

2 Let the Name of the LORD be blessed, *
from this time forth / for evermore.

3 From the rising of the sun to its going down *
let the Name of the / LORD be praised.

4 The LORD is high above all nations, *
and his glory / above the heavens.

5 Who is like the LORD our God, who sits enthroned on high, *
but stoops to behold the heavens / and the earth?

6 He takes up the weak out of the dust *
and lifts up the poor from / the ashes.

7 He sets them with the princes, *
with the princes of / his people.

8 He makes the woman of a childless house *
to be a joyful mother / of children. *[Ant.]*

**Hallelujah* may be omitted from the first verse of the psalm when the antiphon ends with *Hallelujah*; the verse then begins: *Give praise,* you servants....

114

In Advent

The moun - tains and the hills shall break forth be - fore him in - to
sing - ing, and all the trees of the for - est shall clap their hands, for
be - hold, our Lord and Rul - er is com - ing to reign for ev - er,
hal - le - lu - jah.

In Easter Season

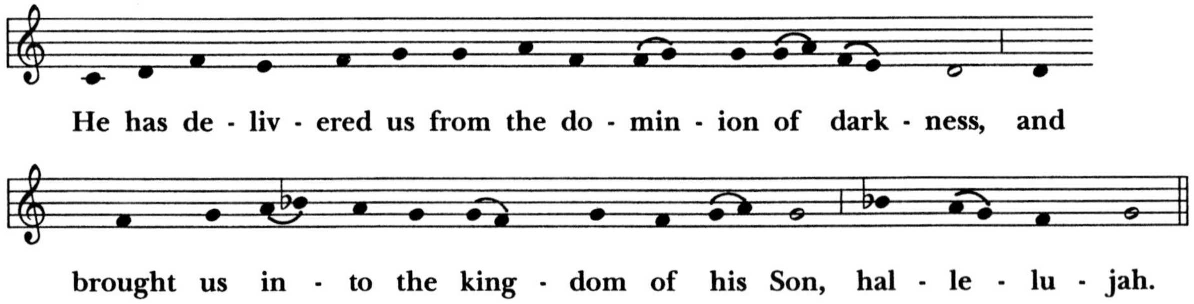
He has de - liv - ered us from the do - min - ion of dark - ness, and
brought us in - to the king - dom of his Son, hal - le - lu - jah.

On other Sundays and Weekdays

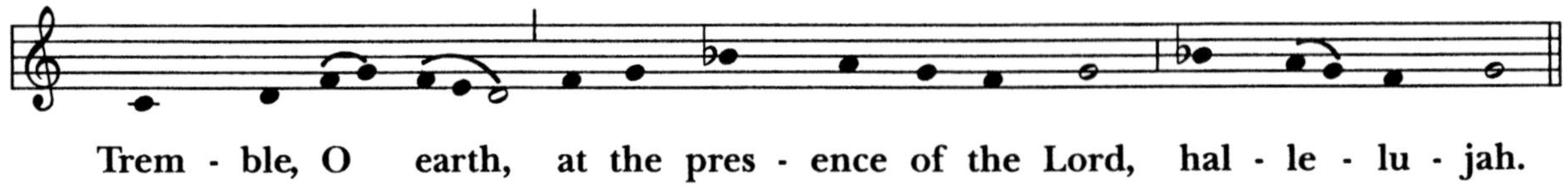
Trem - ble, O earth, at the pres - ence of the Lord, hal - le - lu - jah.

Psalm 114 *In exitu Israel* *Tonus Peregrinus*

*1 *Hal*lelujah!
When Israel / came out of Egypt, *
the house of Jacob from a people / of strange speech,

2 Judah became / God's sanctuary *
and Israel his / dominion.

3 The sea / beheld it and fled; *
Jordan turned / and went back.

4 The / mountains skipped like rams, *
and the little hills / like young sheep.

5 What ailed you, / O sea, that you fled? *
O Jordan, that / you turned back?

6 You moun/tains, that you skipped like rams? *
you little hills / like young sheep?

7 Tremble, O earth, at / the presence of the Lord, *
at the presence of the God / of Jacob,

8 Who turned the hard rock into / a pool of water *
and flint-stone into / a flowing spring. *[Ant.]*

**Hallelujah* may be omitted from the first verse of the psalm when the antiphon ends with *Halleluja* the verse then begins: *When Is - rael / came....*

In Advent

The LORD is our law - giv - er, the LORD is our King; he him - self will

come and save us, hal - le - lu - jah.

In Easter Season

We have turned from the wor - ship of i - dols to serve the liv - ing God,

hal - le - lu - jah.

On other Sundays and Weekdays

Our God is in heav - en; what - ev - er he wills to do he does,

hal - le - lu - jah.

Psalm 115 *Non nobis, Domine* *Tonus Peregrinus*

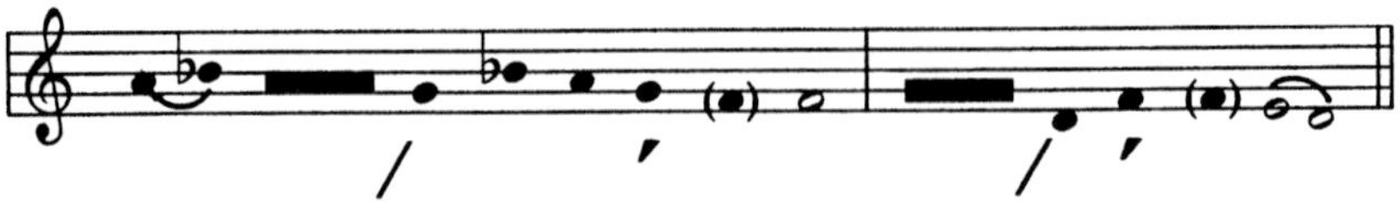

1 *Nöt* to us, O LORD, not to us,
but to / your Name give glóry; *
because of your love and because of / your fáithfulnëss.

2 —/ Why should the héathen say, *
"Where / then ís their Göd?"

3 Our / God is in héaven; *
whatever he wills / to dó he dӧes.

4 Their idols / are silver ánd gold, *
the work / of húman hӓnds.

5 They have / mouths, but they cánnot speak; *
eyes have they, but / they cánnot see;

6 They have / ears, but they cánnot hear; *
noses, but / they cánnot smell;

7 They have hands, but they cannot feel;
/ feet, but they cánnot walk; *
they make no sound / with théir thrӧat.

8 Those who / make them are líke them, *
and so are all who put / their trúst in thëm.

9 O Isra/el, trust in thé LORD; *
he is their help / and théir shiëld.

10 O house of Aar/on, trust in thé LORD, *
he is their help / and théir shiëld.

11 You who fear the / LORD, trust in thé LORD; *
he is their help / and théir shiëld.

12 The LORD has been mindful of us, / and he will bléss us; *
he will bless the house of Israel;
he will bless the house / of Aárӧn;

13 He will / bless those who féar the LORD, *
both small and / great tógethër.

14 May the LORD / increase you móre and more, *
you and your chil/dren áfter yӧu.

15 May you / be blessed by thé LORD, *
the maker of hea/ven ánd ëarth.

16 The heaven of / heavens is thé LORD's, *
but he entrusted the earth to / its péoplës.

17 The / dead do not práise the LORD, *
nor all those who go down / intó silënce;

18 But / we will bless thé LORD, *
from this time forth for evermore.
Hal/lelújäh! *[Ant.]*

116

In Advent

Be - hold, our God shall come with pow - er to en - light - en the eyes of
his ser - vants, hal - le - lu - jah.

In Easter Season

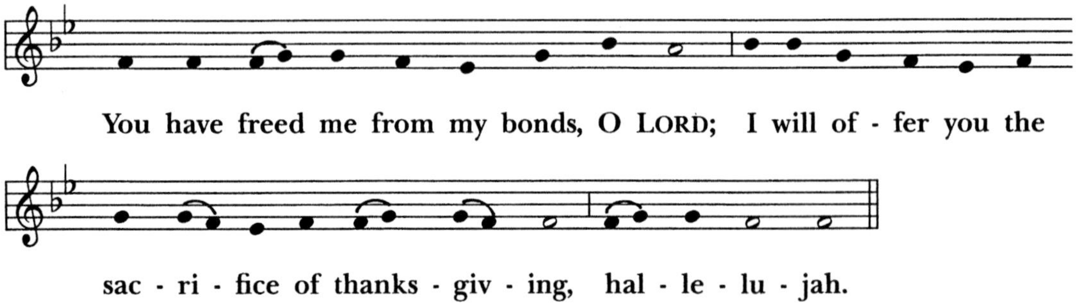
You have freed me from my bonds, O LORD; I will of - fer you the
sac - ri - fice of thanks - giv - ing, hal - le - lu - jah.

On other Sundays and Weekdays

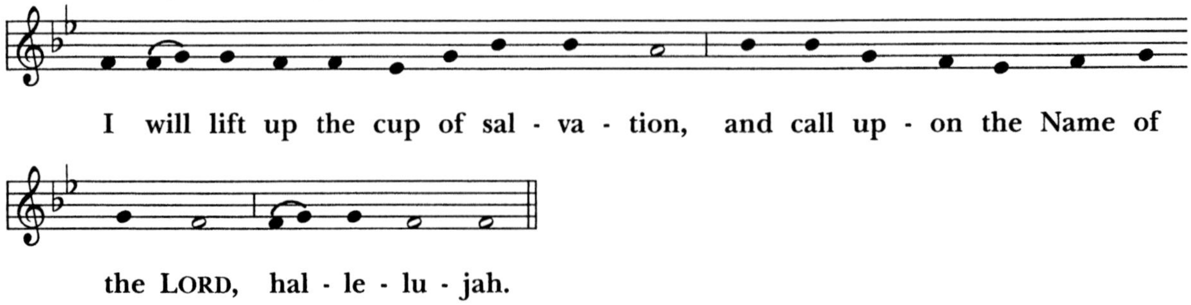
I will lift up the cup of sal - va - tion, and call up - on the Name of
the LORD, hal - le - lu - jah.

Psalm 116 *Dilexi, quoniam* *Tone VIII.1*

1 *I love* the LORD, because he has heard the voice of my supplicátion, *
because he has inclined his ear to me whenever I / called upón him.

2 The cords of death entangled me;
the grip of the grave took hóld of me; *
I came to / grief and sórrow.

3 Then I called upon the Name of the LÓRD: *
"O LORD, I / pray you, sáve my life."

4 Gracious is the LORD and ríghteous; *
our God is full / of compássion.

5 The LORD watches over the ínnocent; *
I was brought very low, / and he hélped me.

6 Turn again to your rest, Ó my soul, *
for the LORD has / treated yóu well.

7 For you have rescued my lífe from death, *
my eyes from tears, and my / feet from stúmbling.

8 I will walk in the presence of the LÓRD *
in the land / of the líving.

9 I believed, even when I said,
"I have been brought véry low." *
In my distress I said, "No one / can be trústed."

10 How shall I repay the LÓRD *
for all the good things / he has dóne for me?

11 I will lift up the cup of salvátion *
and call upon the / Name of thé LORD.

12 I will fulfill my vows to the LÓRD *
in the presence of / all his péople.

13 Precious in the sight of the LÓRD *
is the death / of his sérvants.

14 O LORD, I am your sérvant; *
I am your servant and the child of your handmaid;
you have / freed me fróm my bonds.

15 I will offer you the sacrifice of thanksgíving *
and call upon the / Name of thé LORD.

16 I will fulfill my vows to the LÓRD *
in the presence of / all his péople,

17 In the courts of the LÓRD's house, *
in the midst of you, O Jerusalem.
/ Hallelújah! *[Ant.]*

117

In Advent

On the throne of Da - vid, and ov - er his king - dom, he shall reign for
ev - er, hal - le - lu - jah.

In Easter Season

The king - dom of the world has be - come the king - dom of our LORD
and of his Christ, hal - le - lu - jah.

On other Sundays and Weekdays

The faith - ful - ness of the LORD en - dures for ev - er,

hal - le - lu - jah.

Psalm 117 *Laudate Dominum* *Tone VII.3*

1 *Praise the*—LORD, all you nations; *
laud him, all you peoples.

2 For his loving-kindness toward us is great, *
and the faithfulness of the LORD endures for ever.
Hallelujah! *[Ant.]*

118

In Lent

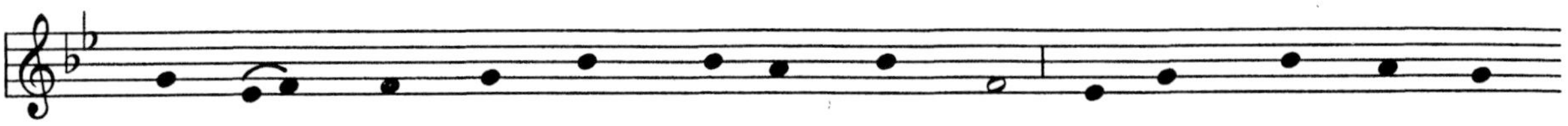
The stone which the build - ers re - ject - ed has be - come the chief

cor - ner - stone. This is the LORD's do - ing, and it is

mar - vel - ous in our eyes.

In Easter Season

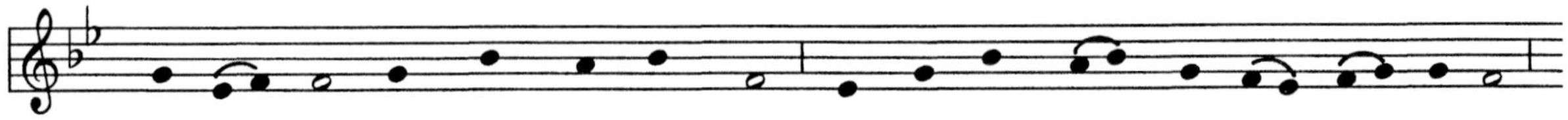
On this day the LORD has act - ed; We will re - joice and be glad in it,

hal - le - lu - jah.

On other Sundays and Weekdays

Give thanks to the LORD, for he is good; his mer - cy en - dures

for ev - er. †

Psalm 118 *Confitemini Domino* Tone VIII.1

1 *Give thanks* to the LORD, for hé is good; *
his mercy en/dures for éver.

2 †*Let Is*rael nów proclaim, *
"His mercy en/dures for éver."

3 Let the house of Aaron nów proclaim, *
"His mercy en/dures for éver."

4 Let those who fear the LORD nów proclaim, *
"His mercy en/dures for éver."

5 I called to the LORD in mý distress; *
the LORD answered by / setting mé free.

6 The LORD is at my side, therefore I wíll not fear; *
what can any/one do tó me?

7 The LORD is at my side to hélp me; *
I will triumph over / those who háte me.

8 It is better to rely on the LÓRD *
than to put / any trúst in flesh.

9 It is better to rely on the LÓRD *
than to put any / trust in rúlers.

10 All the ungodly encómpass me; *
in the name of the LORD I / will repél them.

11 They hem me in, they hem me in on évery side; *
in the name of the LORD I / will repél them.

12 They swarm about me like bees;
they blaze like a fíre of thorns; *
in the name of the LORD I / will repél them.

13 I was pressed so hard that I almost féll, *
but the LORD / came to mý help.

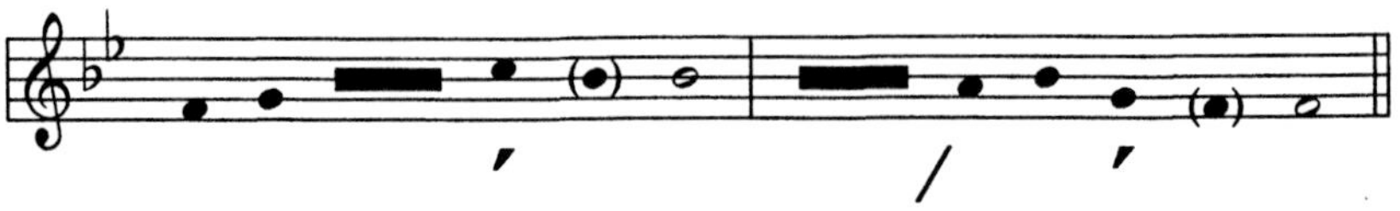

14 The LORD is my strength and my song, *
and he has become / my salvation.

15 There is a sound of exultation and victory *
in the tents / of the righteous:

16 "The right hand of the LORD has triumphed! *
the right hand of the LORD is exalted!
the right hand of the / LORD has triumphed!"

17 I shall not die, but live, *
and declare the / works of the LORD.

18 The LORD has punished me sorely, *
but he did not hand me / over to death.

19 Open for me the gates of righteousness; *
I will enter them;
I will offer / thanks to the LORD.

20 "This is the gate of the LORD; *
he who is right/eous may enter."

21 I will give thanks to you, for you answered me *
and have become / my salvation.

22 The same stone which the builders rejected *
has become / the chief cornerstone.

23 This is the LORD's doing, *
and it is mar/velous in our eyes.

24 On this day the LORD has acted; *
we will rejoice / and be glad in it.

25 Hosannah, LORD, hosannah! *
LORD, / send us now success.

26 Blessed is he who comes in the name of the Lord; *
we bless you from the / house of the LORD.

27 God is the LORD; he has shined upón us; *
form a procession with branches up to the horns / of the áltar.

28 "You are my God, and I will thánk you; *
you are my God, and I / will exált you."

29 Give thanks to the LORD, for hé is good; *
his mercy en/dures for éver. *[Ant.]*

119:1–8

In Easter Season

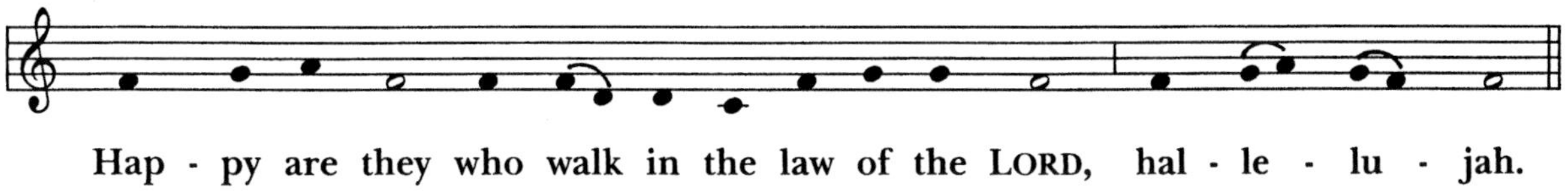
Hap - py are they who walk in the law of the LORD, hal - le - lu - jah.

On other Sundays and Weekdays

Hap - py are they who walk in the law of the LORD.

Psalm 119 Aleph *Beati immaculati* *Tone VI*

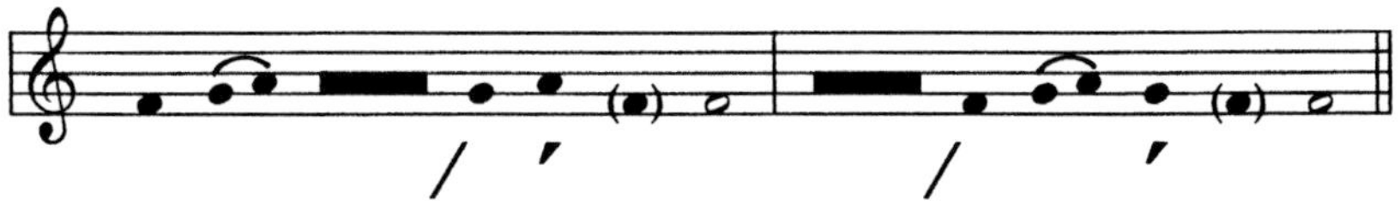

1 *Happÿ* are those whose way / is blámeless, *
who walk in / the läw óf the LORD!

2 Happy are they who observe / his décrees *
and seek him / with äll théir hearts!

3 Who never / do ány wrong, *
but always / walk ïn hís ways.

4 You laid down your / commándments, *
that we should / fullÿ keep them.

5 Oh, that my ways were / made só direct *
that I might / keep yöur státutes!

6 Then I should not / be pút to shame, *
when I regard all / your cömmándments.

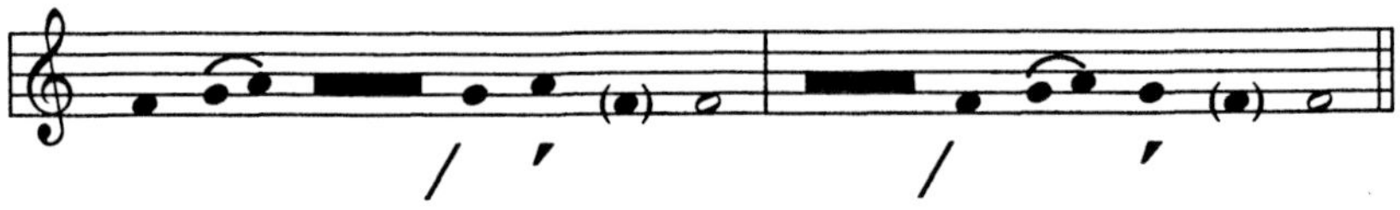

7 I will thank you with / an únfeigned heart, *
when I have learned your / righteöus júdgments.

8 I will keep / your státutes; *
do not utter/ly försáke me. *[Ant.]*

119:9–16

In Easter Season

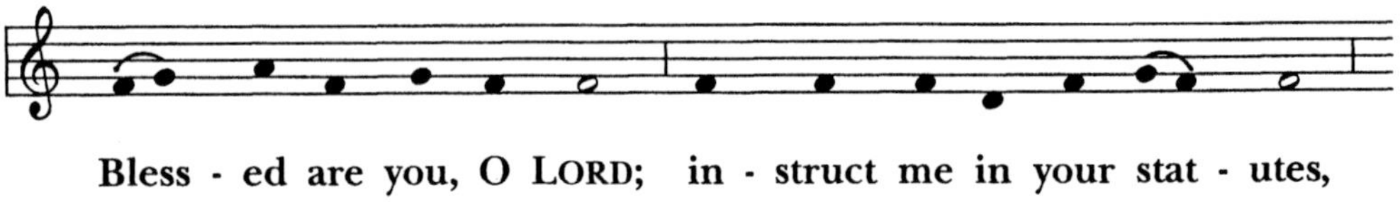

Bless - ed are you, O LORD; in - struct me in your stat - utes,

hal - le - lu - jah.

On other Sundays and Weekdays

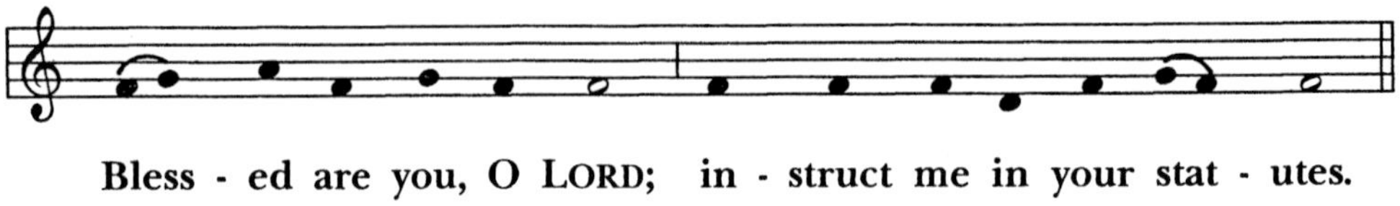

Bless - ed are you, O LORD; in - struct me in your stat - utes.

Psalm 119 Beth *In quo corrigit?* *Tone VI*

9 *How shäll* a young / man cléanse his way? *
By / keepïng tó your words.

10 With my whole heart / I séek you; *
let me not stray from / your cömmándments.

11 I treasure your pro/mise ín my heart, *
that I may not / sin ägáinst you.

12 Blessed / are yóu, O LORD; *
instruct me / in yöur státutes.

13 With my lips / will Í recite *
all the judg/ments öf yóur mouth.

14 I have taken greater delight in the way / of yóur decrees *
than in all man/ner öf ríches.

15 I will meditate on your / commándments *
and give atten/tion tö yóur ways.

16 My delight is in / your státutes; *
I will not / forgët yóur word. *[Ant.]*

119:17–24

In Easter Season

O - pen my eyes, O LORD, that I may see the won - ders of your law,

hal - le - lu - jah.

On other Sundays and Weekdays

O - pen my eyes, O LORD, that I may see the won - ders of your law.

Psalm 119 Gimel *Retribue servo tuo* *Tone VI*

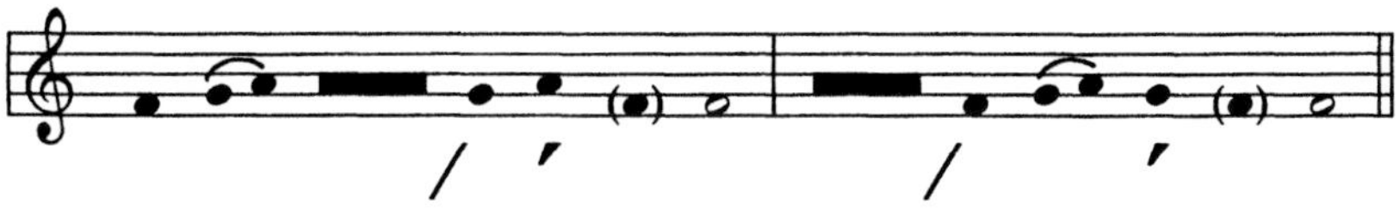

17 *Deal böun*tifully with / your sérvant, *
that I may / live änd kéep your word.

18 Open my eyes, / that Í may see *
the won/ders öf yóur law.

19 I am a stran/ger hére on earth; *
do not hide your com/mandmënts fróm me.

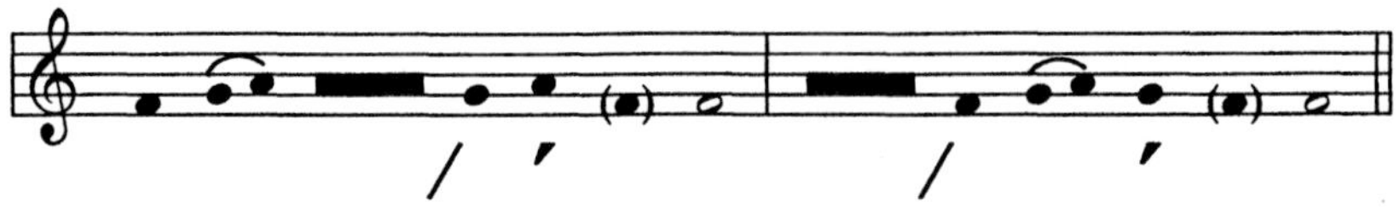

20 My soul is consumed / at áll times *
with longing / for yöur júdgments.

21 You have rebuked / the ínsolent; *
cursed are they who stray from / your cömmándments!

22 Turn from me / shame ánd rebuke, *
for I / have këpt yóur decrees.

23 Even though rulers sit and plot / agáinst me, *
I will meditate / on yöur státutes.

24 For your decrees / are mý delight, *
and they / are mÿ cóunselors. *[Ant.]*

119:25–32

In Easter Season

I will run the way of your com - mand - ments, for you have set my heart
at lib - er - ty, hal - le - lu - jah.

On other Sundays and Weekdays

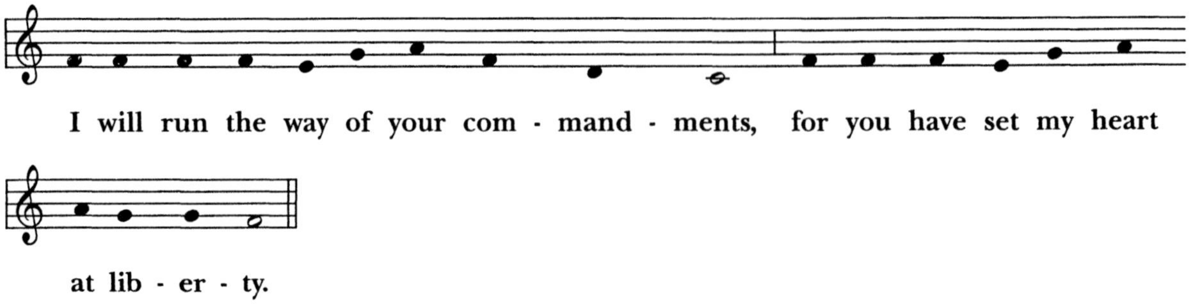
I will run the way of your com - mand - ments, for you have set my heart
at lib - er - ty.

Psalm 119 Daleth *Adhaesit pavimento* *Tone VI*

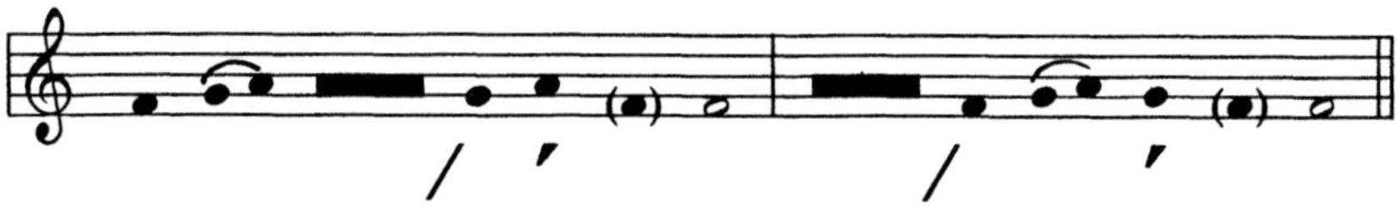

25 *My söul* cleaves / to thé dust; *
give me life accord/ing tö yóur word.

26 I have confessed my ways, and / you ánswered me; *
instruct me / in yöur státutes.

27 Make me understand the way of your / commándments, *
that I may meditate on / your märvélous works.

28 My soul melts away / for sórrow; *
strengthen me accord/ing tö yóur word.

29 Take from me the way / of lýing; *
let me find / grace thröugh yóur law.

30 I have chosen the way / of fáithfulness; *
I have set your judg/ments bëfóre me.

31 I hold fast / to yóur decrees; *
O LORD, let me not / be püt tó shame.

32 I will run the way of your / commándments, *
for you have set my / heart ät líberty. *[Ant.]*

119:33–40

In Easter Season

Give me un - der - stand - ing, O LORD, and I shall keep your law,

hal - le - lu - jah.

On other Sundays and Weekdays

Give me un - der - stand - ing, O LORD, and I shall keep your law.

Psalm 119 He *Legem pone* *Tone I.1*

33 *Teach me,* O LORD, the way of your statutes, *
and I shall / keep it to the end.

34 Give me understanding, and I shall keep your law; *
I shall keep / it with all my heart.

35 Make me go in the path of your commandments, *
for / that is my desire.

36 Incline my heart to your decrees *
and / not to unjust gain.

37 Turn my eyes from watching what is worthless; *
give me / life in your ways.

38 Fulfill your promise to your servant, *
which you make to / those who fear you.

39 Turn away the reproach which I dread, *
because your / judgments are good.

40 Behold, I long for your commandments; *
in your righteous/ness preserve my life. *[Ant.]*

In Easter Season

My hope, O LORD, is in your judg - ments, hal - le - lu - jah.

On other Sundays and Weekdays

My hope, O LORD, is in your judg - ments.

Psalm 119 Waw *Et veniat super me* *Tone VIII.1*

41 *Let your* loving-kindness come to me, O LORD, *
and your salvation, according / to your promise.

42 Then shall I have a word for those who taunt me, *
because I / trust in your words.

43 Do not take the word of truth out of my mouth, *
for my hope is / in your judgments.

44 I shall continue to keep your law; *
I shall keep it for ev/er and ever.

45 I will walk at liberty, *
because I study / your commandments.

46 I will tell of your decrees before kings *
and / will not be ashamed.

47 I delight in your commandments, *
which / I have always loved.

48 I will lift up my hands to your commandments, *
and I will meditate / on your statutes. *[Ant.]*

119:49–56

In Easter Season

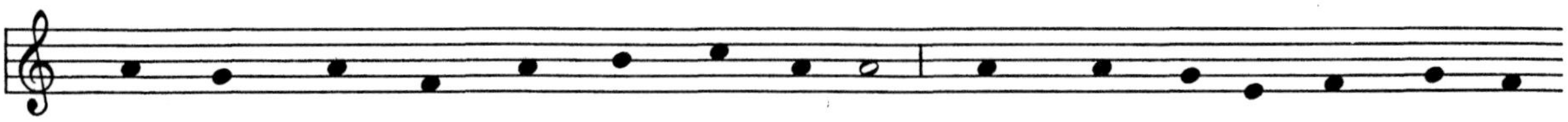
Your stat - utes have been like songs to me, when - ev - er I have lived as

a strang - er, hal - le - lu - jah.

On other Sundays and Weekdays

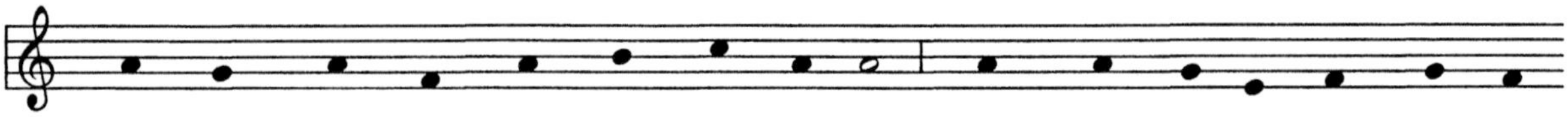
Your stat - utes have been like songs to me, when - ev - er I have lived as

a strang - er.

Psalm 119 Zayin *Memor esto verbi tui* *Tone I.3*

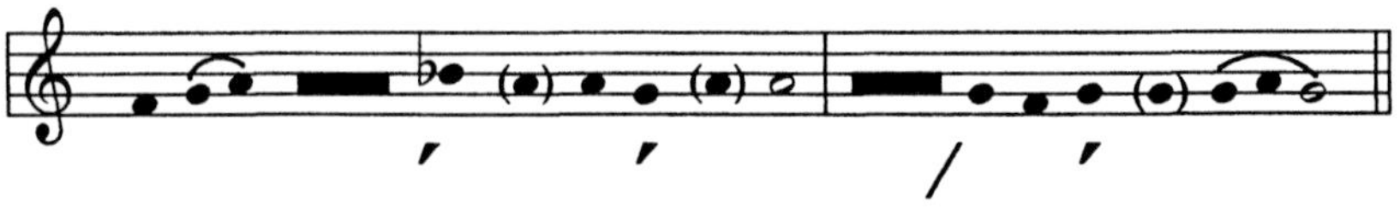

49 *Remem*ber your word to your servant, *
because you have / given me hope.

50 This is my comfort in my trouble, *
that your / promise gives me life.

51 The proud have derided me cruelly, *
but I have not / turned from your law.

52 When I remember your judgments of old, *
O LORD, I / take great comfort.

53 I am filled with a burning rage, *
because of the wicked / who forsake your law.

54 Your statutes have been like songs to me *
wherever I have lived / as a stranger.

55 I remember your Name in the night, O LORD, *
and / dwell upon your law.

56 This is how it has been with me, *
because I have kept / your commandments. *[Ant.]*

119:57–64

In Easter Season

I have con - sid - ered my ways, and turned my feet toward your de - crees,

hal - le - lu - jah.

On other Sundays and Weekdays

I have con - sid - ered my ways, and turned my feet toward your de - crees.

Psalm 119 Heth *Portio mea, Domine* *Tone IV.1*

57 *You* only are my / portion, O LORD; *
I have pro/mised to keep your words.

58 I entreat / you with all my heart, *
be merciful to me accord/ing to your promise.

59 I have con/sidered my ways *
and turned my / feet toward your decrees.

60 I hasten and / do not tarry *
—/ to keep your commandments.

61 Though the cords of the wick/ed entangle me, *
I do / not forget your law.

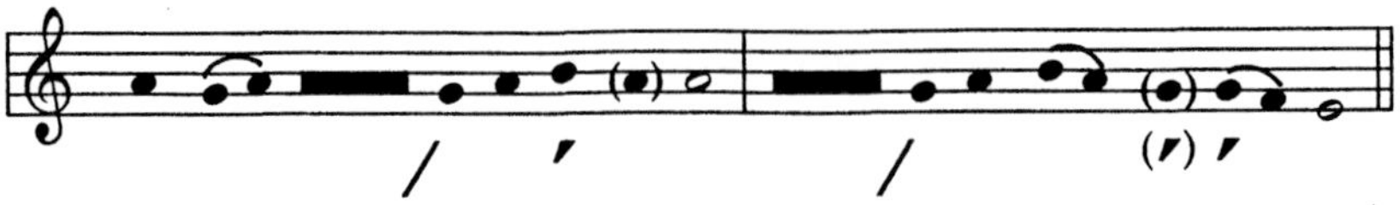

62 At midnight I will / rise to give you thanks, *
because / of your righteous judgments.

63 I am a companion of / all who fear you *
and of those / who keep your commandments.

64 The earth, O LORD, is / full of your love; *
instruct / me in your statutes. *[Ant.]*

119:65–72

In Easter Season

The law of your mouth is dear - er to me than thou - sands in

gold and sil - ver, hal - le - lu - jah.

On other Sundays and Weekdays

The law of your mouth is dear - er to me than thou - sands in

gold and sil - ver.

Psalm 119 Teth *Bonitatem fecisti* *Tone II.1*

65 *O LORD,* you have dealt graciously with your sérvant, *
according / to yóur word.

66 Teach me discernment and knówledge, *
for I have believed in your / commándments.

67 Before I was afflicted I wént astray, *
but now / I kéep your word.

68 You are good and you bríng forth good; *
instruct me in / your státutes.

69 The proud have smeared mé with lies, *
but I will keep your commandments with / my whóle heart.

70 Their heart is gróss and fat, *
but my delight / is ín your law.

71 It is good for me that I have been afflícted, *
that I might learn / your státutes.

72 The law of your mouth is dearer to mé *
than thousands in gold / and sílver. *[Ant.]*

119:73–80

In Easter Season

Let your lov - ing - kind - ness be my com - fort, as you have prom - ised

to your ser - vant, hal - le - lu - jah.

On other Sundays and Weekdays

Let your lov - ing - kind - ness be my com - fort, as you have prom - ised

to your ser - vant.

Psalm 119 Yodh *Manus tuae fecerunt me* *Tone VII.3*

73 *Your hands* have made me and fashioned me; *
give me understanding, that I may learn your commandments.

74 Those who fear you will be glad when they see me, *
because I trust in your word.

75 I know, O LORD, that your judgments are right *
and that in faithfulness you have afflicted me.

76 Let your loving-kindness be my comfort, *
as you have promised to your servant.

77 Let your compassion come to me, that I may live, *
for your law is my delight.

78 Let the arrogant be put to shame, for they wrong me with lies; *
but I will meditate on your commandments.

79 Let those who fear you turn to me, *
and also those who know your decrees.

80 Let my heart be sound in your statutes, *
that I may not be put to shame. *[Ant.]*

119:81–88

In Easter Season

I have put my hope in your word, hal - le - lu - jah.

On other Sundays and Weekdays

I have put my hope in your word.

Psalm 119 Kaph *Defecit in salutare* *Tone VII.3*

81 *My soul* has longed for your salvation; *
I have put my hope in your word.

82 My eyes have failed from watching for your promise, *
and I say, "When will you comfort me?"

83 I have become like a leather flask in the smoke, *
but I have not forgotten your statutes.

84 How much longer must I wait? *
when will you give judgment against those who persecute me?

85 The proud have dug pits for me; *
they do not keep your law.

86 All your commandments are true; *
help me, for they persecute me with lies.

87 They had almost made an end of me on earth, *
but I have not forsaken your commandments.

88 In your loving-kíndness, revíve me, *
   that I may keep the decrées of yóur mouth. *[Ant.]*

119:89–96

In Easter Season

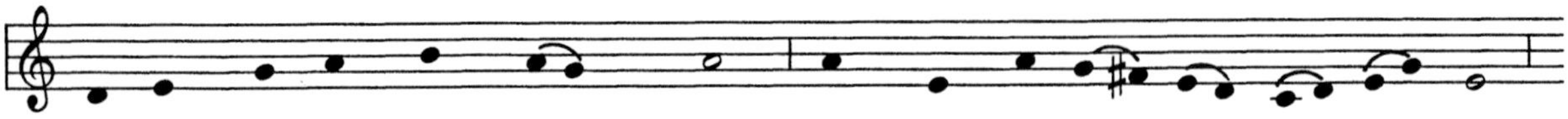

I stud - y your com - mand - ments, be - cause by them you give me life,

hal - le - lu - jah.

On other Sundays and Weekdays

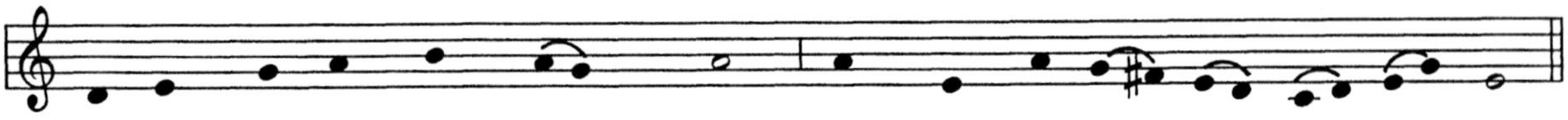

I stud - y your com - mand - ments, be - cause by them you give me life.

Psalm 119 Lamedh *In aeternum, Domine* *Tone IV.4*

89 *O LÖRD,* your word is / everlásting; *
   it stands / firm in the héavens.

90 Your faithfulness remains from one generation / to anóther; *
   you established / the earth, and ít abides.

91 By your decree these con/tinue tó this day, *
   for all / things are your sérvants.

92 If my delight had not / been in yóur law, *
   I should have perished / in my afflíction.

93 I will never forget / your commándments, *
   because / by them you gíve me life.

94 I am yours; oh, that / you would sáve me! *
for I stud/y your commándments.

95 Though the wicked lie in wait for me / to destróy me, *
I will apply / my mind to yóur decrees.

96 I see that all things come / to an énd, *
but your com/mandment has nó bounds. *[Ant.]*

119:97–104

In Easter Season

How sweet, O LORD, are your words to my taste, hal - le - lu - jah.

On other Sundays and Weekdays

How sweet, O LORD, are your words to my taste.

Psalm 119 Mem *Quomodo dilexi!* *Tone VI*

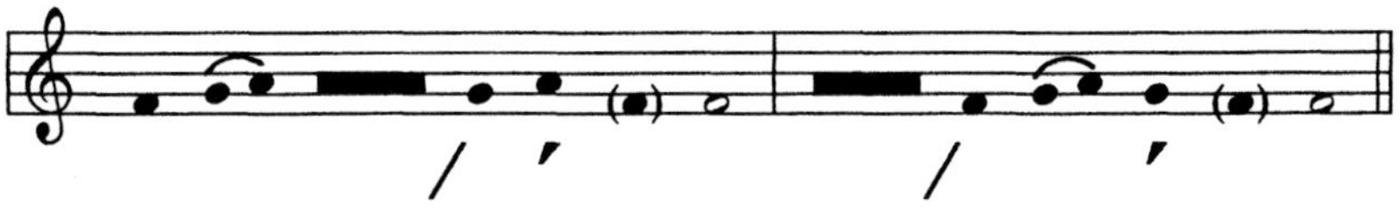

97 *Oh, höw—*/I lóve your law! *
all the day long it / is ïn mý mind.

98 Your commandment has made me wiser than / my énemies, *
and it is / alwäys wíth me.

99 I have more understanding than all / my téachers, *
for your decrees / are mÿ stúdy.

100 I am wiser than / the élders, *
because I observe / your cömmándments.

101 I restrain my feet from ev/ery évil way, *
that / I mäy kéep your word.

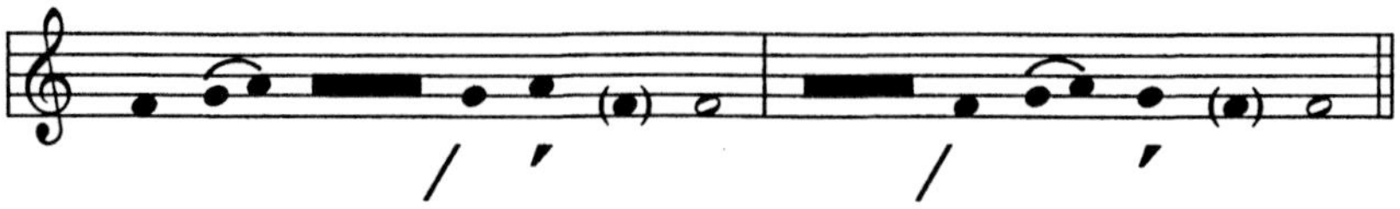

102 I do not shrink from / your júdgments, *
because you your/self häve táught me.

103 How sweet are your words / to mý taste! *
they are sweeter than ho/ney tö mý mouth.

104 Through your commandments I gain un/derstánding; *
therefore I hate / everÿ lýing way. *[Ant.]*

119:105–112

In Easter Season

Your word is a lan - tern to my feet, and a light up - on my path,

hal - le - lu - jah.

On other Sundays and Weekdays

Your word is a lan - tern to my feet, and a light up - on my path. †

Psalm 119 Nun *Lucerna pedibus meis* *Tone II.1*

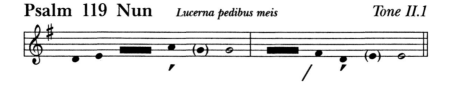

105 *Your word* is a lantern tó my feet *
and a light / upón my path.

106 †*I have* sworn and am detérmined *
to keep your right/eous júdgments.

107 I am deeply tróubled; *
preserve my life, O LORD, accord/ing tó your word.

108 Accept, O LORD, the willing tribute of my lips, *
and teach me / your judgments.

109 My life is always in my hand, *
yet I do not / forget your law.

110 The wicked have set a trap for me, *
but I have not strayed from your / commandments.

111 Your decrees are my inheritance for ever; *
truly, they are the joy / of my heart.

112 I have applied my heart to fulfill your statutes *
for ever / and to the end. *[Ant.]*

119:113–120

In Easter Season

Sus - tain me, O LORD, ac - cord - ing to your prom - ise, that I may live,

hal - le - lu - jah.

On other Sundays and Weekdays

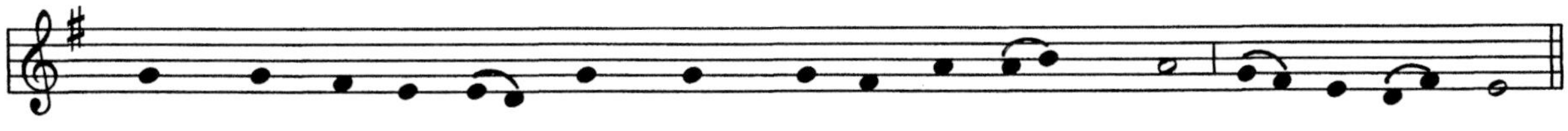

Sus - tain me, O LORD, ac - cord - ing to your prom - ise, that I may live.

Psalm 119 Samekh *Iniquos odio habui* *Tone II.1*

113 *I hate* those who have a divided heart, *
but your law / do I love.

114 You are my refuge and shield; *
my hope / is in your word.

115 Away from me, you wicked! *
I will keep the command/ments of my God.

116 Sustain me according to your promise, that I may live, *
and let me not be disappoint/ed in my hope.

117 Hold me up, and I shall be safe, *
and my delight shall be ever in / your statutes.

118 You spurn all who stray from your statutes; *
their deceitful/ness is in vain.

119 In your sight all the wicked of the earth are but dross; *
therefore I / love your decrees.

120 My flesh trembles with dread of you; *
I am afraid of / your judgments. *[Ant.]*

119:121–128

In Easter Season

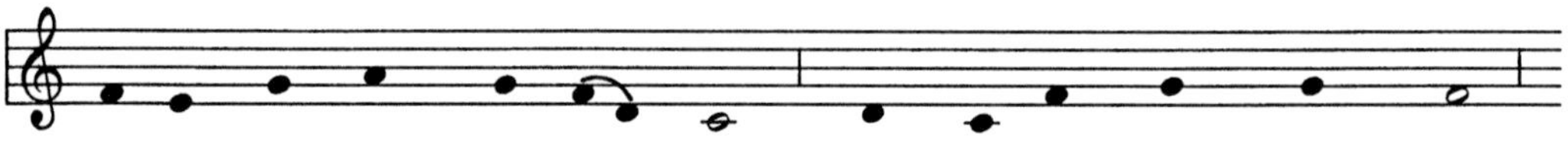
I am your ser - vant, O LORD; grant me un - der - stand - ing,

hal - le - lu - jah.

On other Sundays and Weekdays

I am your ser - vant, O LORD; grant me un - der - stand - ing.

Psalm 119 Ayin *Feci judicium* *Tone VI*

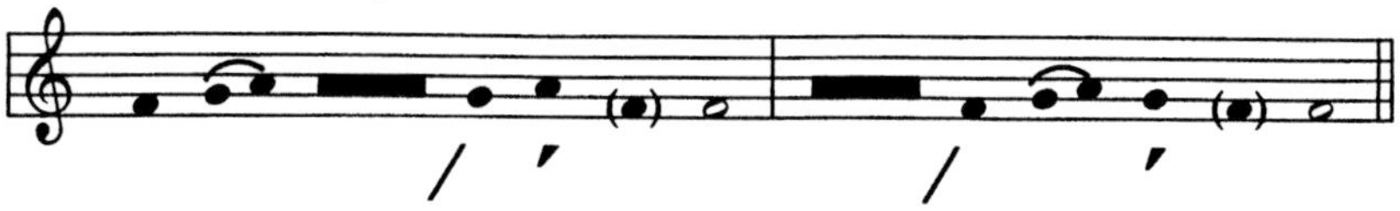

121 *I häve* done what / is júst and right; *
do not deliver me to / my öppréssors.

122 Be surety for / your sérvant's good; *
let not the / proud öppréss me.

123 My eyes have failed from watching for your / salvátion *
and for your / righteöus prómise.

124 Deal with your servant according to your lov/ing-kíndness *
and teach / me yöur státutes.

125 I am your servant; grant me un/derstánding, *
that I / may knöw yóur decrees.

126 It is time for you / to áct, O LORD, *
for they have / brokën yóur law.

127 Truly, I love your / commándments *
more than / gold änd précious stones.

128 I hold all your commandments to / be ríght for me; *
all paths of / falsehöod Í abhor. *[Ant.]*

119:129–136

In Easter Season

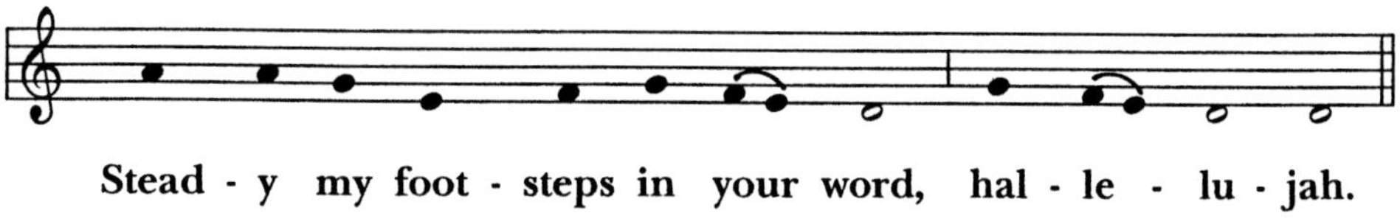
Stead - y my foot - steps in your word, hal - le - lu - jah.

On other Sundays and Weekdays

Stead - y my foot - steps in your word.

Psalm 119 Pe *Mirabilia* *Tone I.1*

129 *Your de*—crees are wonderful; *
therefore I obey / them with all my heart.

130 When your word goes forth it gives light; *
it gives understanding / to the simple.

131 I open my mouth and pant; *
I long for / your commandments.

132 Turn to me in mercy, *
as you always do to / those who love your Name.

133 Steady my footsteps in your word; *
let no iniquity have do/minion over me.

134 Rescue me from those who oppress me, *
and I will keep / your commandments.

135 Let your countenance shine upon your servant *
and teach / me your statutes.

136 My eyes shed streams of tears, *
because people / do not keep your law. *[Ant.]*

119:137–144

In Easter Season

The right - eous - ness of your de - crees, O LORD, is ev - er - last - ing,

hal - le - lu - jah.

On other Sundays and Weekdays

The right - eous - ness of your de - crees, O LORD, is ev - er - last - ing.

Psalm 119 Sadhe *Justus es, Domine* *Tone V.1*

137 *You are* righteous, O LÓRD, *
and upright áre your júdgments.

138 You have issued yóur decrees *
with justice and in pérfect fáithfulness.

139 My indignation has consúmed me, *
because my enemies fórget yóur words.

140 Your word has been tested to the úttermost, *
and your sérvant hólds it dear.

141 I am small and of little accóunt, *
yet I do not forgét your commándments.

142 Your justice is an everlasting jústice *
and your láw is thé truth.

143 Trouble and distress have come upón me, *
yet your commándments are mý delight.

144 The righteousness of your decrees is everlásting; *
grant me understánding, that Í may live. *[Ant.]*

119:145–152

Antiphon

I call to you, O LORD; for in your word is my trust.

Psalm 119 Qoph *Clamavi in toto corde meo* *Tone I.4*

145 *I cȁll*—wíth my whóle heart; *
answer me, O LORD, that I may / keep your státutes.

146 I call to you;
oh, that yóu would sáve me! *
I will / keep your décrees.

147 Early in the morning I crý out tó you, *
for in / your word ís my trust.

148 My eyes are open ín the night wátches, *
that I may meditate up/on your prómise.

149 Hear my voice, O LORD, according to your lóving-kíndness; *
according to your / judgments, gíve me life.

150 They draw near who in malice pérsecúte me; *
they are very / far from yóur law.

151 You, O LÓRD, are néar at hand, *
and all your com/mandments áre true.

152 Long have I knówn from yóur decrees *
that you have established / them for éver. *[Ant.]*

119:153–160

Antiphon

Plead my cause, O LORD, and re - deem me.

Psalm 119 Resh *Vide humilitatem* *Tone I.4*

153 *Behold* my affliction and deliver me, *
for I do / not forget your law.

154 Plead my cause and redeem me; *
according to your / promise, give me life.

155 Deliverance is far from the wicked, *
for they do not stud/y your statutes.

156 Great is your compassion, O LORD; *
preserve my life, according / to your judgments.

157 There are many who persecute and oppress me, *
yet I have not / swerved from your decrees.

158 I look with loathing at the faithless, *
for they / have not kept your word.

159 See how I love your commandments! *
O LORD, in your mer/cy, preserve me.

160 The heart of your word is truth; *
all your righteous judgments en/dure for evermore. *[Ant.]*

119:161–168

Antiphon

Great peace have they who love your law.

Psalm 119 Shin *Principes persecuti sunt* *Tone III.4*

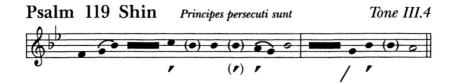

161 *Rulers* have persecuted me without a cause, *
but my heart stands in awe / of your word.

162 I am as glad because of your promise *
as one who / finds great spoils.

163 As for lies, I hate and abhor them, *
but your law / is my love.

164 Seven times a day do I praise you, *
because of your right/eous judgments.

165 Great peace have they who love your law; *
for them there is / no stumbling block.

166 I have hoped for your salvation, O LORD, *
and I have fulfilled your / commandments.

167 I have kept your decrees *
and I have loved / them deeply.

168 I have kept your commandments and decrees, *
for all my ways are / before you. *[Ant.]*

119:169–176

Antiphon

Let your hand be read - y to help me, for I have cho - sen your

com - mand - ments.

Psalm 119 Taw *Appropinquet deprecatio* *Tone III.4*

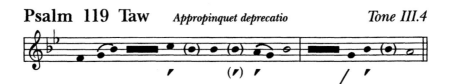

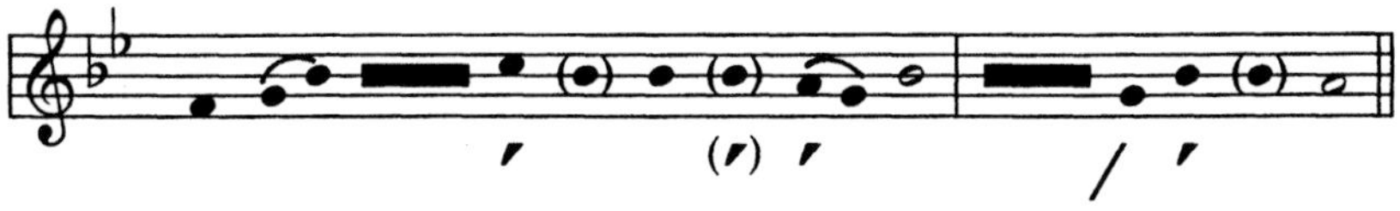

169 *Let my* cry come before you, O LORD; *
give me understanding, accord/ing to your word.

170 Let my supplication come before you; *
deliver me, according to / your promise.

171 My lips shall pour forth your praise, *
when you teach me / your statutes.

172 My tongue shall sing of your promise, *
for all your commandments / are righteous.

173 Let your hand be ready to help me, *
for I have chosen your / commandments.

174 I long for your salvation, O LORD, *
and your law / is my delight.

175 Let me live, and I will praise you, *
and let your judg/ments help me.

176 I have gone astray like a sheep that is lost; *
search for your servant,
for I do not forget your / commandments. *[Ant.]*

120

Antiphon

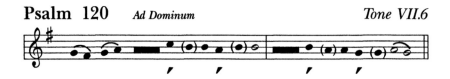

I called to the LORD, and he an - swered me.

Psalm 120 *Ad Dominum* *Tone VII.6*

1 *Whën Ï* was in trouble, I cálled to thé LORD; *
I called to the LÓRD, and he ánswered më.

2 Deliver me, O LÓRD, from lýing lips *
and fróm the decéitful töngue.

3 What shall be done to you, and whát more bésides, *
O yóu decéitful töngue?

4 The sharpened árrows of á warrior, *
alóng with hot glówing cöals.

5 How hateful it is that I must lódge in Méshech *
and dwell among the ténts of Kédär!

6 Too lóng have I hád to live *
among the énemiés of pëace.

7 I am ón the síde of peace, *
but when I speak of it, théy are fór wär. *[Ant.]*

121

Antiphon

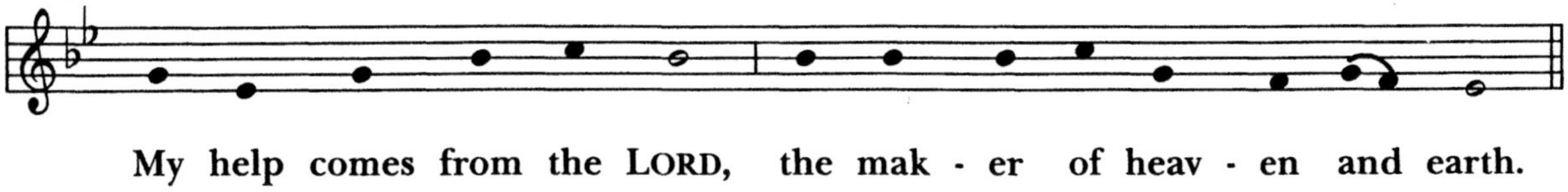
My help comes from the LORD, the mak - er of heav - en and earth.

Psalm 121 *Levavi oculos* *Tone V.1*

1 *I lift* up my eyes to the hills; *
from where is my help to come?

2 My help comes from the LORD, *
the maker of heaven and earth.

3 He will not let your foot be moved *
and he who watches over you will not fall asleep.

4 Behold, he who keeps watch over Israel *
shall neither slumber nor sleep;

5 The LORD himself watches over you; *
the LORD is your shade at your right hand.

6 So that the sun shall not strike you by day, *
—nor the moon by night.

7 The LORD shall preserve you from all evil; *
it is he who shall keep you safe.

8 The LORD shall watch over your going out and your coming in, *
from this time forth for evermore. *[Ant.]*

122

Antiphon

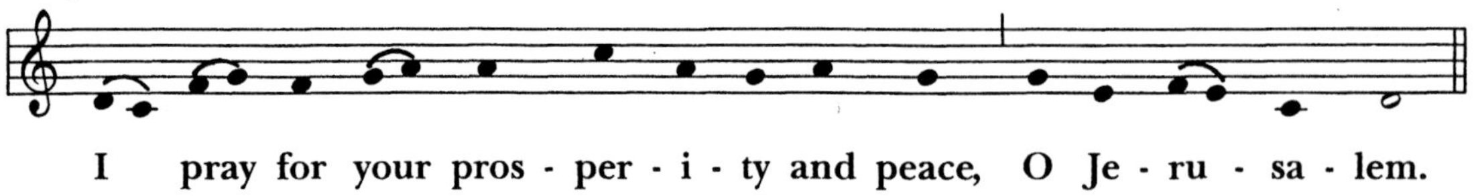
I pray for your pros - per - i - ty and peace, O Je - ru - sa - lem.

Psalm 122 *Laetatus sum* *Tone I.2*

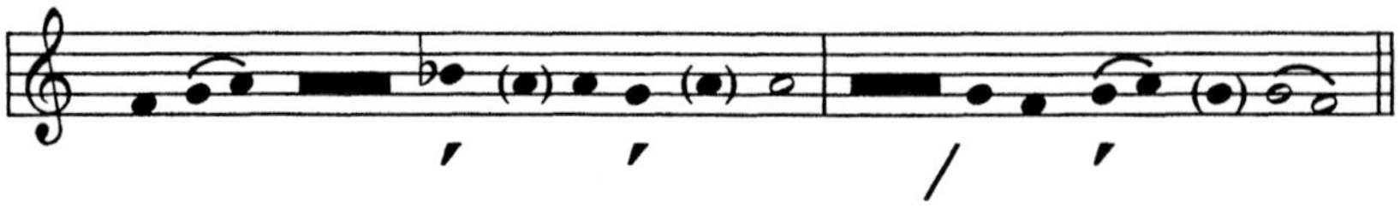

1 *I was*—glad when they said to me, *
"Let us go to the / house of the LORD."

2 Now our feet are standing *
within your gates, / O Jerusalem.

3 Jerusalem is built as a city *
that is at u/nity with itself;

4 To which the tribes go up,
the tribes of the LORD, *
the assembly of Israel,
to praise the / Name of the LORD.

5 For there are the thrones of judgment, *
the thrones of the / house of David.

6 Pray for the peace of Jerusalem: *
"May they pros/per who love you.

7 —Peace be within your walls *
and quietness with/in your towers.

8 For my brethren and companions' sake, *
I pray for / your prosperity.

9 Because of the house of the LORD our God, *
I will / seek to do you good." *[Ant.]*

123

Antiphon

Our eyes look to the LORD our God, un - til he show us his mer - cy.

Psalm 123 *Ad te levavi oculos meos* *Tone VI*

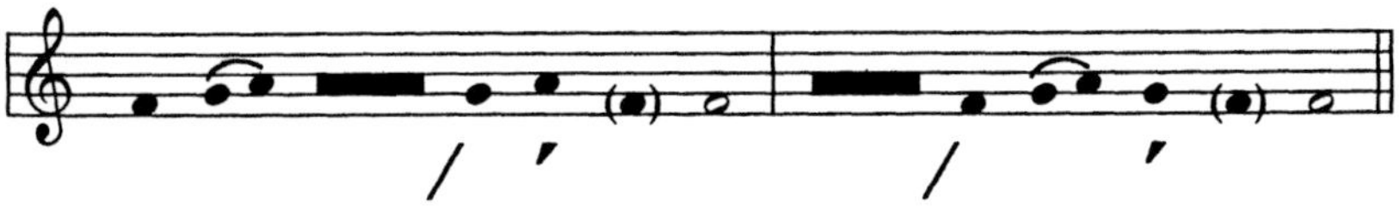

1 *To yöu* I / lift úp my eyes, *
to you enthroned / in thë héavens.

2 As the eyes of servants look to the hand of / their másters, *
and the eyes of a maid to the hand / of hër místress,

3 So our eyes look to / the LÓRD our God, *
until he show / us hïs mércy.

4 Have mercy upon us, O LORD, / have mércy, *
for we have had more than e/nough öf cóntempt.

5 Too much of the scorn of the in/dolént rich, *
and of the de/risiön óf the proud. *[Ant.]*

124

Antiphon

Our help is in the Name of the LORD.

Psalm 124 *Nisi quia Dominus* *Tone IV.1*

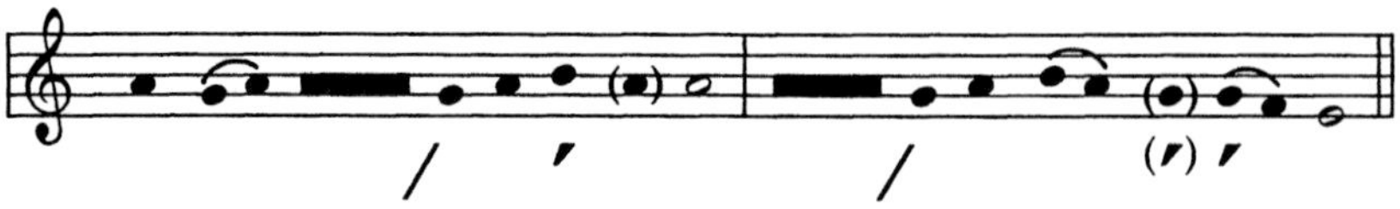

1 *If the* LORD had not / been on our side, *
let / Israel now say;

2 If the LORD had not / been on our side, *
when ene/mies rose up against us;

3 Then would they have swallowed us / up alive *
in their fierce / anger toward us;

4 Then would the waters have / overwhelmed us *
and the / torrent gone over us;

5 Then would the / raging waters *
have / gone right over us.

6 Blessed / be the LORD! *
he has not given us over to / be a prey for their teeth.

7 We have escaped like a bird from the snare / of the fowler; *
the snare is bro/ken, and we have escaped.

8 Our help is in the Name / of the LORD, *
the ma/ker of heaven and earth. *[Ant.]*

125

Antiphon

The LORD stands round a - bout his peo - ple.

Psalm 125 *Qui confidunt* *Tone II.1*

1 *Those who* trust in the LORD are like Mount Źion, *
which cannot be moved, but stands fast / for éver.

2 The hills stand about Jerúsalem; *
so does the LORD stand round about his people,
from this time forth / for évermore.

3 The scepter of the wicked shall not hold sway over the land allotted to the júst, *
so that the just shall not put their hands / to évil.

4 Show your goodness, O LORD, to those whó are good *
and to those who / are trúe of heart.

5 As for those who turn aside to crooked ways,
the LORD will lead them away with the evildóers; *
but peace be up/on Ísrael. *[Ant.]*

126

Antiphon

Those who sowed with tears will reap with songs of joy.

Psalm 126 *In convertendo* *Tone I.1*

1 *When the* LORD restored the fortunes of Zion, *
then were / we like those who dream.

2 Then was our mouth filled with laughter, *
and our / tongue with shouts of joy.

3 Then they said among the nations, *
"The LORD has / done great things for them."

4 The LORD has done great things for us, *
and / we are glad indeed.

5 Restore our fortunes, O LORD, *
like the watercourses / of the Negev.

6 —Those who sowed with tears *
will / reap with songs of joy.

7 Those who go out weeping, carrying the seed, *
will come again with joy, / shouldering their sheaves. *[Ant.]*

127

Antiphon

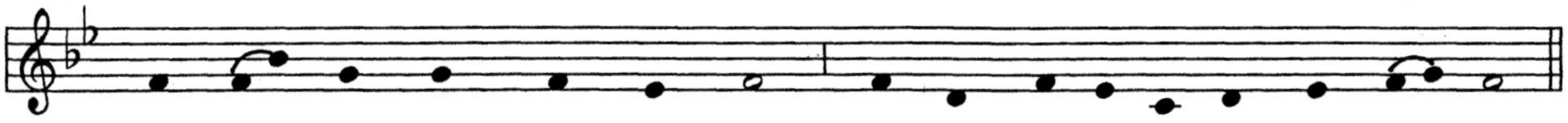
Un - less the LORD builds the house, their la - bor is in vain who build it. †

Psalm 127 *Nisi Dominus* *Tone VIII.1*

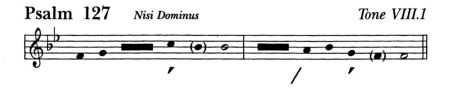

1 *Unless* the LORD búilds the house, *
their labor is in / vain who búild it.

2 †*Unless* the LORD watches over the cíty, *
in vain the watchman / keeps his vígil.

3 It is in vain that you rise so early and go to béd so late; *
vain, too, to eat the bread of toil,
for he gives to / his belóved sleep.

4 Children are a heritage from the LÓRD, *
and the fruit of the / womb is á gift.

5 Like arrows in the hand of a wárrior *
are the chil/dren of óne's youth.

6 Happy is the man who has his quiver fúll of them! *
he shall not be put to shame
when he contends with his en/emies ín the gate. *[Ant.]*

128

Antiphon

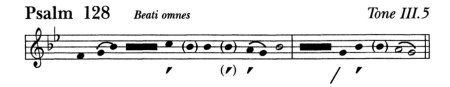

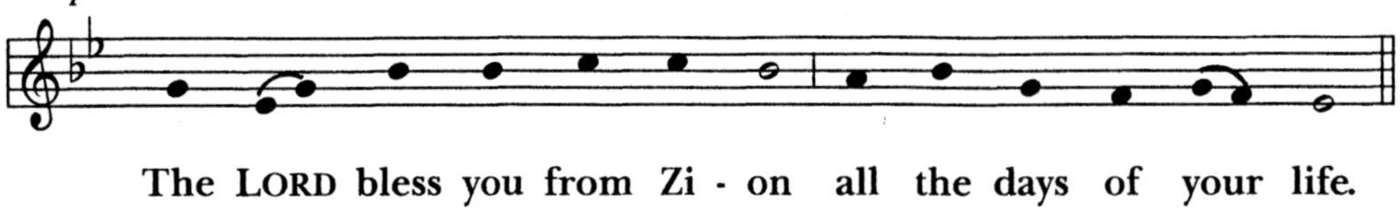
The LORD bless you from Zi - on all the days of your life.

Psalm 128 *Beati omnes* *Tone III.5*

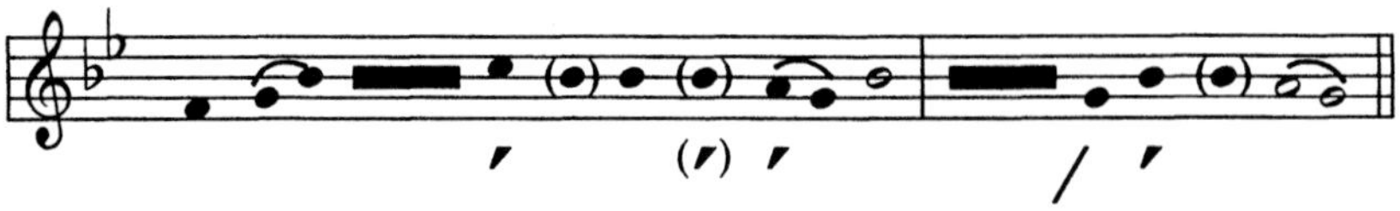

1 *Happy* are they all who fear the LORD, *
and who follow / in his ways!

2 You shall eat the fruit of your labor; *
happiness and prosperity / shall be yours.

3 Your wife shall be like a fruitful vine within your house, *
your children like olive shoots round about / your table.

4 The man who fears the LORD *
shall thus in/deed be blessed.

5 The LORD bless you from Zion, *
and may you see the prosperity of Jerusalem all the days / of your life.

6 May you live to see your children's children; *
may peace be up/on Israel. *[Ant.]*

129

Antiphon

My op - pres - sors shall not pre - vail a - gainst me.

Psalm 129 *Saepe expugnaverunt* *Tone II.1*

1 *"Greatly* have they oppressed me since my youth," *
let Isra/el now say;

2 "Greatly have they oppressed me since my youth, *
but they have not prevailed / against me."

3 The plowmen plowed upon my back *
and made / their furrows long.

4 The LORD, the Righteous One, *
has cut the cords of / the wicked.

5 Let them be put to shame and thrown back, *
all those who are enemies / of Zion.

6 Let them be like grass upon the housetops, *
which withers before it / can be plucked;

7 Which does not fill the hand of the reaper, *
nor the bosom of him / who binds the sheaves;

8 So that those who go by say not as much as,
"The LORD prosper you. *
We wish you well in the Name / of the LORD." *[Ant.]*

130

Antiphon

With the LORD there is mer - cy, and with him there is plen - teous
re - demp - tion.

Psalm 130 *De profundis* *Tone III.5*

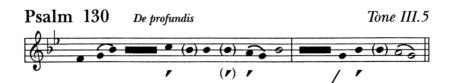

1 *Out of* the depths have I called to you, O LORD;
LORD, hear my voice; *
let your ears consider well the voice of my sup/plication.

2 If you, LORD, were to note what is done amiss, *
O Lord, / who could stand?

3 For there is forgiveness with you; *
therefore you / shall be feared.

4 I wait for the LORD; my soul waits for him; *
in his word / is my hope.

5 My soul waits for the LORD,
more than watchmen for the morning, *
more than watchmen for / the morning.

6 O Israel, wait for the LORD, *
for with the LORD there / is mercy;

7 With him there is plenteous redemption, *
and he shall redeem Israel / from all their sins. *[Ant.]*

131

Antiphon

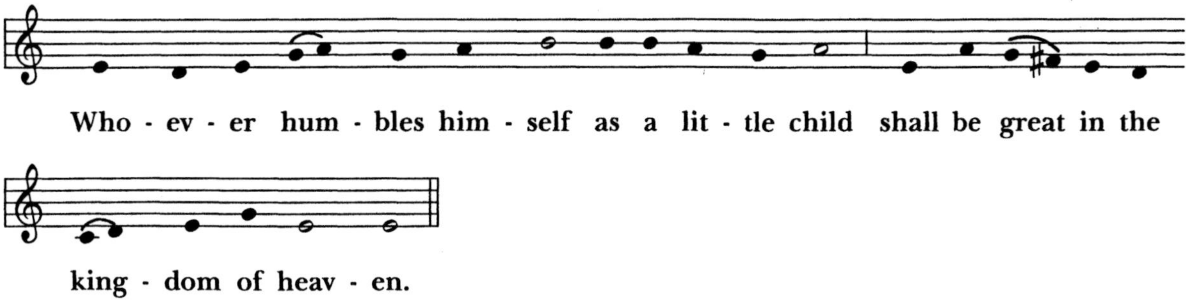
Who - ev - er hum - bles him - self as a lit - tle child shall be great in the
king - dom of heav - en.

Psalm 131 *Domine, non est* *Tone IV.6*

1 *O LORD,* I / am not proud; *
I have no haughty looks.

2 I do not occupy myself / with great matters, *
or with things that are too hard for me.

3 But I still my soul and make it quiet,
like a child up/on its mother's breast; *
my soul is quieted within me.

4 O Israel, / wait upon the LORD, *
from this time forth for evermore. *[Ant.]*

Antiphon

The LORD has cho - sen Zi - on; he has de - sired her for his
hab - i - ta - tion.

Psalm 132 *Memento, Domine* *Tone I.7*

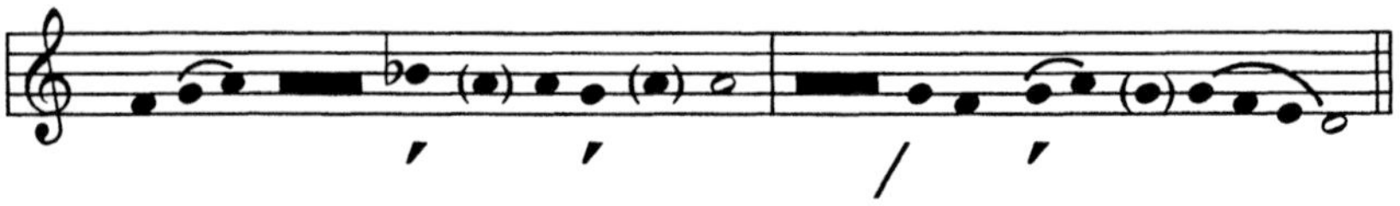

1 *LORD, re*—member David, *
and all the / hardships he endured;

2 How he swore an oath to the LORD *
and vowed a vow to the Mighty / One of Jacob:

3 "I will not come under the roof of my house, *
nor climb up / into my bed;

4 I will not allow my eyes to sleep, *
nor let my / eyelids slumber;

5 Until I find a place for the LORD, *
a dwelling for the Mighty / One of Jacob."

6 "The ark! We heard it was in Ephratah; *
we found it in the / fields of Jearim.

7 Let us go to God's dwelling place; *
let us fall upon our knees be/fore his footstool."

8 Arise, O LORD, into your resting-place, *
you and the / ark of your strength.

9 Let your priests be clothed with righteousness; *
let your faithful / people sing with joy.

10 For your servant David's sake, *
do not turn away the face of / your Anointed.

11 The LORD has sworn an oath to David; *
in truth, he / will not break it.

12 "A son, the fruit of your body *
will I / set upon your throne.

13 If your children keep my covenant
and my testimonies that I shall teach them, *
their children will sit upon your / throne for evermore."

14 For the LORD has chosen Zion; *
he has desired her for his / habitation:

15 "This shall be my resting-place for ever; *
here will I dwell, for / I delight in her.

16 I will surely bless her provisions, *
and satis/fy her poor with bread.

17 I will clothe her priests with salvation, *
and her faithful people / will rejoice and sing.

18 There will I make the horn of David flourish; *
I have prepared a lamp for / my Anointed.

19 As for his enemies, I will clothe them with shame; *
but as for / him, his crown will shine." *[Ant.]*

133

Antiphon

Oh, how good and pleas - ant it is, when breth - ren live to - geth - er

in un - i - ty! †

Psalm 133 *Ecce, quam bonum!* *Tone VI*

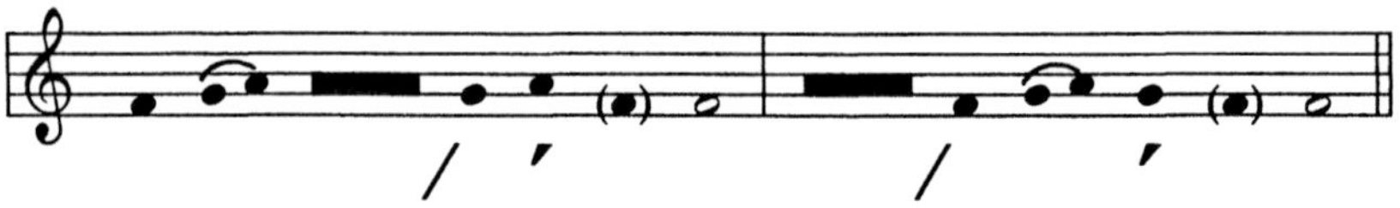

1 *Oh, hŏw* good and pleas/ant ít is, *
   when brethren live togeth/er ĭn únity!

2 †*It ĭs* like fine oil / upón the head *
   that runs / down ŭpón the beard,

3 Upon the beard / of Aáron, *
   and runs down upon the col/lar ŏf hís robe.

4 It is like the dew / of Hérmon *
   that falls upon the / hills ŏf Zíon.

5 For there the LORD has ordained / the bléssing: *
   —/life fŏr évermore. *[Ant.]*

134

In Easter Season

The LORD who made heaven and earth bless you out of Zi - on,

hal - le - lu - jah.

On other Sundays and Weekdays

Lift up your hands in the ho - ly place and bless the LORD.

Psalm 134 *Ecce nunc* *Tone I.1*

1 *Behold* now, bless the LORD, all you servants of the LORD, *
you that stand by night in the / house of the LORD.

2 Lift up your hands in the holy place and bless the LORD; *
the LORD who made heaven and earth bless you / out of Zion. *[Ant.]*

135

In Easter Season

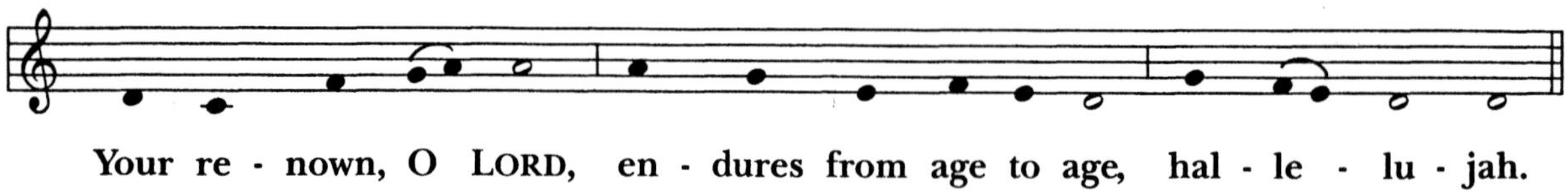

Your re - nown, O LORD, en - dures from age to age, hal - le - lu - jah.

On other Sundays and Weekdays

Praise the LORD, for the LORD is good; sing prais - es to his Name for
it is love - ly, hal - le - lu - jah.

Psalm 135 *Laudate nomen* *Tone I.1*

*1 *Hallelujah!*
Praise the Name of the LORD; *
give praise, you / servants of the LORD,

2 You who stand in the house of the LORD, *
in the courts of the / house of our God.

3 Praise the LORD, for the LORD is good; *
sing praises to his Name, for / it is lovely.

4 For the LORD has chosen Jacob for himself *
and Israel for his / own possession.

5 For I know that the LORD is great, *
and that our Lord / is above all gods.

6 The LORD does whatever pleases him, in heaven and on earth, *
in the / seas and all the deeps.

**Hallelujah* may be omitted from the first verse of the psalm when the antiphon ends with *Hallelujah*; the verse then begins: *Praise the*—Name of the LORD; *

7 He brings up rain clouds from the ends of the earth; *
he sends out lightning with the rain,
and brings the winds out / of his storehouse.

8 It was he who struck down the firstborn of Egypt, *
the firstborn / both of man and beast.

9 He sent signs and wonders into the midst of you, O Egypt, *
against Pharaoh and / all his servants.

10 He overthrew many nations *
and put / mighty kings to death:

11 Sihon, king of the Amorites,
and Og, the king of Bashan, *
and all the king/doms of Canaan.

12 He gave their land to be an inheritance, *
an inheritance for Isra/el his people.

13 O LORD, your Name is everlasting; *
your renown, O LORD, en/dures from age to age.

14 For the LORD gives his people justice *
and shows compassion / to his servants.

15 The idols of the heathen are silver and gold, *
the / work of human hands.

16 They have mouths, but they cannot speak; *
eyes have they, / but they cannot see.

17 They have ears, but they cannot hear; *
neither is there any / breath in their mouth.

18 Those who make them are like them, *
and so are all who / put their trust in them.

19 Bless the LORD, O house of Israel; *
O house of / Aaron, bless the LORD.

20 Bless the LORD, O house of Levi; *
you who fear / the LORD, bless the LORD.

21 Blessed be the LORD out of Zion, *
who dwells in Jerusalem.
/Hallelujah! *[Ant.]*

136

On the Twelve Days of Christmas

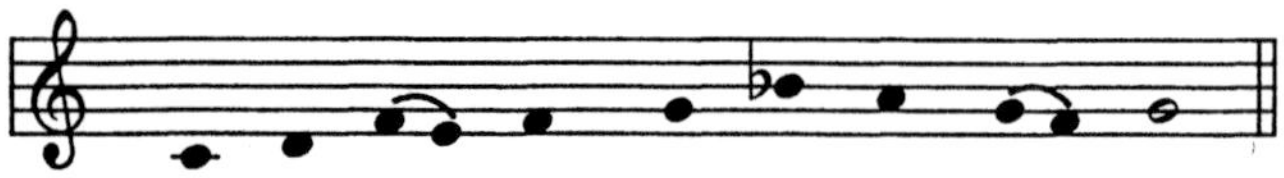

Out of E - gypt have I called my Son.

In Lent

Give thanks to the LORD who does great won - ders, for his mer - cy

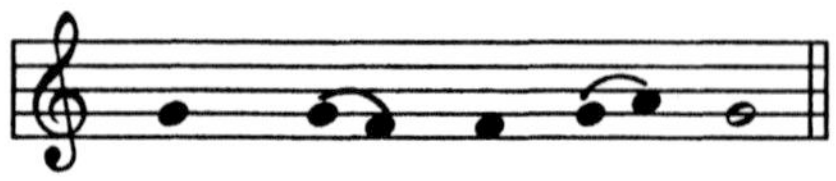

en - dures for ev - er.

In Easter Season

With a might - y hand and a stretched - out arm, he brought Is - ra - el

out of E - gypt, hal - le - lu - jah.

On other Sundays and Weekdays

Great and won - der - ful are your deeds, O Lord God Al - migh - ty.

Psalm 136 *Confitemini* *Tonus Peregrinus*

1 *Gïve* thanks to / the LORD, for hé is good, *
for his mercy endures / for évër.

2 Give / thanks to the Gód of gods, *
for his mercy endures / for évër.

3 Give / thanks to the Lórd of lords, *
for his mercy endures / for évër.

4 Who on/ly does great wónders, *
for his mercy endures / for évër.

5 Who by wis/dom made the héavens, *
for his mercy endures / for évër.

6 Who spread out the earth / upon the wáters, *
for his mercy endures / for évër.

7 Who / created gréat lights, *
for his mercy endures / for évër.

8 —/The sun to rúle the day, *
for his mercy endures / for évër.

9 The moon and the stars / to govern thé night, *
for his mercy endures / for évër.

10 Who struck down the / firstborn of Égypt, *
for his mercy endures / for évër.

11 And brought out Isra/el from amóng them, *
for his mercy endures / for évër.

12 With a mighty / hand and a strétched-out arm, *
for his mercy endures / for évër.

13 Who divided / the Red Sea ín two, *
for his mercy endures / for évër.

14 And made Israel to / pass through the mídst of it, *
for his mercy endures / for évër.

15 But swept Pharaoh and his army / into the Réd Sea, *
for his mercy endures / for évër.

16 Who led his peo/ple through the wílderness, *
for his mercy endures / for évër.

17 —/Who struck down gréat kings, *
for his mercy endures / for évër.

18 —/And slew mightý kings, *
for his mercy endures / for évër.

19 Sihon, / king of the Ámorites, *
for his mercy endures / for évër.

20 And Og, / the king of Báshan, *
for his mercy endures / for évër.

21 And gave away their lands / for an inhéritance, *
for his mercy endures / for évër.

22 An inheritance for Is/rael his sérvant, *
for his mercy endures / for évër.

23 Who remembered / us in our lów estate, *
for his mercy endures / for évër.

24 And delivered / us from our énemies, *
for his mercy endures / for évër.

25 Who gives / food to all créatures, *
for his mercy endures / for évër.

26 Give / thanks to the Gód of heaven, *
for his mercy endures / for évër. *[Ant.]*

137

Antiphon

If I for - get you, O Je - ru - sa - lem, let my right hand for - get

its skill.

Psalm 137 *Super flumina* *Tone I.1*

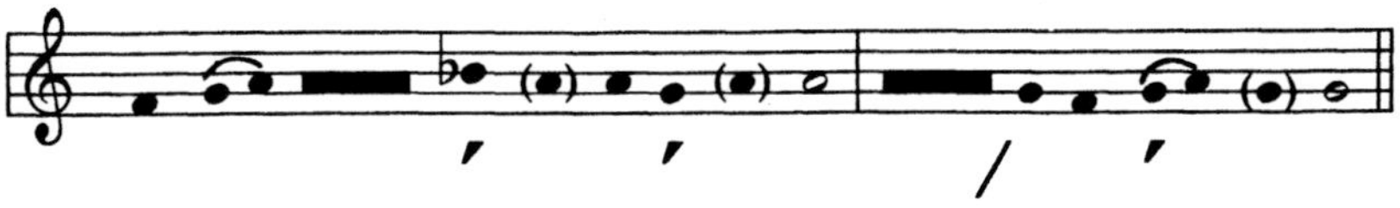

1 *By the* waters of Babylon we sat down and wept, *
when we remembered / you, O Zion.

2 As for our harps, we hung them up *
on the trees in the / midst of that land.

3 For those who led us away captive asked us for a song,
and our oppressors called for mirth: *
"Sing us one of the / songs of Zion."

4 How shall we sing the LORD's song *
up/on an alien soil?

5 If I forget you, O Jerusalem, *
let my right / hand forget its skill.

6 Let my tongue cleave to the roof of my mouth
if I do not remember you, *
if I do not set Jerusalem a/bove my highest joy.

7 Remember the day of Jerusalem, O LORD,
against the people of Edom, *
who said, "Down with it! down with it!
/even to the ground!"

8 O Daughter of Babylon, doomed to destruction, *
happy the one who pays you back
for what / you have done to us!

9 Happy shall he be who takes your little ones, *
and dashes / them against the rock! *[Ant.]*

138

In Advent

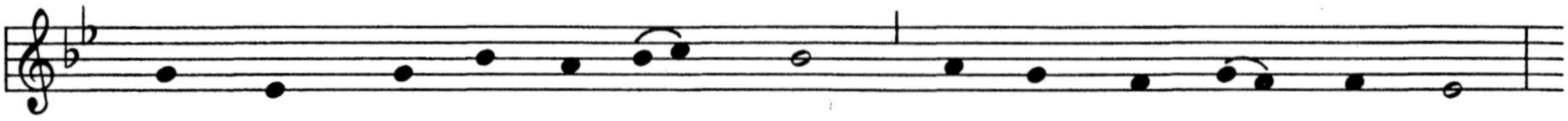

The crook - ed shall be made straight, and the rough pla - ces plain.

Come, O LORD, and do not tar - ry, hal - le - lu - jah.

In Lent

O LORD, your love en - dures for - ev - er; do not a - ban - don the

works of your hands.

In Easter Season

Though I walk in the midst of trou - ble, you keep me safe,

hal - le - lu - jah.

On other Sundays and Weekdays

I will bow down toward your ho - ly tem - ple, and praise your

Name, O LORD.

Psalm 138 *Confitebor tibi* — *Tone V.1*

1 *I will* give thanks to you, O LORD, with my whóle heart; *
before the gods Í will síng your praise.

2 I will bow down toward your holy temple
and práise your Name, *
because of your lóve and fáithfulness;

3 For you have glorified your Náme *
and your wórd abóve all things.

4 When I called, you ánswered me; *
you increased my stréngth withín me.

5 All the kings of the earth will praise yóu, O LORD, *
when they have heard the wórds of yóur mouth.

6 They will sing of the ways of the LÓRD, *
that great is the glóry óf the LORD.

7 Though the LORD be high, he cares for the lówly; *
he perceives the háughty fróm afar.

8 Though I walk in the midst of trouble, you kéep me safe; *
you stretch forth your hand against the fury of my enemies;
your ríght hand shall sáve me.

9 The LORD will make good his purpose for mé; *
O LORD, your love endures for ever;
do not abandon the wórks of yóur hands. *[Ant.]*

139

In Advent

The LORD will sure - ly come and will not tar - ry, and will bring to light

the hid - den things of dark - ness, and will man - i - fest him - self

to all na - tions, hal - le - lu - jah.

In Lent

I, the LORD, search the mind and test the heart, to give to each one as

his deeds de - serve.

In Easter Season

The night shall be as clear as the day, hal - le - lu - jah.

On other Sundays and Weekdays

Search me out, O God, and know my heart; and lead me in the way

that is ev - er - last - ing.

Psalm 139 *Domine, probasti* *Tone III.5*

1 *LORD, you* have searched me out and known me; *
you know my sitting down and my rising up;
you discern my thoughts / from afar.

2 You trace my journeys and my resting-places *
and are acquainted / with all my ways.

3 Indeed, there is not a word on my lips, *
but you, O LORD, know it al/together.

4 You press upon me behind and before *
and lay your hand / upon me.

5 Such knowledge is too wonderful for me; *
it is so high that I cannot / attain to it.

6 Where can I go then from your Spirit? *
where can I flee from / your presence?

7 If I climb up to heaven, you are there; *
if I make the grave my bed, you / are there also.

8 If I take the wings of the morning *
and dwell in the uttermost parts / of the sea,

9 Even there your hand will lead me *
and your right hand / hold me fast.

10 If I say, "Surely the darkness will cover me, *
and the light around me / turn to night,"

11 Darkness is not dark to you;
the night is as bright as the day; *
darkness and light to you / are both alike.

12 For you yourself created my inmost parts; *
you knit me together in / my mother's womb.

13 I will thank you because I am marvelously made; *
your works are wonderful, and / I know it well.

14 My body was not hidden from you, *
while I was being made in secret
and woven in the depths / of the earth.

15 Your eyes beheld my limbs, yet unfinished in the womb;
all of them were written in your book; *
they were fashioned day by day,
when as yet there / was none of them.

16 How deep I find your thoughts, O God! *
how great is / the sum of them!

17 If I were to count them, they would be more
in number than the sand; *
to count them all, my life span would need / to be like yours.

18 Oh, that you would slay the wicked, O God! *
You that thirst for blood, / depart from me.

19 They speak despitefully against you; *
your enemies take / your Name in vain.

20 Do I not hate those, O LORD, who hate you? *
and do I not loathe those who rise up / against you?

21 I hate them with a perfect hatred; *
they have become my / own enemies.

22 Search me out, O God, and know my heart; *
try me and know / my restless thoughts.

23 Look well whether there be any wickedness in me *
and lead me in the way that is e/verlasting. *[Ant.]*

Antiphon

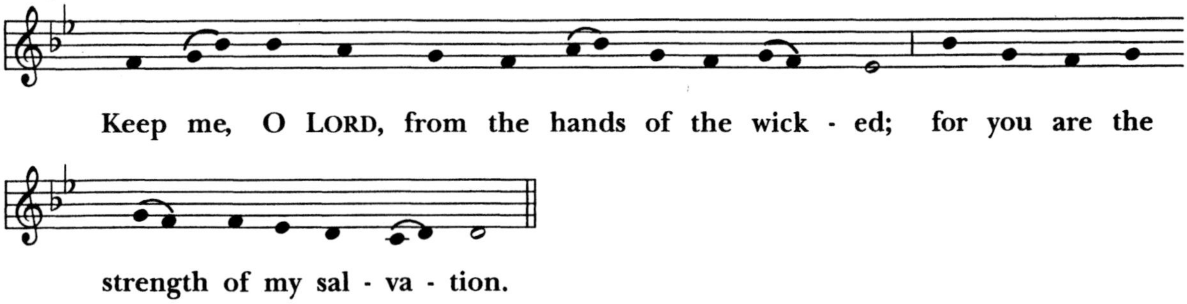
Keep me, O LORD, from the hands of the wick - ed; for you are the
strength of my sal - va - tion.

Psalm 140 *Eripe me, Domine* *Tone III.5*

1 *Deli*ver me, O LORD, from evildoers; *
protect me from / the violent.

2 Who devise evil in their hearts *
and stir up strife / all day long.

3 They have sharpened their tongues like a serpent; *
adder's poison is un/der their lips.

4 Keep me, O LORD, from the hands of the wicked; *
protect me from the violent,
who are determined / to trip me up.

5 The proud have hidden a snare for me
and stretched out a net of cords; *
they have set traps for me / along the path.

6 I have said to the LORD, "You are my God; *
listen, O LORD, to my sup/plication.

7 O Lord GOD, the strength of my salvation, *
you have covered my head in the day / of battle.

8 Do not grant the desires of the wicked, O LORD, *
nor let their evil / plans prosper.

9 Let not those who surround me lift up their heads; *
let the evil of their lips o/verwhelm them.

10 Let hot burning coals fall upon them; *
let them be cast into the mire, never to / rise up again."

11 A slanderer shall not be established on the earth, *
and evil shall hunt down / the lawless.

12 I know that the LORD will maintain the cause of the poor *
and render justice to / the needy.

13 Surely, the righteous will give thanks to your Name, *
and the upright shall continue / in your sight. *[Ant.]*

141

Antiphon

Let my prayer be set forth in your sight as in - cense, the lift - ing up

of my hands as the even - ing sac - ri - fice.

Psalm 141 *Domine, clamavi* *Tone VIII.1*

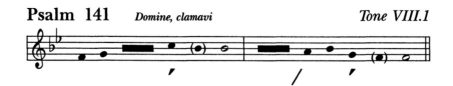

1 *O LORD,* I call to you; come to me quickly; *
hear my voice / when I cry to you.

2 Let my prayer be set forth in your sight as incense, *
the lifting up of my hands as the / evening sacrifice.

3 Set a watch before my mouth, O LORD,
and guard the door of my lips; *
let not my heart incline to / any evil thing.

4 Let me not be occupied in wickedness with evildoers, *
nor eat / of their choice foods.

5 Let the righteous smite me in friendly rebuke;
let not the oil of the unrighteous anoint my head; *
for my prayer is continually a/gainst their wicked deeds.

6 Let their rulers be overthrown in stony places, *
that they may / know my words are true.

7 As when a plowman turns over the earth in furrows, *
let their bones be scattered at the / mouth of the grave.

8 But my eyes are turned to you, Lord GOD; *
in you I take refuge;
do not strip / me of my life.

9 Protect me from the snare which they have laid for me *
and from the traps of the / evildoers.

10 Let the wicked fall into their own nets, *
while / I myself escape. *[Ant.]*

142

In Holy Week

The be - tray - er had giv - en them a sign, say - ing, the one I shall kiss

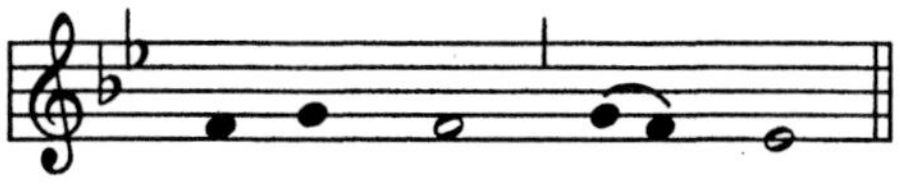

is the man; seize him.

On other Sundays and Weekdays

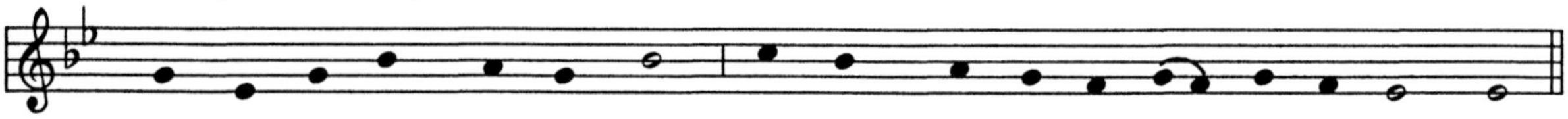

You are my ref - uge, O LORD; my por - tion in the land of the liv - ing.

Psalm 142 *Voce mea ad Dominum* *Tone V.1*

1 *I cry* to the LORD with my vóice; *
to the LORD I make loud súpplicátion.

2 I pour out my complaint befóre him *
and tell him áll my tróuble.

3 When my spirit languishes within me, you knów my path; *
in the way wherein I walk they have hídden a tráp for me.

4 I look to my right hand and find no one who knóws me; *
I have no place to flee to, and nó one cáres for me.

5 I cry out to yóu, O LORD; *
I say, "You are my refuge,
my portion in the lánd of the líving."

6 Listen to my cry for help, for I have been brought véry low; *
save me from those who pursue me,
for théy are too stróng for me.

7 Bring me out of prison, that I may give thanks to yóur Name; *
when you have dealt bountifully with me,
the righteous will gáther aróund me. *[Ant.]*

143

In Holy Week

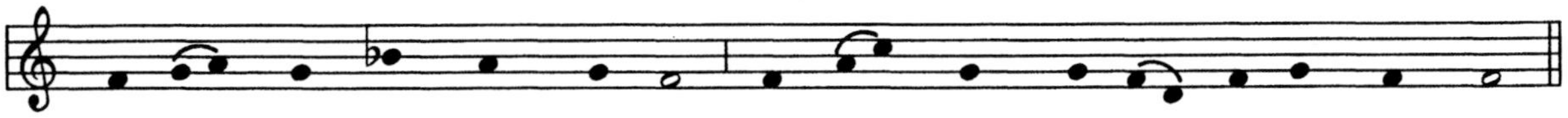

My spir - it faints with - in me; my heart with - in me is des - o - late.

On other Sundays and Weekdays

I spread out my hands to you, O LORD; do not hide your face from me.

Psalm 143 *Domine, exaudi* *Tone VI*

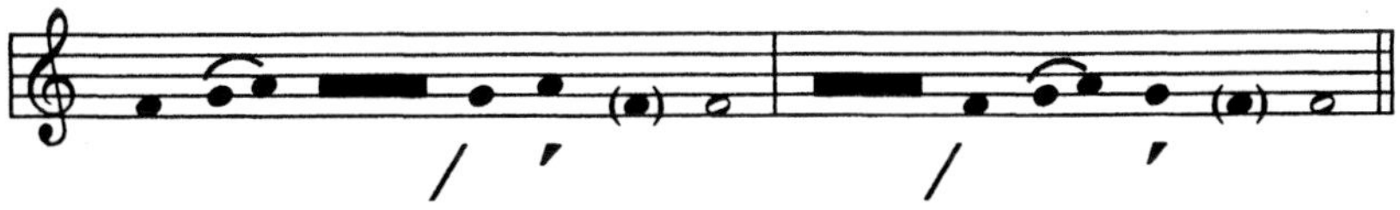

1 *LORD, hëar* my prayer,
and in your faithfulness heed my sup/plicátions; *
answer me / in yöur ŕighteousness.

2 Enter not into judgment with / your sérvant, *
for in your sight shall no one liv/ing bë jústified.

3 For my enemy has sought my life;
he has crushed / me tó the ground; *
he has made me live in dark places like those / who äre lóng dead.

4 My spirit faints / withín me; *
my heart within / me ïs désolate.

5 I remember the time past;
I muse up/on áll your deeds; *
I consider the / works öf yóur hands.

6 I spread out / my hánds to you; *
my soul gasps to you / like ä thírsty land.

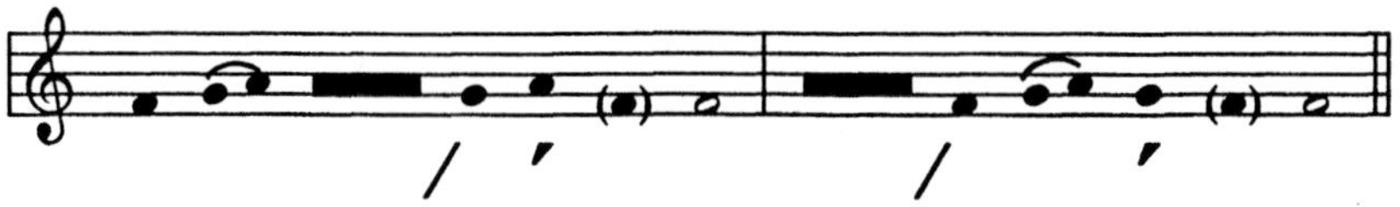

7 O LORD, make haste to answer me; my spir/it fáils me; *
do not hide your face from me
or I shall be like those who / go döwn tó the Pit.

8 Let me hear of your loving-kindness in the morning,
for I put / my trúst in you; *
show me the road that I must walk,
for I lift / up mÿ sóul to you.

9 Deliver me from my ene/mies, Ó LORD, *
for I flee to / you för réfuge.

10 Teach me to do what pleases you, for / you áre my God; *
let your good Spirit lead / me ön lével ground.

11 Revive me, O LORD, for / your Náme's sake; *
for your righteousness' sake, bring me / out öf tróuble.

12 Of your goodness, destroy my enemies
and bring all / my fóes to naught, *
for truly I / am yöur sérvant. *[Ant.]*

144

Antiphon

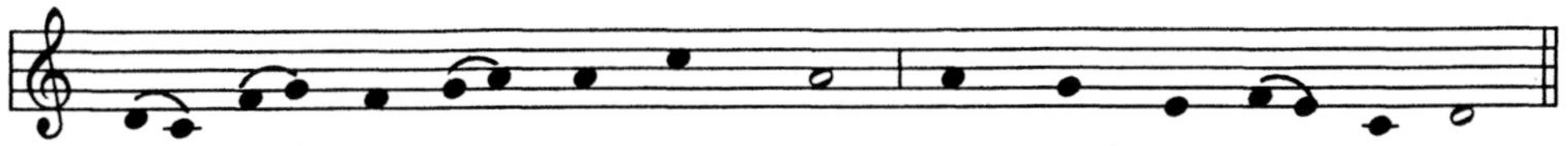
God is my help and for - tress, my shield in whom I trust.

Psalm 144 *Benedictus Dominus* *Tone I.2*

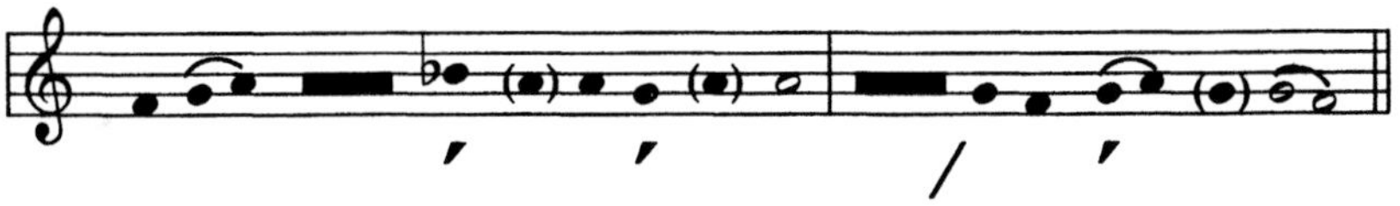

1 *Blessed*—be the LORD my rock! *
who trains my hands to fight and my fin/gers to battle;

2 My help and my fortress, my stronghold and my deliverer, *
my shield in whom I trust,
who subdues the / peoples under me.

3 O LORD, what are we that you should care for us? *
mere mortals that / you should think of us?

4 We are like a puff of wind; *
our days are like a / passing shadow.

5 Bow your heavens, O LORD, and come down; *
touch the mountains, / and they shall smoke.

6 Hurl the lightning and scatter them; *
shoot out your ar/rows and rout them.

7 Stretch out your hand from on high; *
rescue me and deliver me from the great waters,
from the hand of / foreign peoples,

8 Whose mouths speak deceitfully *
and whose right hand is / raised in falsehood.

9 O God, I will sing to you a new song; *
I will play to you / on a ten-stringed lyre.

10 You give victory to kings *
and have rescued Da/vid your servant.

11 Rescue me from the hurtful sword *
and deliver me from the hand of / foreign peoples,

12 Whose mouths speak deceitfully *
and whose right hand is / raised in falsehood.

13 May our sons be like plants well nurtured from their youth, *
and our daughters like sculptured corners / of a palace.

14 May our barns be filled to overflowing with all manner of crops; *
may the flocks in our pastures increase by thousands and
tens of thousands;
may our cat/tle be fat and sleek.

15 May there be no breaching of the walls, no going into exile, *
no wailing / in the public squares.

16 Happy are the people of whom this is so! *
happy are the people whose / God is the LORD! *[Ant.]*

145

On the Twelve Days of Christmas

One gen - er - a - tion shall praise your works to an - oth - er, O LORD,

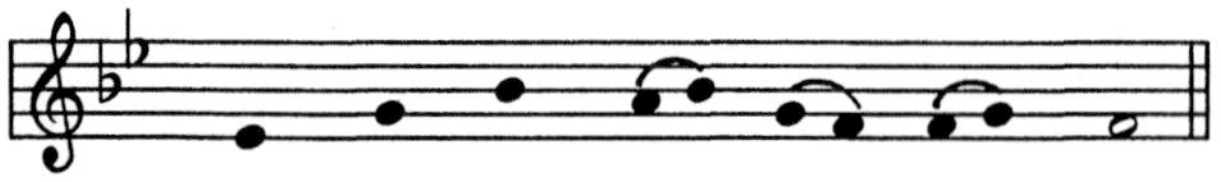

and shall de - clare your pow - er.

In Lent

The LORD ful - fills the de - sire of those who fear him; he hears their cry

and helps them.

In Easter Season

Let all flesh bless God's ho - ly Name for ev - er and ev - er,

hal - le - lu - jah.

On other Sundays and Weekdays

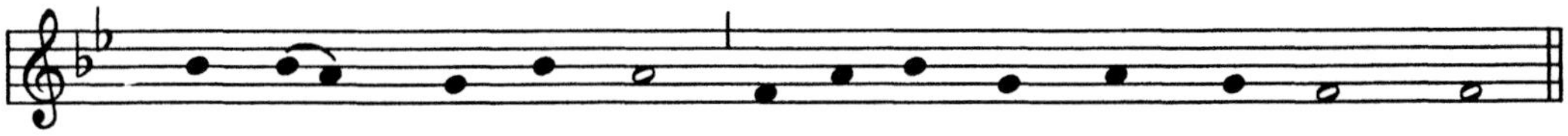
Your king - dom, O LORD, is an ev - er - last - ing king - dom.

Psalm 145 *Exaltabo te, Deus* *Tone VIII.2*

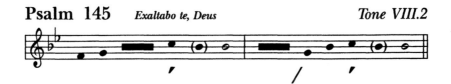

1 *I will* exalt you, O Gód my King, *
and bless your Name for ev/er and éver.

2 Every day will I bléss you *
and praise your Name for ev/er and éver.

3 Great is the LORD and greatly to be práised; *
there is no end / to his gréatness.

4 One generation shall praise your works to anóther *
and shall de/clare your pówer.

5 I will ponder the glorious splendor of your májesty *
and / all your márvelous works.

6 They shall speak of the might of your wóndrous acts, *
and I will tell / of your gréatness.

7 They shall publish the remembrance of your great góodness; *
they shall sing / of your ŕighteous deeds.

8 The LORD is gracious and full of compássion, *
slow to anger and / of great kíndness.

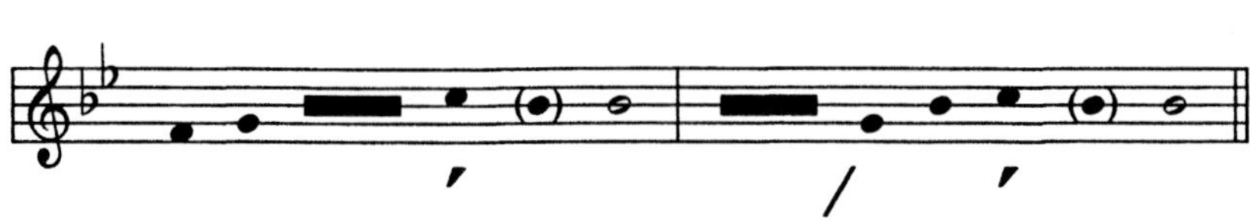

9 The LORD is loving to éveryone *
and his compassion is / over áll his works.

10 All your works praise yóu, O LORD, *
and your faithful / servants bléss you.

11 They make known the glory of your kíngdom *
and speak / of your pówer;

12 That the peoples may know of your pówer *
and the glorious splendor / of your kíngdom.

13 Your kingdom is an everlasting kíngdom; *
your dominion endures through/out all áges.

14 The LORD is faithful in áll his words *
and merci/ful in áll his deeds.

15 The LORD upholds all thóse who fall; *
he lifts up those / who are bówed down.

16 The eyes of all wait upon yóu, O LORD, *
and you give them their food / in due séason.

17 You open wíde your hand *
and satisfy the needs of every / living créature.

18 The LORD is righteous in áll his ways *
and lov/ing in áll his works.

19 The LORD is near to those who call upón him, *
to all who call up/on him fáithfully.

20 He fulfills the desire of those who féar him; *
he hears their / cry and hélps them.

21 The LORD preserves all those who lóve him, *
but he destroys / all the wícked.

22 My mouth shall speak the praise of the LÓRD; *
let all flesh bless his holy Name for ev/er and éver. *[Ant.]*

146

In Advent

Tell it out a - mong the na - tions, and say; "Be - hold, he comes, our
God and Sav - ior," hal - le - lu - jah.

In Easter Season

The LORD shall reign for ev - er; your God, O Zi - on, through - out all
gen - er - a - tions, hal - le - lu - jah.

On other Sundays and Weekdays

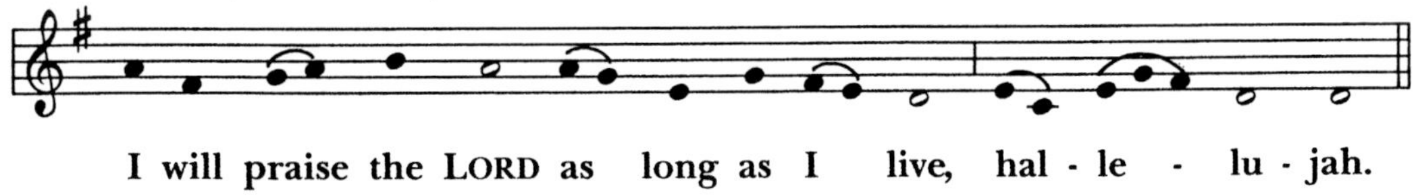
I will praise the LORD as long as I live, hal - le - lu - jah.

Psalm 146 *Lauda, anima mea* *Tone VII.1*

*1 *Hallelujah!*
Praise the LORD, O my soul! *
I will praise the LORD as long as I live;
I will sing praises to my God while I have my being.

2 Put not your trust in rulers, nor in any child of earth, *
for there is no help in them.

3 When they breathe their last, they return to earth, *
and in that day their thoughts perish.

**Hallelujah* may be omitted from the first verse of the psalm when the antiphon ends with *Hallelujah*; the verse then begins: Praise the—LORD, O my soul! *

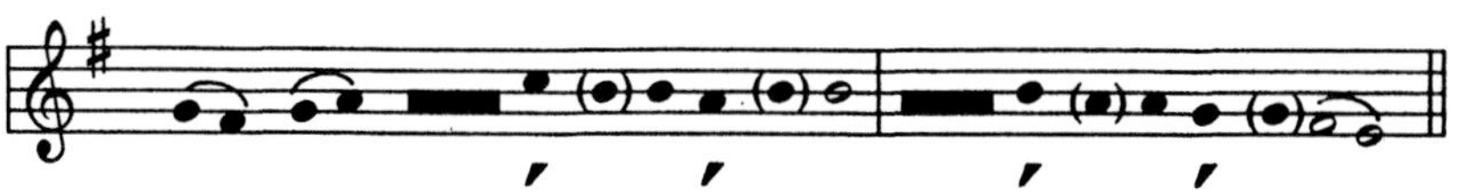

4 Happy are they who have the God of Jácob fór their help! *
whose hope is ín the LÓRD their Göd;

5 Who made heaven and earth, the seas, and áll that is ín them; *
who keeps his prómise for évër;

6 Who gives justice to thóse who áre oppressed, *
and food to thóse who húngër.

7 The LORD sets the prisoners free;
the LORD opens the éyes of thé blind; *
the LORD lifts up thóse who are bówed döwn;

8 The LORD loves the righteous;
the LORD cáres for the stránger; *
he sustains the orphan and widow,
but frustrates the wáy of the wíckëd.

9 The LORD shall réign for éver, *
your God, O Zion, throughout all generations.
Hállelújäh! *[Ant.]*

147

In Advent

On that day, the moun - tains shall drop down new wine, and the hills

shall flow with milk and hon - ey, hal - le - lu - jah.

In Easter Season

Praise your God, O Zi - on; for he has es - tab - lished peace on your

bor - ders, hal - le - lu - jah.

On other Sundays and Weekdays

How pleas - ant it is to hon - or God with praise, hal - le - lu - jah.

Psalm 147 *Laudate Dominum* *Tone VIII.1*

1 *Halle*lujah!
How good it is to sing praises to our God! *
how pleasant it is to / honor him with praise!

2 The LORD rebuilds Jerusalem; *
he gathers the ex/iles of Israel.

3 He heals the brokenhearted *
and / binds up their wounds.

4 He counts the number of the stars *
and calls them / all by their names.

5 Great is our LORD and mighty in power; *
there is no limit / to his wisdom.

6 The LORD lifts up the lowly, *
but casts the / wicked to the ground.

7 Sing to the LORD with thanksgiving; *
make music to our / God upon the harp.

8 He covers the heavens with clouds *
and prepares / rain for the earth;

9 He makes grass to grow upon the mountains *
and green / plants to serve mankind.

10 He provides food for flocks and herds *
and for the young / ravens when they cry.

11 He is not impressed by the might of a horse; *
he has no pleasure in the / strength of a man;

12 But the LORD has pleasure in those who féar him, *
in those who await his / gracious fávor.

13 Worship the LORD, O Jerúsalem; *
praise your / God, O Źion;

14 For he has strengthened the bars of yóur gates; *
he has blessed your chil/dren withiń you.

15 He has established peace on your bórders; *
he satisfies you / with the fínest wheat.

16 He sends out his command to the éarth, *
and his word runs / very swíftly.

17 He gives snów like wool; *
he scatters hoar/frost like áshes.

18 He scatters his hail like bréad crumbs; *
who can / stand agáinst his cold?

19 He sends forth his word and mélts them; *
he blows with his wind, / and the wáters flow.

20 He declares his word to Jácob, *
his statutes and his judg/ments to Ísrael.

21 He has not done so to any other nátion; *
to them he has not revealed his judgments.
/ Hallelújah! *[Ant.]*

In Advent

Be - hold, I send my mes - sen - ger, and he shall pre - pare your way

be - fore your face, hal - le - lu - jah.

In Easter Season

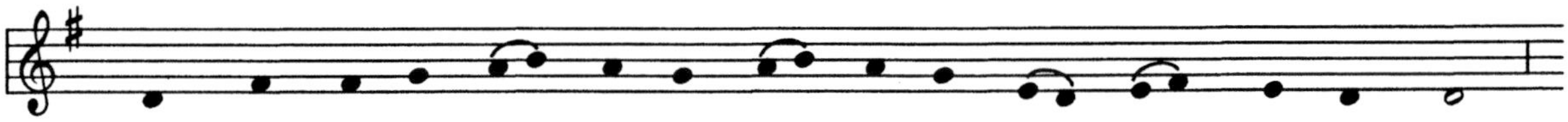

The Name of the LORD is ex - alt - ed a - bove heav - en and earth,

hal - le - lu - jah.

On other Sundays and Weekdays

Praise the LORD from the heav - ens; praise the LORD from the earth,

ha - le - lu - jah.

Psalm 148 *Laudate Dominum* *Tone VII.3*

*1 *Hallelujah!*
Praise the LÓRD from the héavens; *
—práise him ín the heights.

2 Praise him, all you ángels óf his; *
—práise him, áll his host.

**Hallelujah* may be omitted from the first verse of the psalm when the antiphon ends with *Hallelujah*; the verse then begins: Präise thë—LÓRD from....

3 —Praise him, sun and moon; *
praise him, all you shining stars.

4 Praise him, heaven of heavens, *
and you waters above the heavens.

5 Let them praise the Name of the LORD; *
for he commanded, and they were created.

6 He made them stand fast for ever and ever; *
he gave them a law which shall not pass away.

7 Praise the LORD from the earth, *
you sea-monsters and all deeps;

8 Fire and hail, snow and fog, *
tempestuous wind, doing his will;

9 —Mountains and all hills, *
fruit trees and all cedars;

10 Wild beasts and all cattle, *
creeping things and wingèd birds;

11 Kings of the earth and all peoples, *
princes and all rulers of the world;

12 —Young men and maidens, *
old and young together.

13 Let them praise the Name of the LORD, *
for his Name only is exalted,
his splendor is over earth and heaven.

14 He has raised up strength for his people
and praise for all his loyal servants, *
the children of Israel, a people who are near him.
Hallelujah! *[Ant.]*

149

In Advent

Lo, there comes a might - y Proph - et; and he a - lone shall re - new

Je - ru - sa - lem, hal - le - lu - jah.

In Easter Season

Let the faith - ful re - joice in tri - umph, hal - le - lu - jah.

On other Sundays and Weekdays

Let the chil - dren of Zi - on be joy - ful in their King, hal - le - lu - jah.

Psalm 149 *Cantate Domino* *Tone I.1*

*1 *Halle*lujah!
Sing to the LORD a new song; *
sing his praise in the congregation / of the faithful.

2 Let Israel rejoice in his Maker; *
let the children of Zion be / joyful in their King.

3 Let them praise his Name in the dance; *
let them sing praise to him with / timbrel and harp.

4 For the LORD takes pleasure in his people *
and adorns the / poor with victory.

5 Let the faithful rejoice in triumph; *
let them be / joyful on their beds.

**Hallelujah* may be omitted from the first verse of the psalm when the antiphon ends with *Hallelujah*; the verse then begins: *Sing to* the LORD a new song; *

6 Let the praises of God be in their throat *
and a two-edged / sword in their hand;

7 To wreak vengeance on the nations *
and punishment / on the peoples;

8 To bind their kings in chains *
and their no/bles with links of iron;

9 To inflict on them the judgment decreed; *
this is glory for all his faithful people.
/Hallelujah! *[Ant.]*

150

In Advent

Zi - on is our strong ci - ty; a Sav - ior will God ap - point with - in her

for walls and bul - warks.

On the Twelve Days of Christmas

O - pen wide the gates, for God him - self is with us, hal - le - lu - jah.

In Easter Season

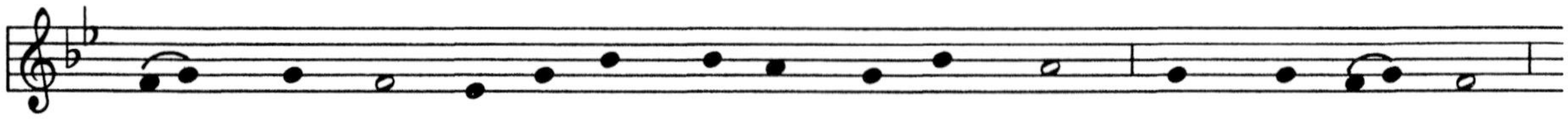

Wor - ship God who is seat - ed up - on the throne, say - ing, A - men,

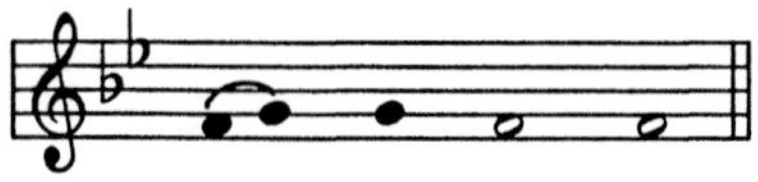

hal - le - lu - jah.

On other Sundays and Weekdays

Praise the Lord for his ex - cel - lent great - ness, hal - le - lu - jah.

Psalm 150 *Laudate Dominum* *Tone VIII.2*

*1 *Halle*lujah!
Praise God in his holy temple; *
praise him in the firmament / of his power.

2 Praise him for his mighty acts; *
praise him for his ex/cellent greatness.

3 Praise him with the blast of the ram's-horn; *
praise / him with lyre and harp.

4 Praise him with timbrel and dance; *
praise / him with strings and pipe.

5 Praise him with resounding cymbals; *
praise him with loud-/clanging cymbals.

6 Let everything that has breath *
praise the LORD.
/ Hallelujah! *[Ant.]*

**Hallelujah* may be omitted from the first verse of the psalm when the antiphon ends with *Hallelujah*; the verse then begins: *Praise God* in his....

Appendix

Appendix

*Tones with their endings used in this Psalter.

Tone 1

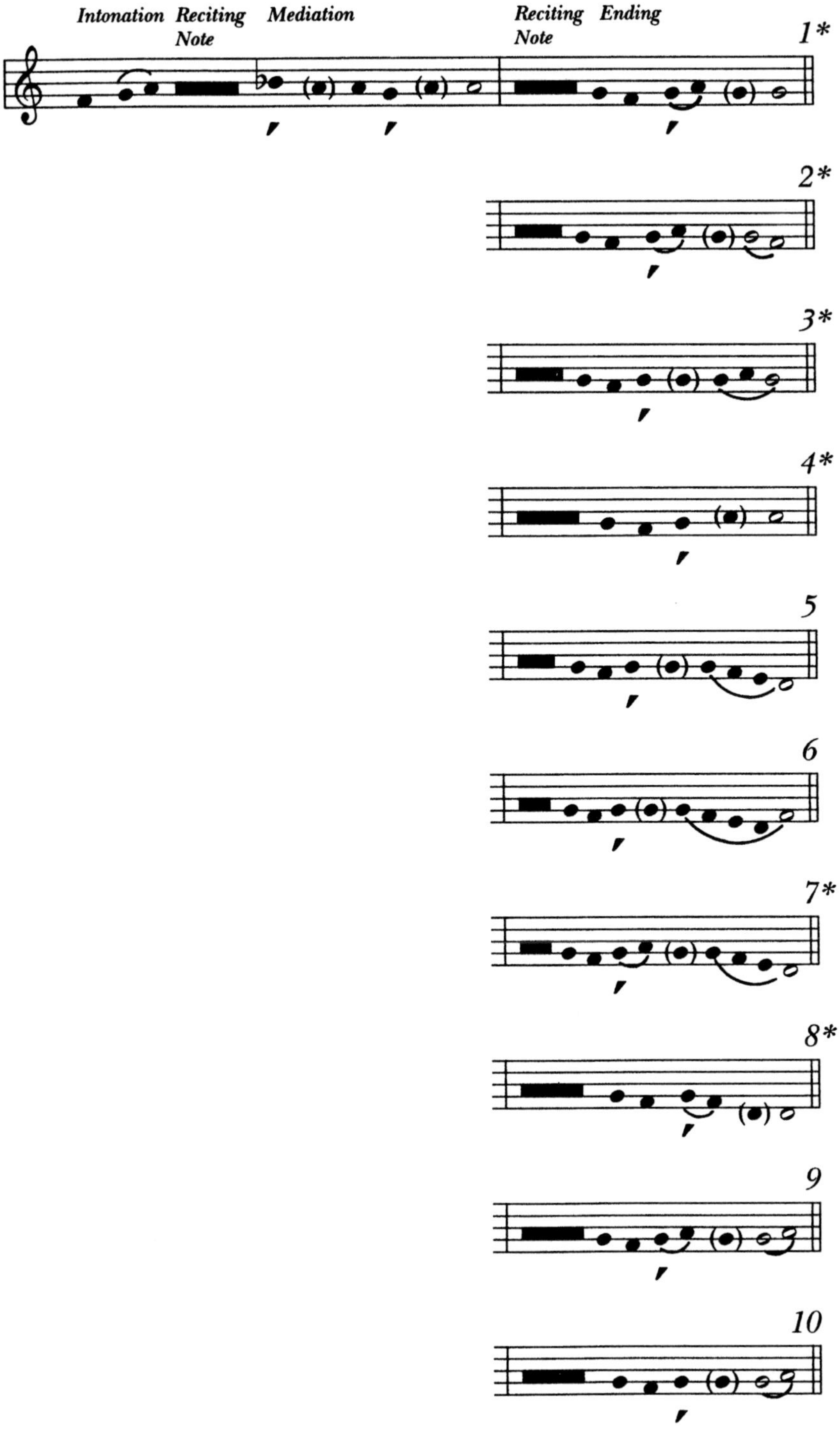
Intonation
Reciting Note
Mediation
Reciting Note
Ending
1*
2*
3*
4*
5
6
7*
8*
9
10

Tone 2

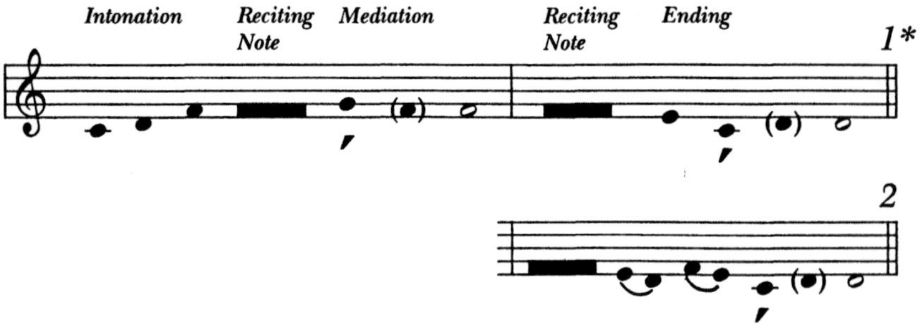
Intonation
Reciting Note
Mediation
Reciting Note
Ending
1*
2

Tone 3

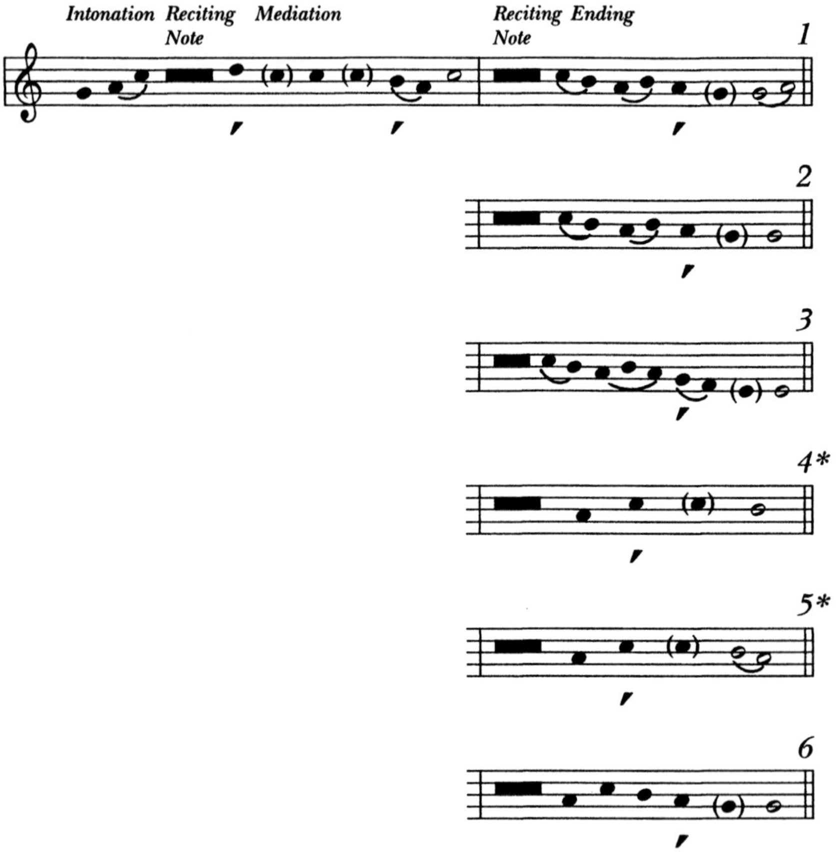
Intonation
Reciting Note
Mediation
Reciting Note
Ending
1
2
3
4*
5*
6

Tone 4

Intonation
Reciting Note
Mediation
Reciting Note
Ending
1*
2*
3
4*
5*
6*
7
8
9

Tone 5

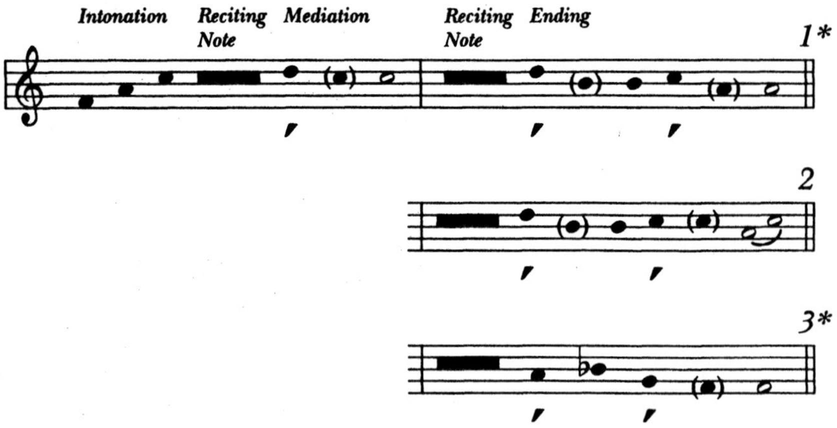
Intonation
Reciting Note
Mediation
Reciting Note
Ending
1*
2
3*

Tone 6

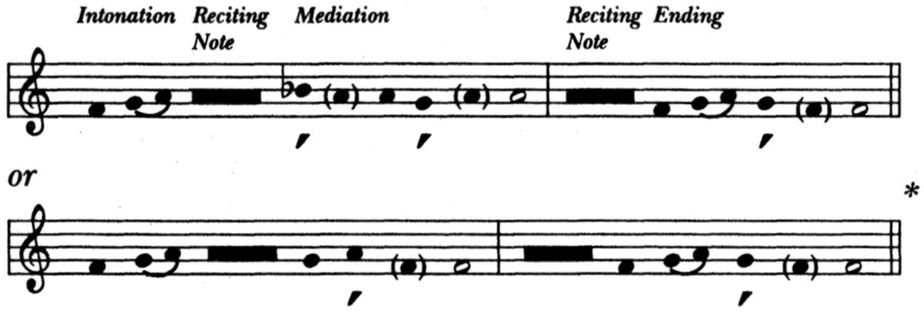
Intonation
Reciting Note
Mediation
Reciting Note
Ending
or
*

Tone 7

Intonation
Reciting Note
Mediation
Reciting Note
Ending
1*
2
3*
4
5
6*
7*

Tone 8

Intonation
Reciting Note
Mediation
Reciting Note
Ending
1*
2*
3*
4*
5*

Tonus Peregrinus

Intonation
Reciting Note
Mediation
Reciting Note
Ending
1*

or